Vickie & Lee,

Apply the principles in this book early in life and you'll come out way ahead. God bless you and your baby!

Walter [illegible]

What others are saying about this book:

"After reading this book you will agree that you will be equipped with the information you need to have a clearer perspective on how to deal with your finances, your family and your faith. This book is full of practical insights that will deepen your walk of faith or begin your journey in the right direction. Walter Woodrick does not compromise when it comes to faith in Christ being your first priority. His book will help you understand where you are financially, and then help you put your priorities in order."

Dr. Charles Stanley
Senior Pastor, First Baptist Church Atlanta
Founder and President of In Touch Ministries

"Woodrick's new book is a keen study in how to manage 'Life's Priorities' in a context that is God-centered. A must read for adults of all ages."

Rick Hattersley, Panama City News Herald

"Sound advice to families who are searching for the basic fundamentals for successful living."

Allan Bense, Florida House of Representatives,
Speaker-designate

"Walter has a remarkable gift of being able to really connect with an audience."

Dr. Douglas C. Pennington, Senior Pastor
Lynn Haven United Methodist Church

More of what others are saying:

"Thanks for the opportunity to be involved. I really think you've done a nice job on the book and pray that God will use it to bless the body of Christ. Be sure to let me know prior to your appearances on Oprah and Letterman."

STEVE MOORE, MONEY MATTERS RADIO TALK SHOW HOST, CROWN FINANCIAL MINISTRIES

"This book teaches you about money, family, and God. It's perfect for busy professionals, single parents, those approaching retirement, and gift-giving grandparents."

"SISTER" BLACKMON MILLIGAN, ATTORNEY, PRIOR FEDERAL PROSECUTOR, PRIOR STATE PROSECUTOR

"Walter is able to share insights and suggestions which are down-to-earth and practical, informed by sound professional competencies, grounded in important core values, and tempered by experience."

RAYFORD WOODRICK, (RETIRED) UNITED METHODIST CLERGY MINISTER OF MISSIONS, ST. MATTHEW'S UNITED METHODIST CHURCH

We want to hear from you. If you'd like to send us your comments after reading this book, please send them to us by visiting:

www.walteronline.com

Finances, Family… and Faith

"An Understandable Guide to Life's Priorities"

by

Walter L. Woodrick, CFP®

Priority Publishing Company
Lynn Haven, FL

www.walteronline.com

Finances, Family… and Faith

An Understandable Guide to Life's Priorities

By Walter L. Woodrick, CFP®

Published by:
Priority Publishing Company
1602 New Jersey Avenue
Lynn Haven FL 32444
www.priority-publishing.com
(850) 248-9606

Photography by Robert Dobbs, Dobbs Photography, Panama City, FL
Cover Design by Lightbourne, Inc.

ISBN 0-9754749-0-1
Personal Finance
Self-Help
Spiritual

Printed in the United States of America

TABLE OF CONTENTS

Introduction

Where Finances, Family... and Faith Got Its Start

Sunday morning, summer of 1976. My mother is throwing a football with me in the front yard. I was six years-old....

My mother at one time was a good athlete. She had been the Mississippi state record holder in high school for the 50- and 75-yard dashes in the mid 1960's. It was a sunny and quiet morning, and we were both very happy to be outside breaking in my new Nerf® football and to be spending some time with each other. You know what a Nerf® is, don't you? It's a foam-like ball that is very soft and easy to squeeze. It's also a great chewable toy for your dog, and it's very heavy once it gets wet because it absorbs water like a sponge. She had just bought the ball for me the day before, so it was in perfect condition... no scratches or chunks missing from it... and I remember it flew through the air with tremendous ease and beauty. She was a little bit downhill from me in the front yard of our middle-class one-story brick home in Hattiesburg, Mississippi, and I threw a pass to her that probably would have been the perfect height for my dad since he was 6'1", but my mom stood about 5'4". Those nine inches sure did make a difference in shaping me as a person.

The spiraling Nerf® football whistled through her raised hands and, for the first time in its short life, bounced into the rough grass. It made one of those crazy first bounces that footballs do, and my mom turned to retrieve it. As the ball continued to roll down the hill, I realized that we needed to hurry and get to the ball before it rolled into the street. The street was in a quiet residential area, but there was a gutter that had an opening just large enough for a football to roll into and disappear forever. I sprinted past my mother and reached down just as the ball was rolling over the curb into the street. I missed it by inches and the new ball then rolled into the rain gutter at the edge of the street. It was like the gutter had an invisible vacuum drawing the ball into its mouth. It fell down into the bottom of the four-foot deep basin, never to be seen again. My six-year old stomach completely turned inside out, and I felt like an irreversible tragedy had just occurred.

I turned to my mother, tears streaming down my six-year-old face, and said, with anger and disappointment, "Look what *you* did!" I was mad at her for not catching the ball in the first place - and then for not getting to the ball before it entered its eternal resting place at the bottom of the gutter. I remember, as vividly as if it happened yesterday, that she said to me in a consoling voice, "It's okay, son, we can go get another one." And my reply to her solution was, "We can't afford to get another one!"

I understand that at this moment you're probably thinking, "I can't believe this guy has written a book because he lost a $3 football!" So, please let me explain. The reason this event sticks out in my mind is because it was the first time I ever communicated with someone that I understood the basics about money and finances; and it will forever be a benchmark and reference point in my adult life where I make a living as a prudent money manager (this can also be jokingly defined as being monetarily anal retentive).

Back then, I knew that, at least in my family, money was fairly hard to come by. It required long hours in the local shopping mall at the candle store that my mother owned or it required that my dad be away for long periods of time, as he was a catastrophe insurance adjuster. Whenever there was a flood, earthquake, hurricane, or hail storm, he had to stop what he was doing and leave right then. He was constantly watching the Weather Channel for his next assignment, and when he left, he didn't come back for several months until the job was finished.

I guess somewhere along the way I picked up the basics about money from overhearing conversations between my mom and dad, I saw how hard mom worked at the store unpacking boxes of candles, I picked up on how important money was by seeing how intently dad was watching the weather, or maybe I was actually taught by my mom, dad, or grandmother about some of the basics of money management. The event with the football frequently comes to my mind today when I'm deciding whether to save, invest, or spend money. I feel blessed to know that I've always had an understanding of what is basically the right thing to do with my finances.

This event also sticks out in my mind as the first time I ever really recognized that my dad wasn't around the family very much. I don't know why my dad wasn't there that Sunday morning… I suppose he was either working out of town or on the golf course with his regular Sunday "lunch bunch" golf group. I can only remember throwing the football with my dad one time in my entire life, and I was our school's quarterback all through junior high and high school. I've thrown a football thousands of times, but my dad was not on the receiving end of very many of those passes. Mom was trying to be the bread winner at that time because there hadn't been much work for my dad due to a lack of catastrophes – it's unfortunate, but dad was really hoping somebody somewhere would have some damage done to their property by the weather so he could help pay the bills. Mom was trying to be a father to me that day by taking me out to throw the football; and she was also trying to be the mom who cooks, cleans, and loves her two children. They both drank alcohol to help them cope with their financial situation and struggling marriage. Family experiences like these made a huge impact on me and on how I will structure the time that I spend with my wife and children. Every child deserves a "normal" childhood.

Finally, this event also made a dramatic impact on my Christian faith. My mother and I were out throwing a football on a Sunday morning, and I now know that God wanted our family to be together - in church - spending time with Him. A personal relationship with Christ could have saved my parents' marriage, and it could have helped my parents, as a loving team, teach me how to deal with money, people, family, and situations in life. I now know that God gives me every event in my life to try and show me how much He loves me and to try to draw me closer to Him. My parents, unfortunately, didn't know how to lead me in a walk with Christ at that time. My faith in Christ is the most important aspect of my life and it is the footing upon which I make financial, family, and life decisions.

The loss of that football happened when I was six years old, and it was the first concrete example I had in my past where I can pinpoint the influences that finances, family, and faith had in shaping who I am today; in how I deal with other people; and in how I prioritize issues and responsibilities as a Christian father, husband, and financial planner.

That six year-old from Hattiesburg, Mississippi has grown up to be an economics graduate from Vanderbilt University, a husband, a father of two beautiful daughters, a financial consultant with a major financial services firm as a CFP® licensee, and a Christian trying to live life happily doing what God wants him to do.

Life is very complicated… but it doesn't have to be.

High-speed vs. regular phone line Internet access … digital vs. cable TV… regular TV or HDTV… real estate, stocks, bonds, or cd's… How should we deal with impatient coworkers, employees, or family members? Should we buy from Ebay, garage sales, or just buy it new? Do we spank our children or not? Is leasing or owning a car better? Do we add on to the house or buy a new one? TV preachers – is that really what religion is about? Private school, home school, or public school? What's the best diet? What's the easiest diet? "Make money from your own home" and other "get rich quick" schemes… Will we need to take care of elderly parents or a spouse? Health club membership, a gym at home, or just try and exercise any way possible? Is the world safe enough to travel overseas? Video tapes or DVD's? Christianity or Islam? Jesus or Mohammed? Innately good or bad? Snail mail, email, or no mail?... and on... and on ... and on.

The list of decisions, choices, and information that we are bombarded with is endless; and it changes as we continue to get older, change our preferences, or have a different set of circumstances to deal with. CNN, CNBC, ESPN, the Internet, wireless phones, instant messaging, text messaging, email, voice mail, and paging make us all just the click of a button away from real-time information, police chases, weather disasters, and constant communication. And, just when we think we've got life figured out and we get into a good rhythm, life changes and we have to go all the way back to the drawing board. We can get bogged down in the details of all of life's small decisions, and all of those small decisions accumulate into one big statement that reflects who we are and what we stand for. Or, we can defer to a lifestyle that is based on some certain big-picture assumptions that have been proven to be the timeless ways to handle life's myriad of situations and difficulties - most of which we probably create and bring upon ourselves by trying to find a way to beat the system.

The purpose of this book is to provide you with a thorough yet concise resource to help you in understanding life's priorities - your finances, family, and faith - so that you can free your mind and your time to enjoy other things. I'll use information I've obtained from all the research I've done in the years past to help give you understanding, simplicity, and clarity regarding "the three F's," – finances, family, and faith. I currently have to refer to the many books and manuals I've read in the past to find the information I need. I hope that this book can be a "one-stop shop" that gives you the basic information you'll need to grow in wisdom, peace and knowledge about your finances (whether you're unemployed, working paycheck to paycheck, financially comfortable, or considered a high net worth individual), about your family (regardless of your background or current situation), and about your faith (in whatever stage you may find yourself).

I could probably spend the rest of my life writing in detail about each topic and the subtopics that spring out from "the three F's", but I'm attempting to limit the size of this book to an amount of material that can be read, digested, and reflected upon in a reasonable amount of time. You may feel led to read this book together with other people in a small group, in a Sunday school class, with coworkers, or with your family. A small group might like to create a schedule where the book is read, studied, and discussed over a ten- or twelve-week period. The chapters are structured so that you can read a few pages a day and have everything make sense at the end of the week.

As a CERTIFIED FINANCIAL PLANNER™ practitioner, I have the experience and knowledge to explain to you, in terms you can easily understand, how to handle some of the basic issues you'll encounter in life regarding your finances. In the chapters regarding finances, we'll talk about some typical situations you might find yourself exposed to and how they should be addressed...from making a living, to spending money, to saving and investing money, to giving away money or assets. I'll use information from my professional experiences, trade magazines, personal knowledge, and sources like Crown Financial Ministries and authors like Howard Dayton and the late Larry Burkett. My investment, financial, and estate planning clients have told me that I have a talent for explaining things in a way that makes financial subjects easier for them to understand. I hope you'll be able to agree with them! For those of you who already know or feel comfortable with "the basics," I will also discuss some sophisticated planning and investment concepts to help you reach or fine tune your financial goals.

In the three chapters regarding family, I'll draw from my own life experiences such as my struggles with my parents' divorce when I was eight-years old; living with my grandmother for four years; coping with family members' misuse of alcohol; dealing with the complicated relations in my blended family; and seeing how "normal" families operate by interacting with them in professional, church, and casual settings. I'll combine these experiences with insight from the Bible and authors like Dr. James Dobson (Focus on the Family), Stormie Omartian (*The Power of a Praying Wife/Husband*) and Rick Warren (*The Purpose Driven Life*) to help you with your family relationships.

In the three chapters regarding faith, I hope you'll obtain a solid grasp of the basic terminology and concepts you might encounter in your walk as a Christian. I used to be intimidated by the Bible, and I felt I could never understand it. But then I actually read a chronological Bible. I read it day-by-day, week-by-week, from cover to cover over a one-year period. What a difference a year makes!

You will find that faith is intertwined throughout all of the chapters – whether it's stated or not, as it should also be intertwined in every aspect of our lives. I think you'll find that we share some common bonds in our experiences with our faith. I'm not a pastor's child, I haven't lived a perfect life, I was not raised in a house that taught me about the Bible or God, and I've walked away from God in the past – do you and I have any of these things in common?

There's Just Not Enough Time In The Day

Our society's productivity was greatly increased in the 1990's by the invention of the fax machine. Paperwork that in the past would have spent weeks in the regular mail system could be transmitted instantly to its destination. In the late 1990's we had the tremendous growth of the Internet, email, websites, downloadable forms, and electronic signatures. Again, the amount of time needed to take care of every day business was dramatically reduced. So, with the reduced time it takes to take care of business, why does it seem like we have less and less time to adequately deal with our finances, families, and faith?

In gathering and assimilating all of the information I've received (and continue to receive) through the years, I constantly search for how to gain the right perspective; how to master the proper technique; how to get more out of my day; how to get more out of myself; how to get more out of others; how others have achieved success, respect, or wealth; how to…. well, you get the idea. I've read, listened, watched, and studied in depth about investing, Christianity, prayer, golf, songwriting, music, boating, selling, construction, real estate, insurance, business, personal relationships, raising children, solving conflicts, healing relationships, getting other people to say yes, overcoming situations where people say no, and the list goes on and on. I was hoping to find an author or person who could put everything in one nice, neat package to have it all make sense and stick permanently in my mind. After years of searching and study of many books by numerous authors on diverse topics, my search is over! I have found the solution, and I'll tell you about it in this book. I hope this book will be a great "one-stop shopping place" for you on the subjects of finances, family, and faith. Purchasing, reading, but most importantly, *utilizing* this book could save you the expense of building a library as expansive as mine, the time of reading many different books that bring you to the conclusion that there wasn't much new insight or information, and the storage space for all of that information (in your house or office, as well as in your brain). I've found that if I can take one thing away from a book, a seminar, or a meeting that helps me improve, I feel I've spent my time wisely. I hope you can find *your* "one thing" inside the covers of this book.

Let's Keep It Simple, OK?

When you've finished reading this book, I hope that you will start to see life as uncomplicated as it really should be. In my life, and probably in yours, I've found that it's usually best to follow the "K.I.S.S." principle. If you don't know, K.I.S.S. means "keep it simple, silly."

When I was younger, I thought I was too smart to keep things simple. I made good grades, had an academic scholarship to a major university, and thought I had to know every detail, why it worked that way, and what other options were available. Afterwards, I always looked back at the decisions that were made to find out why another choice might have been better. Now, I've learned enough to know that I see people who have a great deal more intelligence than I do, people such as homemakers, musicians, pastors, teachers, clients… everyday people… not just people with PhD's writing books, teaching classes, and making an impact on a national or international basis. *I've learned that a true sign of intelligence is when someone notices how much he really doesn't know.* Do you think you know a lot, or do you know that you don't know very much? Your willingness to buy and read this book shows that you're smart enough to know there are better ways to handle your finances, family, and faith. This book will help teach you more about each subject - and yourself. Let's get started! I have confidence that after reading this book you will agree that life is very complicated, but it doesn't have to be.

SECTION I

FINANCES

SECTION I - FINANCES

Chapter One

Where Are You Now?

"I get my statements in the mail, but I have no idea how to understand them."
"I don't have a clue about any of our finances; my husband/wife handles that."
"We can't ever seem to get ahead. Something always comes up that we end up spending a lot of money on."
"We can't afford to make a monetary contribution to a church, but we hope to be able to do that in the future."
"We don't believe in insurance. All you do is pay the insurance company, and you never get anything back from what you paid for."
"Whenever I need to know anything about money or finances, I ask my father-in-law/next door neighbor/boss."
"The only thing we'll ever consider investing in is bank certificates of deposit because we don't want to risk any money at all."
"We've got to have a will drawn up, but we've just never had the time to get it done."
"We don't know who to trust with our investments with all the negative things that have happened with the market, companies, and investment companies."

"My husband/wife will be just fine if I were to die. I don't need any more insurance."
"We don't have enough money to go talk to a financial professional."

Do any of these statements sound like something you've said before? How about someone in your family or a coworker? These are common statements that I hear from people who could benefit from reading the first section of this book regarding finances.

"Money makes the world go 'round" is a correct statement, but in no way is money (or finances) supposed to dominate your life. Dalai Lama, from *What Money Really Means* by Thomas M. Kostigen, said, "Money is good. It is important. Without money, daily survival – not to mention further development – is impossible. At the same time, it is wrong to consider money a god or a substance endowed with some power of its own. To think that money is everything, and that just by having lots of it all our problems will be solved is a serious mistake."[1] People are working multiple jobs, filing bankruptcy (in 2001, there was a fourteen percent increase in the number of national bankruptcy filings over the previous year)[2], or working longer (Americans work an average of thirty-six more hours per year – almost a full week – compared to the number of hours worked in 1990)[3] in an attempt to recover from debts and expenses incurred earlier in life or to work towards retirement. These people, had they obtained a basic understanding earlier in life of income, taxes, spending, saving, investing, insuring, and protecting wealth, would be having a much more enjoyable life right now. The typical graduate student leaves school with four credit cards and an average balance of $4,778.[4] The average undergraduate student had an average of $18,900 in student loan debt in 2003. The average student loan debt for undergraduate students has increased sixty-six percent since 1997.[5]

Are you one of those people mentioned above? Do you have "more month than money?" Do you have a basic understanding of how much you need to save and/or invest in order to have a sufficient retirement? Have you planned for a college education for your children? Do you understand your health insurance, life insurance, disability insurance, and retirement benefits offered through your employer? Do you constantly get a large tax refund every year? Do you regularly have to pay additional taxes when you file your return? Have you talked with your family about your estate plan? Have you named guardians for your young children?

The following chapters in Section I should help you obtain a better understanding of some of the issues revealed in the questions outlined above. Each topic that we will discuss could (and probably does) have an entire book written just on that subject, so please remember that I am simply trying to provide you with the basic, vital information to get you pointed in the right direction. This basic information will give you a solid foundation to be able to have an intelligent conversation about your finances with a banker, lawyer, accountant, or financial planner and remove any fear or intimidation that you may have about the topic of finances. I've met with a lot of people who finally decided at the age of sixty that it was time to go find out what they need to know about their finances and how to address any shortcomings. My goal is to educate you so that you know what the issues are in life, what is basically the right or wrong direction, and who you should talk with to help you. Federal Reservc Chairman Alan Greenspan said in recent TV and radio ads, "No matter who you are, making informed decisions about what to do with your money will help build a more stable financial future for you and your family."[6]

Know "What You Have and Who You Owe"

The first step to take is to make a detailed list of your assets and liabilities. I like to refer to this as listing "what you have and who you owe." You'll want to write this information down and bring it with you to your first meeting with your financial professional. Start with an inventory of your most valuable assets (home, other real estate, retirement accounts, investments, vehicles, life insurance cash value) and work down through all of your assets (checking, savings, personal property). Make a column on the left to write the name of the assets that you own and then make a column on the right to record how much each asset is worth. If it's a bank account, you'll know exactly what it's worth on that particular day. It's OK to put an average value if your account fluctuates every month. If the asset is a piece of real estate, record a "best guess" estimate of the realistic amount that you feel you could obtain if you sold the property today. Be as accurate as possible; it doesn't do any good to low-ball the estimate or inflate the value. This is just for your benefit, and you deserve accuracy, don't you?

I find that it's easier to use a blank sheet of paper, but if you'd like a form to fill out to help you, there is a worksheet at the end of this chapter. There are also plenty of resources available to you at the office of your financial professional, your local bank, my website at www.walteronline.com, or other Internet sites to help you make sure that you've got everything accounted for. In addition to knowing how much each asset is worth, you'll need to know how the asset is titled. Another way to say this is to ask, "Whose name is on the asset?" or, "Who owns or has control of the asset?" I usually write this beside the name of the asset. For example, an IRA would be in your name only, but your home would probably be in both yours and your spouse's name, unless the house was owned by one of you prior to marriage. Next to each asset, write down when you bought or acquired that asset and how much you paid for it. If you don't know this information, your financial professional can help you. I would take the time to list any asset that is worth over $500.

Here's an example of what you might have written:

Home - (jointly owned)	$150,000	1999/$120,000
Checking Account - (wife only)	$5,000	
IRA - (husband only)	$50,000	
Vehicle #1 - (jointly owned)	$20,000	2003/$25,000

Be sure you list everything!

"Who you owe," or liabilities, should be listed also. It helps tremendously to know exactly how much you owe, the amount of the payment, when the payment is due, what interest rate you're being charged, and when the loan will be paid off. This includes your home mortgage, car loan(s), credit cards, personal loans, student loans, open lines of credit, etc. All of this information can generally be found on your most recent statement.

An example of "who you owe" may be something like this:

Mortgage ($800 per month, 7% interest, paid off 12/2020)	$110,000
Vehicle #1 Loan ($340 per month, 8% interest, paid off 1/2006)	$12,000
Credit Card #1 (19% interest, $40 minimum payment)	$10,000

Again, be sure you list everything! If your monthly payment to a liability such as a credit card varies, you won't really know when that loan will be paid off, so do the best you can to estimate. A representative at a local bank or your financial professional can help you find out how to address this issue.

Next, add up the market value (what your asset would sell for if you tried to sell it in the newspaper) of all your assets. This is your "Total Assets" value. Once you have that number, add up the total amount of the payoff figures on all of your liabilities. Once you have that number, subtract your liabilities from your assets, and you'll get your "Total Net Worth." This number is basically what you are worth on paper, and it may be negative if you owe a lot of money on credit cards, close to $0 if you're just getting started, and a large positive number if you're approaching retirement or have been a good manager of your finances.

Take some time now to go ahead and answer question #1 at the end of this chapter. Use the worksheet to try and make a rough outline of your assets, your liabilities, and your resulting net worth. This number does not have to be exact, but accuracy does help in the long run. Your financial professional can help you fine-tune your figures. When you get done with that, come back to the section below, and we'll move on to the next step, "Work on a Budget."

Work on a Budget

Ok, now you know basically how much you're worth. How does it feel? Are you encouraged or discouraged? Keep the faith because we'll talk about how to help make things better! If you've found your net worth to be negative because you owe more than the value you have in assets, then your budget will probably show you where you can try to start taking steps to save or make money to move your net worth to a positive dollar amount.

In order to get a firm grasp on what you're spending, you'll need to track your expenses for about three months. If you use checks and credit cards for most of your purchases, you can probably look back at your last three months' statements and see where you spent your money. If you use cash to make purchases, you'll probably need to track your next three months (unless you can remember where you spent every dime or you kept every receipt). Carry a piece of paper with you and write down everything you spend or keep the receipts for the next three months.

If you have major expenses that you pay once or twice per year that weren't paid in the three months you're looking at (such as car insurance, homeowners insurance, property taxes, etc), be sure you include a monthly average amount for that expense. For example, if your car insurance is $600 per year, and you pay that every January, make sure your budget reflects a $50 per month outlay for car insurance ($600 annual expense divided by twelve months equals $50 per month). Missing one of these major expenses can really throw a wrench in a well-intended budget! Use the worksheet provided in question #2 at the end of this chapter to help you work on your budget. You can also visit www.crown.org and utilize their expense tracking and budgeting tools that are available. The worksheet along Crown's budgeting programs and forms will help you find out how much you should be spending on each category or expense based on your income. Remember, this book is trying to make you aware of the issues and to equip you to find the right people or places to carry things further.

Again, start with your largest monthly expenses first… mortgage or rent, property taxes, homeowner's insurance (fire, wind, theft, etc), flood insurance (if you're in a flood zone), and mortgage insurance. Mortgage insurance is typically paid if you owe more than 80% of the value of your home to your mortgage company. For example, if your home is worth $100,000 and your mortgage balance is $90,000, you have a 90% "loan to value" ratio and you are probably paying mortgage insurance. These first items may already be included in your monthly mortgage payment, so look at your mortgage statement for an itemization. Your next largest expense may be tithes and offerings to your church, a car loan, car insurance, gasoline for your car, electricity, cable TV, natural gas for your house, water/sewer, credit card debt, student loans. Be sure you get everything!

If you find that you are spending more every month than you bring in, don't worry about it as it's not a big deal. I'm just joking with you; you should be worried! You've got some work to do… but you probably already know that, don't you? However, you're not alone. The average American today spends more than he makes as evidenced by the high number of bankruptcies, foreclosures, repossessions, and credit repair agencies. This is a hole that we Americans are digging for ourselves that is only going to get deeper unless we take aggressive steps to put an end to it. Statistics show that more and more people know less and less about money. High school students in 2002 scored an average of 50.2% on financial literacy tests versus a score of 57.3% in 1997.[7] I'm glad you're doing all you can to help yourself. Reading this book is a great start!

So that we can see what a healthy picture of income and expense looks like, let's talk about Mr. Bill Smith. We'll use the sample budget percentages provided by Crown Financial Ministries as our guide, but I have modified them slightly based upon my experience.

Bill is an extremely nice but fictional guy who is thirty-five years old and works at a large company that pays him a steady salary of $50,000 per year. Let's track his salary from the time the check is processed at his employer until it ends up in his savings account.

(One quick side note here... these illustrations have some detail that may cause some people to be tempted to skim over them. Please, do yourself a favor and look at each item line by line. Take your time, make notes in the margin, compare the illustrations to your situation, and really try to understand what's going on and why. Get your most recent pay stub out and compare your deductions to Bill's deductions. Note: If you make $25,000 per year, you can basically divide all these numbers in half... if you make $100,000 per year, you can basically multiply these numbers times two. Even if you don't entirely grasp what's being talked about, the time you spend trying will get you that much closer to understanding! We will discuss what each item means later, but this illustration is to help you see the big picture. Hang in there and take your time. You can do it!)

Example of Bill Smith's Monthly Income and Expenses:

Annual Income	$50,000
Monthly Income ($50,000 ÷ 12)	$4,166.66/mo
Gross pay reported on check (per month)	$4,166.66
Less *Pre-Tax Deductions* taken out of paycheck:	
401(k) (10% of gross salary)	$416.66
Health Insurance	$100.00
Dental Insurance	$30.00
Disability Insurance	$50.00
Taxable Income Remaining	$3,570.00

Less *After-Tax Deductions* taken out of paycheck:	
Life Insurance ($100,000 coverage)	$10.00
Federal Income Tax (15% paid to IRS)	$535.00
Social Security Tax (1/2 of 6.2% = 3.1%)	$130.00
Medicare Tax (1/2 of 1.45%)	$30.00
Take-Home Pay	**$2,865.00**

After Bill gets his take-home pay of $2,865.00 per month in his checking account, the math continues:

Less:	
Donation to Church (10% of gross pay– *rounded*)	$415.00
Net Spendable Income	**$2,450.00**
Less:	
Housing (typically 38% of **Net Spendable Income**. This is the number above in bold print and includes Mortgage/Rent, Insurance, Property Taxes, Electricity, Gas, Water, Lawn, Phone, Maintenance, Cable TV, Pest Control, etc.)	$931.00
Groceries (15% of Net Spendable Income)	$368.00
Transportation (15% of Net Spendable Income and includes car payments, gas and oil, auto insurance, licenses and taxes, maintenance/repair/replace)	$368.00
Debts (6% of Net Spendable Income and this includes credit card payments, student loans, personal loans. This does not include your house payment or car loans – which is where Americans are having trouble.)	$147.00

Entertainment/Recreation (8% of Net Spendable Income and includes eating out, baby-sitters, activities/trips, vacation, pets, recreation, music) $196.00
Clothing (6% of Net Spendable Income) $147.00
Miscellaneous (6% of Net Spendable Income) $147.00
Savings (6% of Net Spendable Income – *rounded*) $146.00

(If Bill had children, he should budget approximately 5-7% of his Net Spendable Income on childcare, diapers, etc. He would have to reduce his other expenses by that same percentage to retain a balanced budget. For example, he might choose to reduce his miscellaneous expenses by 3% and his clothing by 3% in order to have 6% of his Net Spendable Income available to spend on children.)

Net Spendable Income less expenses **$0**

That $0 sure makes it look like Bill has absolutely zero dollars left at the end of the month, but look a little closer. Bill deposited $146 into a savings account to go along with the money he had already placed in the account for emergencies from previous months. He's also put $416.66 into his 401(k) to invest for retirement. A balanced budget means that every dollar is accounted for and has a purpose. When every dollar is accounted for, you're living with a balanced budget!

Can you see any way to get your budget working as well as Bill has his budget working for him? The numbers and descriptions don't tell the full story of how people like Bill go through the same hunger pains that you do... hunger pains to "keep up with the Joneses" and to have the newest TV, to go on great vacations, to drive the latest car, to have the best looking clothes, etc. My pastor has said frequently that people who try to keep up with the Joneses find themselves always going out to borrow more money than the Joneses. The Bible says, *"Just as the rich rule the poor, so the borrower is servant to the lender."*[8] How many people do you know (or are you actually this person) who have to work hard at their job(s), and can't take a vacation because they'd get behind in their bills? Life is too short to be strapped to making monthly payments to car loans, credit cards, personal loans, student loans, mortgages, "90-day same as cash" loans, and "no interest" promotions. People like Bill know that having a successful financial life is about making sacrifices and being aware that the benefit of buying something today means that you won't have that money in the future. Not only will you not have the money you spent, you will not have the interest that money could have earned through the years until you needed it. If you have something today, it probably means you won't have something in the future, unless it is an appreciating (it goes up in value, not down) asset. Money can be used today, or it can be used tomorrow, and it should ideally be there for you in either time when you need it. A balanced budget and a financial plan help you know how much needs to go towards which item.

Did you know that $1,000 spent on a vacation today, could have grown to be over $6,700 in twenty years based on that money growing at a rate of 10% per year? That means that $5,000 spent today on a vacation, TV, stereo, and clothes could have grown to be over $33,600! That's a pretty expensive vacation when you look at it that way, isn't it? Yes, we need the basic necessities and we need to balance an enjoyable life today with an enjoyable retirement, but we should be prudent, stay within prudent budgeting guidelines, and be able to say "no" when our income and expense says "no way!" *"The wise man saves for the future, but the foolish man spends whatever he gets."* [9]

Things You Need To Do Now

1. **Neatly complete the net worth calculator provided below.** This is simply a list of your assets and their values, followed by a list of your liabilities and their values. This is just a rough estimate. If you're married, combine everything together. Do not worry about being exact. You're just trying to get in the ballpark. Use any blank space to make notes and add up the totals for each line item.

Net Worth Analysis
ASSETS

Asset Name/Description	Approximate Value
All liquid money – checking, savings, money market accounts	______________
Investments (non-retirement)	______________
Home Market Value	______________
Other real estate (investment, vacation, etc.)	______________
Business value (how much could you sell the business for today after deducting for business debts?)	______________
Vehicles, boats, planes (anything transportation or recreation)	______________
Jewelry, household furnishings, etc.	______________
Loans to others (money owed to you)	______________
Other assets	______________
Employer provided retirement plans (profit sharing, 401(k), etc.)	______________
IRA's (traditional, roth)	______________
Educational IRA's and 529 Plans	______________
Cash value of life insurance (*cash value,* not the *death benefit*)	______________
Annuities (fixed and variable)	______________
TOTAL ASSETS	______________

LIABILITIES

Liability Name/Description	**Approximate Balance**
Mortgages on the home (total of 1st, 2nd, or all mortgages)	________________
Mortgages on other real estate	________________
Car loans (total of all car loans)	________________
Credit cards (total of all credit cards – yes, all of them!)	________________
Student loans	________________
Other debts (medical, recent purchases. Anything not included above)	________________
TOTAL LIABILITIES	________________
NET WORTH (TOTAL ASSETS minus TOTAL LIABILITIES)	________________

Were you able to complete this fairly easily? If so, that's great! If not, this book will really help you. How do you feel about your net worth? Embarrassed, confused, surprised, shocked, or impartial are words that might come to mind. How do you think you could change this number?

2. Look back over your last three months, or track the next three months' worth of expenses and write them down neatly in the worksheet below. This worksheet is an example of an average of a three-month period. If you're married, add up income and expense from both spouses. If your spouse doesn't want to cooperate, just estimate as best you can on your own without causing a family ordeal. (We'll talk more about family ordeals and situations like this later in the book.)

CURRENT MONTHLY INCOME AND EXPENSE

INCOME

Gross earned income is your pay before you have any deductions from your paycheck. DO NOT use *take-home pay*. To determine your monthly gross earned income, divide your annual salary by 12 or multiply your hourly wages times 173. For example, $15 per hour x 173 = $2,595/mo

Your gross earned income ________________

Pension or fixed income (You don't have to go to *work* to get it.) ________________

Social Security income (if you're retired, disabled, or a widow(er)) ________________

Business income, profits, commissions *(Use a monthly average.)* ________________

Net rental income *(profits from renting real estate)* ________________

Investment income *(interest, withdrawals from accounts, etc.)* ________________

TOTAL GROSS INCOME ________________

EXPENSES

(Don't forget to include annual expenses such as taxes & insurance and divide them by 12.)

Expenses usually deducted from your paycheck before you get your take-home pay

Federal and state income taxes *(usually noted on your pay stub)* ________________

Payroll taxes *(Social Security, Medicare, etc. See your pay stub.)* ________________

Health, dental, life, disability, long-term care insurance *(if provided through your employer)* ____________________

Your contributions to retirement accounts, stock purchase plans, etc. ____________________

Other expenses on your paycheck ____________________

Total expenses before you get your take-home pay ____________________

Net Spendable Income *(gross income minus expenses incurred before take-home pay)* ____________________

Expenses Incurred after you get your take-home-pay

Charitable donations including religious affiliations ____________________

Housing *(total of items below)* ____________________

- Monthly mortgage(s) or rent ____________
- Monthly average for fire, wind, flood, earthquake, etc. insurance on your home (see your mortgage statement) ____________
- Monthly average for property taxes ____________
- Utilities – electricity, gas, water, TV, phone, cell phone, pager, Internet ____________
- Maintenance & repairs ____________

Groceries *(not "eating out" as that is entertainment. This is for food you prepare and eat at home)* ____________________

Transportation *(total of items below)* ____________________

- Payments ____________
- Gas and oil ____________
- Insurance ____________
- Licenses and taxes ____________
- Maintenance, repair, and replace ____________
- Other ____________

Insurance *(total of items below - be sure you don't double-count these in other places)* __________
- Life Insurance ________
- Health ________
- Other ________

Debts *(credit cards, personal and student loans - not house or car)* __________

Entertainment/Recreation *(total of items below)* __________
- Eating out – This is a toughie! ________
- Baby-sitters (not daycare) ________
- Activities and local trips (zoo, etc.) ________
- Vacation (travel, hotel, etc.) ________
- Pets and other ________

Clothing __________

Savings *(short-term savings – not for retirement or investments)* __________

Medical Expenses *(total of items below)* __________
- Doctor ________
- Dentist ________
- Prescriptions ________
- Other ________

Miscellaneous *(total of items below)* __________
- Toiletries and cosmetics ________
- Beauty and barber ________
- Laundry and cleaning ________
- Allowances ________
- Subscriptions ________
- Gifts (including Christmas) ________
- Cash ________
- Other ________

Investments *(anything not defined as short-term savings)* __________

School and child care *(total of items below)* __________
- Tuition __________
- Materials __________
- Transportation __________
- Day Care (necessary so that you can go to work) __________

Total "after take-home pay" expenses __________

Monthly Surplus or Deficit __________

This is your current way of spending money. How do you feel about this monthly outlay? What can you do to change that?

3. **Make a budget that you would like to stick to for the next six months.** A *budget* is not spending money in the same fashion you have in the past; that's called *tracking expenses*. A *budget* is a defined breakout of expenses and the maximum amount that you will spend on that category for that month. It's a manual. When you've spent your entire month's money that you had allotted for entertainment, no more entertainment until next month. Discipline is the key, and you can do it! Visit www.walteronline.com for some great tools and links to resources (such as www.crown.org) that are available to you to help you determine how much you should be spending on each category, to help you track and manage your expenses, and to help you understand the deeper reasoning behind making these changes. To determine the percentages of your budget, divide your monthly total for an expense by your total gross income for a month. For example, if you spend $825 per month on housing and your gross income per month is $3,750, then you're spending about 22% of your monthly gross income on housing. Basically, your budget should strive to be fairly close to the following percentages of **gross income** for each expense:

Expense	Guideline % of Gross Income	Your Actual % of Gross Income
Gifts to church & charity	10%	________
Income & payroll taxes, etc.	20%	________
Housing	22%	________
Food	8%	________
Transportation	9%	________
Insurance	4%	________
Debts	4%	________
Entertainment & recreation	5%	________
Clothing	3%	________
Savings	4%	________
Medical Expenses	3%	________
Miscellaneous	4%	________
Investments	4%	________
Total Percentages	**100%**	________
School and Child Care	4%	________

(Please note that the School and Child Care category is *in excess* of the 100%. This means that if you have a need for this expense in your budget, you need to reduce some other expenses so that you can make room for this 4%. For example, you may decide to reduce Investments by 2% and Miscellaneous by 2%.) Good luck with getting your budget in order. It sometimes takes years, but it always requires you to take the first step. Take that first step today!

4. **Organize your finances.** If you are computer literate or you're willing to learn, use a financial program like Quicken® or Microsoft Money®. If you are not comfortable with putting your financial information into a computer program, develop a good filing system and a hardcopy of your financial data. Going forward, you should be able to find out your net worth and determine how much you spent last month in less than five minutes. You should also be able to put your hands on a copy of last year's tax return very quickly.

Many thanks to Crown Financial Ministries for their budget outline that I modified in these exercises and the impact that it's clarity had on our family's budget!

SECTION I - FINANCES

Chapter Two

Who Can Help?

Chapter One helped you:

- Take an inventory of your current financial situation
- Track your income and expenses
- Set up a budget.

Now, you're ready to move ahead onto the highway that leads to financial success! This chapter will talk about reasons why you should have someone help guide you down this road to financial security and how financial professionals help people make good financial decisions.

Why Should Someone Ask for Financial Advice?

You've heard the saying "two heads are better than one," and I firmly agree with that principle. Another person's opinion, especially from someone who is qualified to talk specifically about that topic, can do wonders to ensure that you are making prudent and well-informed decisions. Even if you are educated about the issues, are intelligent enough to weigh the pros and cons of the alternatives at hand, and are confident enough to try to tackle life's issues on your own, you can benefit from having an objective sounding board available to discuss things with you and ask you questions about issues you might need to give further thought. The Bible says, *"The way of a fool is right in his own eyes, but a wise man is he who listens to counsel."*[1] In order for someone to be able to *listen* to counsel, they must have first *sought* counsel. Ben Franklin said, "They that will not be counseled, cannot be helped. If you do not hear reason, she will rap you on the knuckles." Charles Schwab, chairman and co-CEO of Charles Schwab Corp., said in January 2003 in the *Wall Street Journal*, "Investors don't know what to believe, so they've taken an understandable course of action: Don't believe anything. In my four decades working with individual investors, I've never seen such a crisis of trust."[2] You must, as a prudent and reasonable person, seek out, listen to, and act on the counsel of a professional.

It is not an embarrassment to admit to a doctor you don't know how to fix your broken leg, heal your sore throat, or perform surgery; nor is it an embarrassment to tell an attorney that you would like some help reviewing the documents you'll be signing when you buy or sell a piece of real estate. When you are in need of surgery, do you call your father-in-law for a second opinion? When your car needs repair, do you ask your pastor to take a peek under the hood? When your air conditioner at your house stops cooling in the middle of August, do you ask your neighbor to see if he can fix it? Sure you don't. You go to the most qualified person that you can afford. As Robert Half once said, "Free advice is worth the price."

I often say that I work with people who don't have the *time*, the *desire*, or the *knowledge* to handle their own investments, financial planning, and estate planning. You probably fall into one, two, or all three of those categories of people. If you have the *time* to handle your finances, then you probably could be using that time enjoying a hobby or directly interacting with your family. Your time should be so valuable to you that can't afford *not* to delegate this aspect of your life. If you have the *desire* to handle your finances, that's great! Channel that desire into becoming educated enough about the subject so that you can have intelligent, time-efficient conversations with your financial professional in order to better understand the advice you're receiving. If you have the knowledge about how to handle your finances, and, believe it or not most people do, then use that *knowledge* to get a basic understanding of your financial issues and to find a financial professional you can trust. After that, try to occupy your mind with other projects to improve your happiness, health, faith, family life, work environment, or productivity.

The prudent and wise thing to do when you have a problem is call the appropriate person or company to deal most effectively with the issue you're addressing at that moment. When it comes to dealing with your money and your finances, you want someone to tell you what's wrong (hopefully in a nice way), to advise how you should address the problem, and to inform you about how much time the meeting will take and what the cost will be. When you've done these things, you've sought advice. The next step requires you to listen to and follow that advice.

The First Step... A Financial Professional

The first step in the right direction on your highway to financial security, if you are *serious* about improving your financial situation, is one that leads you to a relationship with a qualified financial professional. Qualified financial professionals may be found in brokerage firms, insurance companies, banks, independent agencies and broker dealers - just to name a few. They may have titles such as financial consultant, financial professional, financial specialist, financial adviser, insurance agent, stockbroker, or investment counselor, and I will use these words interchangeably throughout the book. They come in all shapes, sizes, ages, and colors. The best financial professional for you is someone who, first and foremost, knows what she's doing. She must also have the time, the desire, and the integrity to find out and do what's best for you. You have the right to shop around for the right adviser, and you have the right to change advisers if you feel you can get a more comfortable relationship along with better quality advice and results from someone else.

Some financial professionals, myself included, take steps over and above their firms' basic training and licensing requirements to become CERTIFIED FINANCIAL PLANNER™ practitioners. A financial professional that has successfully met certain strenuous requirements may also call himself (or herself) a CFP *certificant* or a CFP *professional*. There are many non-CFP professionals in the world who have competently and prudently been advising people for years. In fact, the majority of financial professionals are not CFP certificants. In fact, the majority of financial professionals are not CFP certificants. By the end of 2002, there were only about 40,000 CFP certificants in the United States.[3] Because of the additional knowledge and expertise potentially available from a CFP certificant, it is important that you have some idea of what additional benefits and peace of mind a CFP practitioner may bring to your situation.

A CERTIFIED FINANCIAL PLANNER Practitioner

A CERTIFIED FINANCIAL PLANNER™ certificant is a person who has been awarded the title and certification by successfully completing a series of rigorous financial planning courses and examinations. The courses and exams are then followed by a two-day, ten-hour comprehensive examination administered according to the CERTIFIED FINANCIAL PLANNER™ Board of Standards, Inc., much like the board exam that an attorney or doctor must pass in order to practice his profession.

In other words, a CFP practitioner has training concerning the following subjects:

- Financial Planning
- Income Tax Planning
- Retirement Planning and Employee Benefits
- Estate Planning
- Investment Management
- Insurance

In addition, a person must have a minimum of three years' experience in the financial planning process prior to earning the right to use the CFP certification mark. A person must also have a clean and ethical background that does not have a history of criminal, civil, governmental, or self-regulatory agency proceedings or inquiries. And, beginning in 2007, a person must have a bachelor's degree.

A CFP professional brings additional financial planning knowledge and credentials to work for you along with being held accountable to a higher standard of ethics and responsibilities than traditional financial professionals, consultants, and brokers. There are severe sanctions for those CFP professionals who do not abide by the following principles. These sanctions and penalties are in addition to any actions taken by regulatory agencies and the consultant's firm. The governing board for CFP practitioners requires that the following ethical principles be followed by all CFP certificants. Also included are the benefits to you, the client, of each principle. A CFP certificant must agree to display:

Integrity - Honesty and candor that is not compromised by a consultant's desire for personal gain or advantage. The CFP practitioner must have character deserving of trust and be a person who will put your interests in front of his.

Objectivity - Intellectual honesty, impartiality, and an ability to step back from a situation and analyze it based on the facts at hand, regardless of the ramifications of the decision. The CFP professional must be poised at all times and able to keep his business decisions separate from any emotions.

Competence - Knowledge and skill to provide adequate and timely services to clients; the awareness of when a referral to a specialist may be appropriate; and the commitment to staying on top of changes in the economy, laws, markets, professional regulations, etc. Basically, the CFP professional must know what he's doing!

Fairness - Fair and reasonably priced services are provided and conflicts of interest are disclosed. This requires impartiality, honesty, and an ability to treat others in the same way that you would like to be treated. If someone is fair and treats people fairly, everyone should be happy.

Confidentiality - Your private information is kept private unless legally required to be disclosed. You won t have to worry about other people finding out about your private financial affairs.
Professionalism - A CFP practitioner treats clients and other professionals with dignity and courtesy, regardless of how much someone is worth on paper. You deserve to have someone who can treat you with the highest level of respect.
Diligence - A CFP professional ensures that proper planning and supervision of the services are provided to you in a prompt and thorough manner. The CFP certificant is responsible for making sure that all the details are taken care of and accounted for.

The qualifications and requirements outlined by the CERTIFIED FINANCIAL PLANNER Board of Standards do an excellent job of weeding out anyone who is not qualified to be a CFP professional due to a questionable ethical background, a lack of an ability to communicate an understanding of the required knowledge, an unsatisfactory record with regulatory agencies, a history of client complaints, and an insufficient amount of time in the financial planning business. The end result from having these additional qualifications is that you, the investor – the client - are more protected, better informed, and can more easily decide who is most worthy of earning your trust and your business. The additional knowledge, experience, and continuing education possessed by a CFP practitioner will benefit you over the long run. You can search for a CFP practitioner in your area by visiting http://www.cfp.net.

Now that you know the reasons why you might want to look for a financial professional that is a CFP certificant, let's talk about what a financial professional (whether or not he's a CFP certificant) does and how he gets compensated.

What Does a Financial Professional Do?

I get this question a good bit, and the short answer that I usually give is, "I can advise you on just about any financial issue that you may encounter in your lifetime." Such financial issues may be investing for retirement, college, or future needs; term and cash value life insurance; long-term care insurance (also known as nursing home insurance); estate planning; income tax planning; income structuring and protection; budgeting; business sale; business retirement planning [401(k)'s, 403b's, SIMPLE or SEP IRA's, profit sharing plans, etc]. The details in the remainder of the financial section of the book will give you a better idea of the details regarding what a financial professional does.

How Does a Financial Professional Get Paid?

I'm sure you've heard people say, "You get what you pay for" or, "There's no free lunch." In my experience, this is very true in finding someone to adequately guide you in your finances.

There are three main ways that financial professionals are compensated as an investment and personal financial planning advisors:

- Commission - The investor pays a fee at the time of purchase, could potentially pay a fee at the time of sale, or a combination of both
- Fee based - An annual percentage of the assets under management is deducted from the account
- Hourly - A fee per hour is paid based upon the amount of time the financial professional took to complete a financial plan, a meeting, a phone call, service, etc.

We will talk about specific examples later. These three variations of compensation will vary between professionals, and one pricing method for one person may not be the best one for another person. It is the responsibility of the financial professional to propose to you the most appropriate way to be compensated, and it is up to you to ask further questions, to negotiate further, and to accept or decline the proposal. Also, please keep in mind that any businessperson is in business to earn a *fair and reasonable* living for people that have similar education, qualifications, and experience. They are in business to make a profit. I'm sure you go to work expecting to receive a paycheck for what you do during your workday and you realize that if someone didn't pay for the goods and services that you produce at work, there wouldn't be a paycheck waiting for you on pay day. We're all in favor of finding the best value we can for our dollars, but there is a great deal to be said about loyalty, fairness, and the real meaning of the word *value.*

When my wife and I first moved to Panama City about seven years ago, I was so tight with money you could hear me squeak when I walked. Do you know anyone or are you like this? I would compare prices and benefits, haggle, negotiate, and try to find any opportunity I could to get something as cheaply as possible. An example of this would be my search for a moving van when Wendy and I moved from Tennessee to Florida. A local tire sales and repair shop was also the local representative for a moving van company. I met with them and confirmed a reservation for their largest moving van for a certain date. When that date arrived, they didn't have the right sized van and they couldn't find another truck anywhere near our location. Due to deadlines in Tennessee where I had to go pick up our furniture, I had to do our best with a smaller truck. I was not pleased with the inconvenience and asked them to give me as many blankets and a tow dolly at no charge. They agreed to do so because they felt bad about not having the truck I had reserved. I went to Tennessee and packed that truck so that there wasn't a one single vacant square inch available to put anything else in. The truck was completely full – even the driver's and passenger's seats. But, as I'm sure you can guess, it didn't come close to being large enough for us to take everything. We left a lot of our possessions sitting outside of the house we were leaving and hoped for the best.

We hauled that load to Florida, unloaded it, and returned to the dealer to see what they could do for us. The owner didn't *have* to do anything as he had fulfilled his obligation to give me an operational truck. It was my decision to accept the smaller truck. However, he allowed me to take the truck to Tennessee again so that I could fill it up with the remaining items and return to Florida at little or no cost. He really went out of his way to help me find a truck so that I could get everything to Florida, and I didn't have to spend more money by making two trips in a truck that charges its fee based upon the number of miles it travels. I thanked him at that time, but, to be honest, I still had some hard feelings for all of the headaches.

Several months later, my wife needed new tires on her car. The cost at the tire dealership was about $300, but I could get them at Wal-Mart for $250. Can you guess where I went? I went to Wal-Mart because at that point in my life I was determined to save every dollar I could, regardless of the relationships I had with other people or what they had done for me in the past. I now see the bigger picture, and I hope this story opens your eyes to the point that I'm making.

The owner of that local tire and moving van dealership did exactly what a financial professional should do for you. He went out of his way to understand what I needed. It was not his fault that the national dealership was not able to get a truck to his location that fit my needs, but he took money out of his pocket to help make up for my inconvenience. I should have known at that time that he was the type of person I would like to see prosper in business. He was the type of person that deserves to make a fair and reasonable profit on the goods and services he provides.

In dealing with him since then, he has always made good on his promises, and I'm sure that I could get oil changes, tires rotated and replaced, and general vehicle maintenance at a cheaper cost at large franchises that have such a huge volume of business they can afford to charge a lower price. But I'm convinced that the value I get from him and his business over time will far outweigh the additional cost I pay him for new tires, oil changes, and service. He deserves to make a profit, and I'm glad that I can help him. He certainly has helped my family and me.

Another example of value in today's marketplace would be

Internet access to investment accounts and online trading. These online brokerage firms charge commissions on stock trades that are a great deal less than what a financial professional or a full-service stockbroker would have to charge. But, I've found that people who try to follow the cheapest route often regret forging out into the financial world alone to buy and sell stocks without any professional advice. As you read the following case studies, think about your situation today, as well as what it might be in the future, and see if you fall into the *cheapest alternative at all costs* personality or the *I want the best value* personality.

Real Examples of a Financial Professional at Work

The following are some examples of how a financial professional has helped clients in dealing with their finances. Please note that these are hypothetical situations and are not based on any individual(s). You may feel inclined to think that one of these situations *exactly* describes your life. Even though you may think your situation is exactly like one of these, there are often many small differences that create the need for other remedies and solutions. You'll notice that several terms such as *IRA* and *mutual fund* are used in these scenarios. Rest assured, later in the book we'll talk more about what those words mean and how they affect you later. The main point here is for you to see that a financial professional can wear many hats while guiding a wide variety of clients toward meeting their financial goals.

Young and Single

A single, twenty-four year old female named Janet, earning $24,000 per year, in meeting with her financial professional, learns that she does not have adequate life insurance and that she needs to begin saving for retirement. He helps Janet determine how much life insurance she needs, takes an application, and will deliver the policy to her when the insurance company finishes its review process. Janet then opens a Roth IRA and signs a form to have $150 per month auto-debited from her checking account to be deposited into the Roth IRA. The financial professional then recommends an appropriate investment for her, and she chooses to work with him on a commission basis. He will be paid a commission each time the money is invested in the Roth IRA and will be paid a commission from the life insurance company for selling the life insurance policy. Janet feels that she's received great service from a trustworthy and competent financial professional.

Working Couple With Children

A husband and wife, Jim and Michelle, both age thirty-five and making $40,000 each, meet with their financial professional to talk about planning for retirement, saving for college for their two kids, obtaining the right amount of life insurance, and reducing the amount of income tax they are paying. After talking in detail about their income, expenses, investment experience, risk tolerance, time horizon, anticipated colleges, and their potential income needs during retirement, the financial professional recommends the following:

- In order to increase the amount saved for retirement and to reduce their current income taxes, they should contribute the maximum allowable amount to each person's retirement plan available through their employers. The financial professional does not get paid any money for making this recommendation as he is compensated when money is invested or policies are purchased through him.
- Open Coverdell Education Savings Accounts to save money for college for the two children. Jim and Michelle open the accounts, decide to add $100 to each account monthly, and decide which investment to purchase inside of each account. The financial professional will be paid a commission on the money invested each month.
- Purchase term-life insurance on both of their lives to provide income to the surviving spouse to replace the income lost from the deceased spouse. The insurance company will pay the financial professional a commission for selling the policies.

The family is unable to contribute to Roth or Traditional IRA's or set up any additional investments, as they simply don't have any more money on a monthly basis to invest because they are still making loan payments on the house and their two cars. The financial professional recommends consolidating their car loans into a home equity loan to increase their tax deductions and lower the interest rate they are paying. They will continue paying the same amount to the home equity loan that they were paying to the car loans, and this will allow them to be able to pay the loan off sooner than if they had kept the car loans. When the home equity loan is paid off they can start saving more for retirement. The financial professional does not get paid anything for making this recommendation.

Married Couple Approaching Retirement

Carl and Susan, husband and wife both sixty years old, meet with their financial consultant as they are excited about their approaching retirement date in two years. Carl makes $80,000 per year and has been at the same job for twenty-five years while Susan is a homemaker who raised their two grown children. Carl has a 401(k) in which he deposits $8,000 each year out of his pay and his company matches $.50 for every dollar he puts in the plan ($4,000). As a result, we find that he's saving 15% of his pay when Carl's contribution of $8,000 is added to his company's contribution of $4,000 for a total amount of $12,000 per year. After talking in detail with them about their income, expenses, investment experience, risk tolerance, time horizon, expected retirement expenses, insurance coverages, etc., the financial consultant recommends the following:

- Invest the $50,000 in their money market account in a tax-favored investment to help increase the amount of money they have for retirement. The financial consultant is generally paid a commission by the company managing the investments, and the Carl and Susan will only have to pay an out-of-pocket charge if they take too much money out of the investment within the first few years.

- Apply for and purchase long-term care insurance policies, if they are approved, to protect them from the great expense of nursing home or in-home care that could be $40,000 or more per year. The policies will cost about $3,000 per year and will prevent them from spending over $40,000 per year if they were to need nursing home or in-home care. The insurance company will pay the financial consultant a commission for selling the policies.
- Discuss "rolling over" the $250,000 in Carl's 401(k) to a Traditional IRA when he retires in order to have more control over the investments, improve his diversification, have more flexibility in structuring his income, give his beneficiaries more flexibility if he were to die, and reduce the number of accounts he has to deal with on a regular basis. The financial consultant does not get paid anything at this time for making this recommendation.
- Verify life insurance coverage amounts and beneficiary designations. The financial consultant does not get paid for this analysis.
- Discuss their estate plan and the different documents that an attorney might advise them to consider such as a will, durable power of attorney, living will, physician's directive, and revocable living trust. The financial consultant also gives them the names of three qualified attorneys to speak with concerning their estate plan. The financial consultant does not get paid for this consultation, but the attorney they choose is paid a flat fee or an hourly rate for his work.

Comfortable Couple Wanting To Protect Their Estate

Robert and Debbie, both sixty-nine years old and married to each other, decide to talk further with their financial professional about making sure that their investments, property, and insurance go to their family and charities; not to the IRS, attorneys, or any other undesirable destinations. Robert receives a pension of $3,000 per month from his company where he worked for twenty-five years. He also receives Social Security benefits of $1,400 per month.

Debbie has a small pension from her teaching career of $600 per month, and her Social Security benefit is $1,100 per month. Robert has a Traditional IRA worth approximately $800,000; Debbie has a Traditional IRA worth approximately $400,000; and they are taking $2,000 per month out of each of these IRA's to travel and enjoy their retirement. The financial professional rolled over Robert's company retirement plan, Debbie's 403(b), and Debbie's DROP distribution into the IRA's several years ago and invested the proceeds in a diversified portfolio of investments. Robert and Debbie have been taking the $2,000 per month out of the IRA's for a couple of years, but the accounts have actually grown from their original amounts. They have an investment they purchased ten years ago that is worth $250,000; a home worth $500,000; a condo on the beach worth $400,000; $10,000 in a checking account; $50,000 in a money market; and $1,000,000 in a joint investment account. After more detailed conversations about how they would like their estate distributed when they both pass away, the financial professional makes the following recommendations:

- Consult their attorney to revise their wills and revocable living trust documents in order to take advantage of the recent income and estate tax changes. There is no compensation to the financial professional, but the attorney is paid a flat fee or an hourly rate.
- Consider creating an *Irrevocable Life Insurance Trust* (ILIT) to help funnel as much of their estate to their children with a smaller estate tax that must be paid to the IRS. The financial professional would be paid a commission for selling a life insurance policy used to accomplish this goal. An attorney would be paid a flat fee or an hourly rate for creating the trust, obtaining a tax identification number for the trust, etc.
- Consider naming qualified charities as the beneficiaries of all or part of the IRA's in order to avoid estate and income taxes to the recipient. Consider a *Charitable Remainder Trust* or a *donor-advised fund* as an alternative for some of the assets in the joint brokerage account in order to obtain an immediate income tax deduction, retain an income stream, and donate

money to charity at their death. There is no compensation to the financial professional for this advice.

- Consider purchasing long-term care insurance in order to protect their estate or surviving spouse from the high expenses of nursing home or in-home care.
- Consider implementing an annual gifting program to family members of up to $11,000 per year per spouse if the overall financial plan shows that annual gifts will not sacrifice their standard of living for the rest of their lives. This means that each spouse could give $11,000 to any person he or she chooses without having to file a gift tax return. As a result, they could give their son $22,000 each year - $11,000 from Robert and $11,000 from Debbie.

Surviving Spouse Searching For Direction

Carrie, a seventy year old widow who just lost her husband, talks with her financial professional to try to make sense of the financial situation her husband left for her. In addition to feeling a tremendous amount of loneliness, uncertainty, and sadness, Carrie feels completely lost without her husband at home as a companion and as the financial manager in the family. She brings in a stack of statements that she has never dealt with. She has no idea how to read the statements, has no idea where her income will be coming from, and can't believe that she just never got around to learning anything about their financial situation. Carrie owns a widely diversified and confusing portfolio of investments and some real estate. A couple of life insurance policies on her husband paid her about $300,000 one month after her husband died. After a great deal of conversation about her life with her husband, their children (whom the financial professional suggested attend the next meeting), and her concerns about the future, the financial professional makes the following recommendations:

- Do not make any major financial decisions or investments until she feels capable of understanding the facts and has had time to recover from the shock of his death.
- Over the next several months, Carrie should track her expenses and then create a budget for the future.

- Suggest that Carrie have her estate planning documents reviewed (or written for the first time) by an attorney when she's ready.
- Assist in making sure that any Social Security payments are properly made or changed.
- Review existing investments to see if any immediate action needs to be taken to prevent income or estate tax problems, losses from improper investments, or investments maturing in the near future.
- Open an account to help assist Carrie in getting the investments in joint name moved into her name only.

The financial professional does not receive any compensation for any of the above services at this time. He will attempt to ensure, as time passes, that Carrie has adequate income and will take the time to educate her (and her family if she so desires) about the appropriate investments she needs to keep, sell, or purchase in order to accomplish her goals of living comfortably for the rest of her life and efficiently passing her estate to her family when she dies.

(These recommendations have a great deal more information that could accompany these brief explanations. That further detail is beyond the scope of this book. Please contact your financial professional to obtain further details as I am simply trying to give you a concise understanding of what resources are generally available to you and what you might expect to pay for those resources.)

As you can see, a common thread woven throughout these case studies is that the financial professional asked a great deal of questions and probably spent a lot of time getting to know these people before he made any recommendations to them. This fact-finding process is crucial in any financial planning relationship. If someone doesn't ask you enough questions to make you feel comfortable that he has your best interests at heart, then you have every right to go find another financial professional.

If you feel led to work with a CFP certificant, but you can't find one to work with, either because there isn't one in your area, you aren't satisfied with the choices that you have, or she is not accepting any new clients at that time, use the information provided in this book, along with a good dose of common sense and judgment of character, and find the next best qualified financial consultant that is not a CFP professional. For your sake, please take the time to ask around and find a financial consultant who has been in the financial planning business for at least three years (but preferably more), has a solid reputation, and has a clean record with the securities and insurance regulatory agencies.

A good financial professional will take the time to get to know you, will be qualified and competent enough to have you trust that he knows what he's doing, and will provide you with regular communication and meetings to keep you informed about current and future financial issues that you will need to address. You deserve to have the most qualified people working on your financial team!

Things You Need To Do Now

1. **Make an appointment to meet with two or three financial professionals or CFP practitioners in your area.** Schedule all three appointments *before* you meet with any of them so that you cannot make an immediate decision on any one person without having the chance to compare all of them against each other. Try to complete these appointments during one week, on your day off, or during your lunch hour for a few days in that week. Remember, you are looking for a person who will take the time to get to know you, who will have your best interests at heart, and who will be a good counselor for you and your family for many, many years to come.

SECTION I - FINANCES

Chapter Three

Accumulating Savings

"It has been estimated that 40% of Americans have not put aside funds for an emergency or job change."[1]

In order to move from where you are today towards your future financial goals, you need to work towards *creating* and *maintaining* a comfortable and prudent amount of money in savings.

What Does the Word *Savings* Mean?

The word *savings* is a very important word that is very different from the word *investments*. Savings is an amount of money that can be used for emergencies, major purchases, vacations, job loss, etc. Savings can be removed from an account (please note that I did not say "removed from under the mattress" or "taken out of the freezer" or "pulled out of an old sock in your drawer") at any time without cost, penalty, or tax implications and that has not been subject to any risk.

Generally, you need three to six months' worth of expenses stored in a savings account that hopefully pays you a decent interest rate. For example, if in Chapter One you saw that you spend about $3,000 per month for all of your expenses, then you need anywhere from $9,000 to $18,000 in savings. If you have a job that pays you a steady salary and if you have adequate health, life, disability, auto, and home insurance, you can probably get by with an equivalent of just three months' salary stored in savings. If you don't have a salaried job, if you work on commission, if your employment is not steady or unpredictable, or if you don't have adequate insurance coverage, then you probably need an amount equal to six months' expenses in savings. Also, if you have a tendency to make large purchases at the spur of the moment, you need to have six months (or more) saved. You also need to work on changing the habit of buying things on impulse!

In the past, I didn't feel it was necessary to keep any money in savings as I felt it was "dead money" and that it was costing me money to leave it there by not having it invested in the stock market or paying down other debts. With the bear market that we endured from 2000 – 2002 (*bear* means bad stock market), I was forcefully reminded of a rule that I knew and that I preached, but not one that I practiced 100% of the time. That rule is, "Don't put any money anywhere near the stock market that you may need within three to five years because you may not have time to make it back if it goes down in value." I put my *savings* money in the stock market thinking (like everyone else did) that I could get a quick 20% return and use those profits to pay off more debt or have even more money in savings. The stock market from 2000 to 2003 humbled a lot of people, including me, and I am determined to have those negative financial experiences be positive memories because I learned something from them. In August of 2003, only forty percent of households kept at least three months' worth of living expenses in savings.[2] The lessons I learned and remember for my own good are now being used to help you! I hope that you can live a better financial life by learning from other people's examples and mistakes.

I learned from those tough market times and my error in thinking that I didn't really need to carry an equivalent of three to six months' expenses in savings because I was a financial planner and that I knew what I was doing even though my pay is based on commission. I have vowed to *create* a cash cushion in savings again and I will *retain* it. You should do the same to prevent your family from possibly losing money that you may need within three to five years in the stock market or from having to go into credit card debt to make car repairs, replace air conditioners, repair roofs, take a vacation, pay hospital bills, or miss work.

Cambridge Credit Index reported in May 2003 that 83 percent of people pay less than half of their credit card balance each month..[3] The average American household carries an average of $8,419 in credit card debt.[4] Amerix reported in 2002 that 70 percent of the people enrolled in debt management programs are women..[5]

Should I Pay Off Debt, Accumulate Savings, or Both?

You may be asking, "Should I pay off some (or all) debt *while* I'm adding to savings or should I pay the debt off completely *before* I start adding to savings?" This is a very good question, and the answer requires you to have completed your homework in Chapter One. If you didn't do your homework in Chapter One, please be fair to yourself and your family by stopping and completing it now.

In order to accumulate money in savings, you might have to stop spending in certain areas. You probably realized that in your net worth and budget analysis. Larry Burkett, the late Christian financial counselor for Crown Financial Ministries, always told callers to his radio show - and I fully agree - that before you start paying down debts on credit cards, autos, credit lines, and personal loans, you need to be sure that you realize how you got into debt in the first place. You must then take steps to make sure that those bad habits don't have you adding back to the debt that you spent six months reducing. If your credit card balance is $3,000 and you see on your prior statements that you have a tendency to eat out a great deal, cut back (or stop) eating out. If you have a tendency to reward yourself by going shopping, taking a trip, or buying a large ticket item after you have done a great job of staying within your budget, then you need to learn to reward yourself in other ways.

> You should aggressively pay down any debt that has a fixed interest rate greater than 8% and any variable interest rate debt that has an interest rate greater than 5%

To directly answer the question of whether or not you should pay off debt, accumulate savings, or both, my *rule of thumb* is that you should aggressively pay down any debt that has a *fixed interest rate greater than 8%* and *any variable interest rate debt that has an interest rate greater than 5%*. If the rate is fixed and is below 8%, that's actually a pretty good rate for almost any loan in any interest rate environment. If it's a variable rate that's charging you over 5%, get started today in your attempt to pay it down because a rise in interest rates could get you deeper in financial trouble very quickly. Pay down the debts that have the highest interest rate first because they are the ones that are digging you deeper into debt at a faster pace. Remember, if you have one credit card that's charging you 18% interest on your balance, and another that's charging you 10%, you still need to meet the minimum payments on the lower rate card until you have completely paid off the 18% card. After the card charging you 18% is paid off, you can then start aggressively paying down the card charging you a 10% rate.

It's also a good idea to pay off the credit cards with a smaller balance first because it helps give you some confidence that you're making headway and that there is light at the end of the tunnel. This means that if you have a card that has a $500 balance and one that has an $8,000 balance, pay off the card with the lower balance first to give yourself some confidence that these debts can be paid off. Many small steps add up to make large steps!

Don't pay down debt without having a financial safety net somewhere – either in savings or in being able to charge on your credit card. If, *in an emergency only*, you could still use these credit cards that you're paying down AND if you didn't have any savings to use first, then it's okay to pay these credit cards off aggressively without accumulating money in savings at the same time. You do need somewhere to turn if you had a financial emergency but didn't have any money in savings because you had been paying down debt and not adding money to your savings account. Don't paint yourself into a corner that you can't get out of. Always be sure that you have some resource available to you in case of an emergency.

You may have access to credit cards that are charging "no interest" or "special low rates." It is wise to take advantage of these offers to help you slow the pace at which your interest charges are digging you deeper into debt. Each U.S. household receives approximately fifty credit card solicitations per year and credit card companies are increasing the amount of debt that they will allow their current customers to maintain with them as credit card limits increased by sixteen percent from 2000 to 2001.[6,7] Keep in mind that every time you respond to a new credit card offer in the mail, your credit report will reflect an inquiry on your credit rating. This typically is not good for your beacon score. A *beacon score* is generally the number that lenders evaluate to see if you're likely to pay off the loan they are considering giving to you. The higher the beacon score, the better, and inquiries, late payments, and judgments subtract from your score. A good beacon score is one that is over 740, but this varies by lender. More importantly, however, you must first stop the habits of spending that got you into debt, and then you can set a goal based on the following:

- Your ability to pay down the debt as best you can by using the money you have left every month *after* you pay your vital living expenses OR
- Your desire to pay down the debt based on a target date when you'd like to have the debt paid off.

For example, if you owe $10,000 on a credit card that is charging you 0%, and you're paying $150 per month towards that debt, it will take you ($10,000 balance ÷ $150 payment per month) about sixty-six months to pay that card off completely. If you do the math, sixty-six months is 5.5 years (66 months ÷ 12 months per year). This is if you aren't being charged any interest at all!

However, if you owe $10,000 on a credit card that is charging you 18% (and you may have some credit cards that charge an even higher rate), and your budget shows that you can make payments of $200 per month, then (based on an amortization schedule) you should have that card paid off in about ninety-four months. Ninety-four months divided by twelve months per year means that it will take you almost eight years to pay off that credit card! You would have paid back the original $10,000 that you owed, PLUS $8,800 in interest! Do you see how much of a difference the value of the interest rate they are charging you makes?!

But, if you set a goal to have that card paid off in five years and the credit card company is charging you interest at a rate of 18% per year, you'll need to make monthly payments of around $254. Any extra money that you receive over and above your budgeted income, or any money that you save from paying other bills off or reducing other expenses can be paid toward this credit card at any time and pay it off faster! Any goal in life needs to be S.M.A.R.T., which means your goals need to be:

Specific – clearly define your goal – "I want to pay this card completely off."

Measurable – define some way to measure your progress – "I want to pay $254 per month."

Action-oriented – be sure your goal requires you to do something – "I will cut back on other expenses to be able to have the $254 per month.

Realistic – be sure you set goals that are within reach. Don't set a goal that is too high and unattainable based upon your financial situation. Saying that you want to pay $600 per month doesn't mean anything if you simply don't have that much available cash on hand every month.

Time-bound – set a deadline for your goal – "I want to have this card paid off within five years."

A good goal may look something like this: "I want to pay my credit card off completely within five years by reducing my monthly expenses to $3,000 so that I can send in at least $254 every month."

As with anything, if you have a realistic goal, a well-designed plan, and you are sticking to that plan, then you can have the peace of mind that you're doing your best. This peace of mind will then free up your mind (and your time) to enjoy other aspects of your life.

Things You Need To Do Now

1. **Develop a plan (with the aid of your financial consultant) to pay down any improper debt based upon your current situation.** Write down your plan and your goal. Remember, goals must be S.M.A.R.T.!
2. **Develop a plan to accumulate an appropriate amount of savings to help prevent emergencies, repairs, and major purchases from pulling you down into debt.**
3. **Implement and stick to your plan!**

SECTION I - FINANCES

Chapter Four

Retirement & Social Security

"The best time to start thinking about retirement is before the boss does." – Anonymous

Retirement is probably the most important financial goal for the majority of people, and it is a very complex topic. I will try to make this discussion as easy to understand as possible while giving you enough information for you to be able to have an educated conversation with your financial professional. Please note that I did not say that you should have an educated conversation with just *anyone.* I say this because the *anyone* you choose to speak with may actually know less than you know, but he may do a good job of making you think he knows what he is talking about. This person (and you) may also think that your situations are fairly similar because you make the same amount of money, work at the same company, or live in the same neighborhood; however your goals, life experiences, thresholds for risk, debt situation, health condition, insurance coverage, commitment of faith, and life expectancy may make your situations extremely different. Don't forget that some people have ulterior motives that would make their advice unreliable. Talk with professionals only.

Remember, *before* you start investing for retirement, you really need to have your financial house in order. This means that some debts may need to be paid off, that you need to have addressed and changed the habits that created those debts, and that you need to have an adequate amount of money built up in savings.

What is *Retirement*?

Retirement is the time in life when someone can have a comfortable lifestyle without actually having to go to work. Some people say they'll never retire because they like to work, and some may say they'll never retire because they can't afford to retire. Planning for retirement is important because your health or job skills may force you to retire at some point due to being physically unable to go to work or complete the tasks required at your job. Wouldn't you agree that it makes sense to plan for retirement, even if you don't think you'll need it? Most prudent and wise people like to have an emergency plan or a backup plan that is based upon a worst-case scenario.

Let's say that you think you'll never retire because you love the job you have and you would do it even if you didn't get paid. But what happens if you're used to living on $50,000 per year when you severely break your leg in a car accident and become disabled. Let's also assume, as is the case most of the time, that you don't get much (if any) benefit from the automobile insurance companies that insured those persons involved in the accident. You'd first use your savings to help carry you for a while. Hopefully, if you have both short-term and long-term disability insurance, they will pay you for some period of time, but these payments usually aren't more than sixty percent of your pre-disability income. If your normal income was $50,000 per year, this would mean you could only expect to receive about $30,000. In a good scenario, you're then faced with living on $30,000 when you were used to living on $50,000. To reduce expenses, you could potentially stop doing certain things and be ok that year by doing without. But what about the next year when costs go up more than your income does? The increase in costs is called *inflation*.

Inflation is the evil that most people do not plan for with regards to investing for college, retirement, major purchases, etc. In the same way that the credit card company that charges you eighteen percent requires a lot more money be paid back than a credit card that doesn't charge any interest, expenses today will become a lot more in years to come. Did you know that a stamp used to cost only $.03, and now it's $.37? What if you had retired from your job thinking that stamps would only cost $.03 for the rest of your life? You'd now either be finding a way to do without stamps or you'd be spending a lot more money than you had planned on. Or how about the price of a gallon of milk, or toilet paper, or an automobile? Did you know that most automobiles today cost more than the first house purchased by our World War II veterans when they came home from the war? I often have clients and seminar attendees who say that their last car cost them more than their first home. You must be aware of inflation and its potential impact on your future quality of life! If you don't factor in the fact that costs will be higher in the future, you run the risk of running out of money!

Continuing with our previous example, at some point your disability policy would probably stop paying you due to reaching its policy limits on length of time or total dollars paid out (if you even had a disability policy in the first place). Now where is your income going to come from? Social Security may approve you for some benefits, but how confident are you that this system will still exist or that the amount they pay you would be adequate? We'll talk about our Social Security System later in the chapter, but first we should talk further about the reasons you should invest for retirement.

Why Invest for Retirement?

As discussed above, you need to save for retirement in order to:

- Protect against the unexpected events in life (injuries, loss of job, etc.),
- Make up for the possibility of not having any other source of income (such as Social Security or a company pension) if you cannot or do not want to work (disability, forced retirement,

or regular retirement), and...
- Put away as much as you can for a "rainy day" or a time when your life plans change.

My flight instructor, Joe Romack, trained me to be a private pilot. He said time and time again, "The runway behind you and the air above you won't do you any good." He said this because when you're in trouble in an airplane, you want to see a lot of runway in front of you so that you can slow down and you want a lot of altitude below you so that you can have time to glide to a safe landing spot. Once you give up the runway or altitude, you'll never get it back if your engine is failing. Similarly, the years behind you in which you could have saved for retirement but didn't (for whatever reason) will do you no good. Subsequently, your lifestyle in retirement will reflect that shortfall in such a way that everyone will be able to see it.

The National Council on the Aging asked people age sixty-five and older that considered themselves retired to state the most important reason they decided to retire. The biggest reasons were

72% - Qualified for Social Security
71% - Accumulated savings
50% - Reached a specific age
46% - Family reasons
40% - Decline in health
20% - Pressure from employer

Among those over age sixty-five, fifty-eight percent considered themselves completely retired, twenty-three percent said they were retired and working, and nineteen percent said they were not retired.[1] Why do you want to retire? When do you want to retire? I'm sure your ideal answer is "today" – so let me rephrase the question – "When do you think a realistic goal for a retirement date might be?" *Write down your answer in the margin.*

As you can see above, the biggest reason people retired was because they qualified for Social Security. We'll now talk about what benefits are available and how likely it is that you may be able to collect some type of benefits.

Our Social Security System - A Basic Overview

In order to qualify for some Social Security benefits and be *fully insured*, you need to have at least forty quarters of coverage, or *credits*. This basically means that you need to have worked ten or more years. In 2004, one credit is earned for each $900 in earnings, and you can earn up to four credits per year. As a result, income of $3,600 in 2004 will get four credits credited towards your benefits.[2] You should receive in the mail, about three months before your birthday each year, a detailed report from Social Security that outlines how much you'd qualify to receive at age sixty-two, at full retirement age, and if you were to become disabled. These benefit amounts are based upon how much you've earned in the past, and Social Security provides a detailed breakout on page three of their report that shows your earnings in all prior years. Make sure these numbers are accurate, and report any discrepancies. Your Social Security benefit will be calculated based upon your best thirty-five years of earnings. If you have not received such a report, contact your local Social Security office, call them at (800) 772-1213, or visit their website at http://www.ssa.gov.

It is estimated that seventy percent of retirees take Social Security benefits before age sixty-five.[3] In 1960, thirty-one percent of men aged sixty-five or older were still in the workforce, but in 2000, only eighteen percent were still in the workforce.[4] In 2002, eighteen percent of workers said they plan to retire at age sixty-six or later; in 2003, that number increased by one-third to twenty-four percent of workers.[5] In the past, *normal retirement age* was age sixty-five. Normal retirement age is now increasing based upon when you were born, and people born on or after 1960 won't be eligible for full retirement benefits until age sixty-seven. Currently, people can take a reduced benefit from Social Security as early as age 62. Social Security made these changes because people are living longer today due to improved medical care and medicine. People born in the year 2000 have a record life expectancy of 76.9 years.[6] The average life span in the 1800s was about forty years.

There are significant concerns that Social Security will not be able to survive much longer, and some analysts, using assumptions that are between the worst- and best-case scenarios, expect the system to not be able to make payments to people after the year 2037. The worst-case scenario used in that analysis says that the Social Security trust fund will be depleted as early as 2026.[7] The reason for this concern stems from the fact that more people are taking money out of the Social Security System than there are paying into the system. That's pretty similar to you spending more than you make – your outflow is greater than your inflow. The "baby boom" generation – people born between 1946 and 1964 – account for over twenty-eight percent of the U.S. population. In 2008, the oldest of the baby boom generation will turn sixty-two.[8] This means that over twenty-five percent of the U.S. population will soon be moving out of the workforce. This will increase the strain on our system because the baby boomers will no longer be helping to fund the system, they'll be taking money out.

Refer to Chapter One where we showed Bill Smith's income and expense... the amount deducted from his gross pay that was paid to Social Security was his amount paid in, and almost every person (except some clergy, civil service workers, government employees, farmers, school teachers and railroad workers) has this percentage (currently 7.65% of gross pay) deducted from his pay on the first $87,900 (in 2004) earned per year. Bill's employer pays in another 7.65% of Bill's gross pay towards Bill's Social Security benefit for a total cost of 15.3% for Social Security. If you make more than $87,900 in 2004, Social Security tax is not deducted from the excess amount over $87,900. However, the excess amount does not increase your Social Security benefit when you retire.[9]

I try not to take any expected Social Security benefits into account for anyone under the age of forty.

Currently, there is more money going out of the system than there is going in, and that rate of outflow is expected to increase until it completely wipes out the Social Security system unless dramatic changes are made. As a CFP certificant, I try not to take any expected Social Security benefits into account for anyone under the age of forty. So, if you're under forty years of age (or even close to forty), I wouldn't advise relying on the Social Security System's ability to help pay for your cost of living during retirement. This means that we have to save more money ourselves in order to make up for that income that won't be available to us when we retire. Yes, we will still have the tax deducted from our income, and yes, we may not ever get to see any of that money again.

The report from Social Security also shows the other benefits that could be available in addition to retirement benefits, such as:

<u>Disability benefits</u> – available if you're *fully insured*, under age sixty-five, and have worked for five out of the last ten years under *covered employment*. The amount of the benefit will equal the amount you would receive at normal retirement age and is payable for disabilities that are expected to last at least twelve months or result in death. An interesting statistic showed that there is a seven in ten chance that a person reaching age sixty-five will suffer a disability or cognitive impairment.[10]

For example, Bill Smith is currently thirty-five years old, and he's been working since he was twenty-one (thus he's fully insured). Bill gets hurt and can't return to work. Doctors don't think he'll be able to go back for a couple of years, so Bill applies to Social Security for benefits. He is approved, and based upon his earnings history, they start sending him a disability income check that would be the same amount if he were retiring at full retirement age.

<u>Death benefits</u> – a one-time $255 death benefit is payable to a surviving spouse who is eligible for benefits or to a child/children entitled to benefits based upon your earnings record if you're *currently insured* (at least six quarters of coverage during the thirteen calendar quarters ending with the quarter in which you die, or become entitled to retirement or disability benefits).

For example, Bill Smith gets married and dies after the honeymoon. His wife has also been working for ten years and is thus eligible for benefits. She receives one check for $255 as a one-time death benefit. If Bill was not married and had kids that he was raising by himself, one check for $255 would be paid to his children to share amongst themselves.

Survivor benefits – the surviving spouse will be eligible, if you are currently insured (this is the same requirement as for the death benefit), for monthly payments during the time your children are under sixteen years of age. These children can also receive monthly payments during the time they are under eighteen years of age (or age 18-19 if they are full-time high school or elementary school students).

For example, Bill marries and has two children, and then passes away. His wife will receive a monthly benefit until the children turn sixteen, and then that payment to her stops. The children would also receive a check each month until they are nineteen and out of high school, which Bill's surviving spouse would probably use to help pay living expenses for the children. The amounts payable are based upon how much Bill had earned in the past and had paid in to Social Security. There is a limit to the amount of monthly benefits paid to everyone in the house (the surviving spouse *and* children) called the *family maximum*. This amount is the most that will be paid regardless of the number of children eligible to receive survivor benefits.

Bill's wife would not receive Social Security benefits payable to her from the time the children turn sixteen until she turns age sixty-five. She could elect, if she so desired, to receive a lower payment per month when she turns sixty. This payment would be about twenty percent less than if she waited until she turned age sixty-five. Bill would want to be sure that there was enough life insurance to support his wife from the time the kids are age sixteen until his wife turns at least age sixty if he didn't want her to have to go back to work. His wife could get a monthly benefit at age fifty if she was disabled. If Bill's wife chose to go back to work, she could qualify for a retirement benefit based upon her earnings that could be higher than the benefit she would get based upon his earnings history. She could then take the higher benefit of the two - but she can't take both.

Divorced spouse benefits – A divorced spouse (an ex-wife or ex-husband) is potentially entitled to benefits if he or she was married to a worker for at least ten years before the date the divorce became final, is not married, is over age sixty-two, is not eligible for his or her own benefits that would be greater than one-half of the worker's benefit, and the worker is entitled to retirement or disability benefits.

For example, Bill marries, and fifteen years later divorces a lady named Jane. Jane does not remarry, is not employed (because she had enough money in savings and investments), and thus does not have anything paid into Social Security for her own benefit. When she turns age sixty-two, she can go file for benefits and receive up to one-half of the benefit that Bill would receive based upon his earnings. Bill will still receive his normal benefit.

Having these benefits available is certainly a good thing, but they are by no means meant to be the only financial support that you should have for retirement income, for payments if you become disabled, and payments to your surviving spouse and children if you were to die.[11]

(Contact Social Security to request your detailed statement, or find your statement if you have received it in the past. Then contact your financial consultant or Social Security to discuss your particular situation. There are too many variables in income, marital status, number of children, and age to adequately discuss all the possibilities within the scope of this book. While every attempt has been made to be sure these summaries are accurate, please make your financial decisions regarding Social Security only after you have talked directly to a representative from that agency and your financial professional.)

In summary regarding Social Security, if you're near the age when you could start receiving benefits, you can factor those benefits into your retirement or disability analyses. If you are under the age of forty, I would advise you to operate under a worst-case scenario and do not factor Social Security benefits into your financial plan. Attempt to protect yourself through adequate savings (for emergencies, loss of income for a short time, etc.), investments (to be used for retirement, disability, etc.), and insurance (disability insurance if sick or hurt and can't work; life insurance to protect your surviving spouse and children if they no longer have your income to help support them).

Things You Need To Do Now

1. **Obtain a copy of your Social Security benefits estimate by visiting your local Social Security office, by calling Social Security at 1-800-772-1213, or by visiting their website at www.ssa.gov.**
2. **Have your financial professional run an analysis with and without Social Security benefits that shows how realistic your retirement goal is.** When in doubt, don't plan on having any Social Security benefits!
3. **Make a list of things that you would like to do (or have) in retirement.** Would you like a vacation home, the ability to travel, unlimited amounts of money and time, etc? Shoot for the moon, dare to dream, set your sights high!

SECTION I - FINANCES

Chapter Five

Investing for Retirement through Your Employer

In October of 2001, only four percent of eligible workers put the maximum contribution into their 401(k) plan. [1]

The question of "how should you go about investing for retirement?" has many subsets. One subset is: What type of account? The type of account is important for tax reasons. Another subset is: What type of investment? And still another subset is: How much should be invested?

This information can get complicated if you allow it to do so. Please keep in mind that even some financial professionals who deal with these topics every day still don't firmly grasp all of the details. Digest each section that applies to you; take it sentence by sentence; make notes in the margin; get out your employee information and see what your company offers. Use this section as a guide to help you decipher what opportunities are available to you. Move through this section slowly until you feel you have a decent understanding or call and make an appointment with your financial professional.

Accounts Provided by Employers

401(k) – This is a retirement account into which an employee can make *pre-tax contributions* into an account that has a blend of investment options. The employee selects the investments, and these investments grow tax-deferred until withdrawals are made from the account. I sure dove right off into the deep-end with some of the terms in those sentences, didn't I? Well, here's what I mean. *Pre-tax contributions* are amounts that you decide to have deducted from each paycheck to be deposited into the 401(k) account. Because you don't actually receive the income, you don't have to pay taxes on that money in the year you actually earned it. In short, it saves you taxes in the year you made it and it allows you to save money towards retirement. Both of these points are very positive benefits. The IRS is basically saying, "Don't pay us any tax on the money right now. Put it into a retirement account and let it grow so that you can try and have a decent retirement. We won't charge you any taxes on the growth while it stays inside the account, but we do want you to pay taxes on the money when you actually take it out of the account." In essence, they're saying, "don't pay us now, pay us later." If you take the money out of the account before you're age 59 ½ (with some exceptions), the IRS will charge you regular income tax PLUS a 10% penalty.

In 2004, you can *defer* up to $13,000 per year. If you're over 50 years old, you can defer up to $16,000 because the IRS recently created a *catch-up provision* that allows you to defer an additional $3,000 of income to help you catch up and put more back for retirement since you have fewer years to reach your retirement goals.[2] The employer usually makes some sort of *matching contribution* and, in some cases, will make a *profit sharing contribution*. Both of these contributions by the employer are put into your account without your having to pay income tax on those amounts. Some companies will actually put money into your account, and some will deposit an amount of shares of the company stock that is worth the same amount of money. The most that can be contributed to a 401(k) in 2004 through all available options is

$41,000. The total amount that can be contributed to a 401(k) is scheduled to increase through the years to allow you to save more for retirement. It is very helpful to work for a company that is willing to pay you a decent wage for the job you do today and is also willing to take money out of their profits to put into your retirement account.

So far we've talked about the good points of the 401(k) program. But we all know there's no free lunch, don't we? The restrictions and stipulations regarding a 401(k) are as follows:

- As mentioned above, *withdrawals made before you turn age 59 ½ are taxed just like you would have been taxed if you had been paid directly by your company, PLUS you have to pay a 10% penalty for not keeping the money in the account past age 59 ½.* Exceptions include death, disability, withdrawals due to divorce as evidenced by a qualified domestic relations order, withdrawals made for the payment of deductible medical expenses, withdrawals directly from the 401(k) after you turn age 55, or annuitization under rule 72(t).[3] Please see your financial professional for more specific information about these exceptions.
- *Money contributed by the company may be subject to a vesting schedule.* A *vesting schedule* is a period of time where the money the employer has deposited into your account may not actually be fully yours. The company may vest you at a rate of 20% of the contributions per year. For example, if you leave the company after three years, you may only get 60% of the matching contributions your company made (three years of service x 20% per year vesting). The remaining 40% of the money that was in the account gets returned to the company after you leave. If you had stayed with the company for five years, you would have gotten all of it. Once you've been with a company long enough to be fully vested, all monies (both past and future) are yours to keep. Remember, any money that you have

A vesting schedule is a period of time where the money the employer has deposited into your account may not actually be fully yours.

deferred out of your pay is always your money. Vesting schedules only apply to the money put in your account by the company. The company is helping you greatly by putting this money in your account, and they are hoping that you will stay with them for a long time as a faithful and dedicated employee. A vesting schedule associated with that money helps them give you a monetary reason to stay with them because you'll see your account balance fall if they take back the money that was not vested. Take advantage of their generosity, make the best of your job if you have great benefits, and hang in there for the long term!

- *Investment choices and alternatives inside the 401(k) are provided by the company, and there are usually somewhere between six and twenty-five choices available.* You get to choose which of those choices are most appropriate for you. The number and quality of selections have improved dramatically in a recent attempt to educate employees about proper diversification due to the losses incurred by employees at companies who saw the value of their stock in their 401(k) become worthless. See your financial professional for advice on how to invest your 401(k) money appropriately based on your age, goals, risk tolerance, and investment choices available.

Let's look at an example of how a 401(k) works. Let's assume Bill Smith has a 401(k) at his company, and his paperwork for the 401(k) says something like this: *"Employees may defer up to $13,000 per year or a maximum of 15% of pay, whichever is less. The company will match $1 for $1 on the first 6% of salary deferrals and will make a profit sharing contribution at the end of each year. The profit sharing contributions are subject to a six-year vesting schedule, with 20% being vested each year."*

Let's look at each sentence carefully and see how this 401(k) works.

"Employees may defer up to $13,000 per year or a maximum of 15% of pay, whichever is less." This means that Bill, since he makes $50,000 per year, can defer the lesser of 15% of $50,000 (which is $7,500) or $13,000. Since $7,500 is less than $13,000, the most Bill can deduct from his pay is $7,500. Bill's budget only allows him to defer 10% of his pay, so he's only going to need to defer $5,000. He's not really worried about the maximums right now. The big benefit Bill gets for putting this $5,000 into the 401(k) is that he gets a pre-tax deduction – this means he saves about $1,400 in income taxes based upon his personal tax bracket. (Your tax bracket may be different due to your income, marital status, number of dependents, deductible expenses and tax credits.) If Bill chooses not to defer any money into his 401(k), he would have to pay the $1,400 in income taxes that he would have saved because he did not make the "pre-tax deductions" of $5,000 from his income. Another way to say this is that Bill is putting $5,000 into the 401(k), but since he's saving $1,400 in taxes, it only cost him $3,600 ($5,000 - $1,400). That's a pretty good deal, isn't it?

"The company will match $1 for $1 on the first 6% of salary deferrals..." This means that for every dollar Bill puts into the 401(k), up to 6% of his salary, the company will put in an equal amount in matching contributions. Bill's salary is $50,000, and 6% of that amount is $3,000. Currently, Bill is deferring 10% of his pay ($5,000), and the company will match his contributions only on the first 6% ($3,000). At the end of the year, Bill's 401(k) account will have $5,000 of *his* money plus $3,000 in matching contributions *from the company*. If Bill's budget said that he could only defer 3% of his pay ($1,500), the company would only have to deposit another 3% ($1,500). Remember, this is a *matching* contribution. The company is only going to help Bill as much as he is willing and able to help himself. The company can't match something that doesn't exist or wasn't deposited into the account in the first place. Bill has to put the money into the account in order for it to be matched. Be sure you defer at least the percentage of income that your company will match because matching dollars are a great return on investment without your even having to take any risk!

"...and will make a profit sharing contribution at the end of each year." This means that some amount may be deposited into your 401(k) based upon the profitability of the company. If the company has zero profits, then they probably won't put any money into your account. Also, the company can have profits, but management may decide not to put any money into employees' accounts in order to use it to buy more equipment, land, or new products. Contributions amounts will fluctuate through the years, and in some years there may not be any contributions at all.

Let's assume that Bill's employer says that they've had a good year and they are going to make a 5% profit sharing contribution to each employee's 401(k) account. Since Bill made $50,000, his account will receive the 5% profit sharing contribution, which is $2,500. This doesn't mean that Bill gets 5% of the profits. It means that the company will use some of the profits to deposit an extra 5% of Bill's salary into his 401(k). Bill is very appreciative of his company's willingness to share the profits with him, and he's looking forward to future years when the company will make additional contributions to his account!

"The profit sharing contributions are subject to a six-year vesting schedule, with 20% being vested each year." In this situation, the profit sharing money is not entirely Bill's for the first six years. If Bill leaves the company in the first year, he won't get any of that $2,500 because he didn't meet the first year vesting schedule requirement. If he stays at that job for three years, he may get 60% of that money (three years of employment at 20% vesting per year), which is $1,500. The other $1,000 basically goes back to the company to be used for the other employees. If he stays for greater than five years, all of that $2,500 is his to keep because five years at 20% vesting per year means he's 100% vested. Remember, he always gets to keep the amount he's deferred out of his pay and the matching amount. Vesting schedules are set up in a variety of ways. Be sure to check with your employer and your financial professional about the other features available through your company's specific plan.

To summarize Bill's 401(k), he's deposited some of *his* money out of his paycheck ($5,000), the *company matched* his first 6% ($3,000), and he got a *profit sharing* contribution of $2,500 *from the company*. The total amount deposited into his 401(k) for the year was $10,500. Since $10,500 was deposited into his account, and taking into account the fact that Bill makes $50,000 per year, he now has the net effect of saving 21% of his pay ($10,500 ÷ $50,000). Do you see how all this adds up to help him towards retirement? If Bill had not deferred any of his pay, he would only have gotten the profit sharing contribution of $2,500 from the company. This amount would have only been 5% of his pay ($2,500 ÷ 50,000). As you'll see later, every little bit helps and it all starts with you!

It is very important to get your financial house in order, to put some emergency money into savings, and to start putting money into your 401(k) so that you can take advantage of how your employer is willing to help you save money for retirement. Every day you miss making contributions into your account means you'll ultimately reduce the quality of your retirement. Start saving and investing today!

S.I.M.P.L.E. IRA (Savings Incentive Match Plan for Employees)– This is an account that allows you to make pre-tax contributions from your pay into a SIMPLE IRA account. This money can then be invested according to your wishes. You can have your SIMPLE IRA account at any financial institution of your choice. Your employer may make matching contributions, usually up to 3% of your pay. You don't want to touch this money until you're at least 59 ½ because you'll have to pay regular income taxes PLUS the 10% penalty. However, if you take money out of your SIMPLE IRA within the first two years of opening the account, you'll have to pay regular income taxes PLUS a 25% penalty. Smaller companies with just a few employees and sole proprietorships usually have SIMPLE IRA's. Do not confuse a SIMPLE IRA with other types of IRA's. In 2004, you can defer the lesser of up to $9,000 or 100% of your income from your pay into a SIMPLE IRA. If you are over 50 years old, you can defer an additional $1,500. In 2005, those numbers change to $10,000 and $2,000, respectively. Be sure your boss knows you appreciate her willingness to put some of the company's money into your account when they deposit the matching contribution!

S.E.P. IRA (Simplified Employee Pension) – This is an account in which the employer makes contributions into a SEP IRA account for you. You generally don't contribute any of your pay into this account as the employer makes the entire contribution. A SEP IRA is similar to a profit sharing contribution in that it can vary each year, and it can be anywhere from 0 to 25% of your pay up to a maximum of $41,000 in 2004. The maximum dollar amount is scheduled to increase in future years to help you save more for retirement. You can choose how you want to invest the money once it's in your account, and you can have your SEP IRA account at any financial institution. You don't want to touch this money until you're over age 59 ½ due to having to pay regular income taxes PLUS the 10% penalty. Thank your employer for taking money out of their profits to put into your retirement account!

Pension Plan or "Defined Benefit Plan" – The employer makes contributions into this account for you, which grow through the years on a tax-deferred basis. This money builds up in the account and can be used to pay you a monthly pension after you retire. This account is different from the plans we've talked about so far, because you are not in control of how the money is invested. The company is in control of how the money is invested. The employer is required to be prudent in its decisions, but there is a great deal of flexibility available to the employer. If the employer makes good decisions and the investments go up in value, then everyone's happy. There are times when the employer makes good decisions and the investments go down in value. There are also times when the employer makes bad decisions and the investments perform badly also. History shows that employees tend to file lawsuits on the basis that the money was mismanaged when this final situation occurs. As a result of these lawsuits and the liability the employer assumes when making the investment decisions, we are seeing fewer and fewer of these types of plans.

If you leave the company before you retire (as with any of the above accounts), you can roll the value of your share of the pension plan into a Traditional IRA. If you leave the company and do not roll the money to an IRA, the company continues to invest your money as it sees fit. After you reach retirement age, you can ask the company to send you a monthly check over a period of time that you choose. This period of time may be for the rest of your life (called *single life*), for the rest of either you or your spouse's life (called *joint life*), or for your life with a certain number of guaranteed years (called *life with period certain*). You basically get a printout each year that tells you how much your portion of the pension plan is worth. You want to be able to trust that your employer is making good investment decisions, and you'll want to be able to sleep at night believing that they will be able to pay you a pension after you retire. See your financial consultant or your employer for more details.

403(b)'s – Typically, this is an account offered by non-profit or government employers such as hospitals, school systems, churches, etc. It allows you to contribute pre-tax money out of your income (like a 401(k) or SIMPLE IRA) into an account that grows tax-deferred. These deferral amounts are always your money, are subject to the same age rules as the 401(k), and can be rolled over to an IRA if you leave your employer or retire. You can defer up to $13,000 of your pay in 2004, and the *catch-up provision* for those ages 50 or over is an additional $3,000. You are in control of how the money is invested within the options the retirement plan provides you.

Deferred Compensation Plans (Deferred Comp or 457 plans) – This is a retirement savings vehicle that allows you to have money deducted from your pay on a pre-tax basis. This money is placed in an account where it is invested according to your wishes based on the investment choices available to you. This plan is generally available only through employers that are state or local government entities or are tax-exempt organizations. In 2004, employees can contribute the lesser of 100% of salary or $13,000. This deferral amount is increasing in order to help people save more for retirement to $14,000 in 2005, $15,000 in 2006, and is indexed for inflation after 2007 in $500 increments. Catch-up provisions also apply, so check with your financial professional or your employer if you are age 50 or over and desire to contribute the maximum.

All of the above retirement savings plans, accounts, or vehicles are called *qualified retirement plans*. This means that they are registered with the IRS, which allows you to save pre-tax dollars, have them grow tax-deferred, and then take them out any time after age 59 ½ and pay taxes on the amount withdrawn at your regular income tax rate at that time without any penalties. Your hope is that your tax bracket will be lower after you retire so that you pay less tax on the money at that time than if you had paid income taxes in the year it was actually earned at work.

<u>FRS DROP Plans</u> – Specific to my home state of Florida, the Florida Retirement System Deferred Retirement Option Program (FRS DROP) provides a lump-sum retirement benefit to state government, state university, state community college, and county-level government employees who elect to enroll in the program. Some city and special districts participate in the FRS, but participation is not mandatory. The DROP program was implemented to give employees an added retirement benefit by giving them a lump-sum payment, in addition to their monthly pension, upon retiring.

If you work for a participating employer, you are eligible to enroll in the DROP program when you have at least thirty years of service OR when you become eligible for "full, unreduced benefits based upon your age and/or service." Once you become eligible for the DROP program and your application to enter DROP is approved, you can enter the program and continue it for a maximum of five years (some employees may be able to extend their DROP period past the five years, so check with your employer about your position's eligibility). Every month that you are in the

DROP program, the state deposits an amount equal to what you would have been paid by your pension if you had retired. This money is deposited into an interest bearing account (called the FRS Trust Fund) that compounds monthly at an annual rate of 6.5%. The amount of the monthly deposit into the FRS Trust Fund will increase every July based upon any cost of living adjustments (COLA). The deposits are not taxed as income, and you still have your regular income to live on while you're still working at your job. You can stay in the program for a maximum of five years and can leave at any time you so desire without a penalty, other than the fact that your benefit will be smaller than if you had stayed in the program for the full five years. You must decide if you want to enter the DROP program within a twelve-month period that begins when you first reach your normal retirement date unless you are eligible to postpone your decision under one of four *deferred election* circumstances. You do not have to enter DROP if you do not want to do so.

When you decide to retire and *stop going to work*, the DROP program ends. Remember, you can only be in the DROP program for a maximum of five years. You can then:

- Take a lump sum payment and pay taxes on the money,
- You can perform a *direct rollover* to a Traditional IRA and defer income taxes on the full amount, or
- You can do a combination of both.

Remember, you'll have to pay regular income taxes on any amount you receive that is not rolled over into an IRA. If you roll over your account balance to an IRA, you can then choose to set up a withdrawal plan from the rollover IRA account to help supplement your income that you'll be getting directly from the Florida Retirement System. It is not uncommon for employees to have $150,000 eligible to roll over if they stay in the program for the full five years. Visit http://www.frs.state.fl.us for more information.[4]

What Happens if You Quit, Get Fired, Retire, or the Company Ceases Operations?

In all of the above plans, whatever amount you have contributed out of your pay *plus* whatever amount your company has given you that is vested, *plus (or minus)* whatever the investment performance has generated is yours to take with you. You generally have three choices to make:

1) *Leave the money inside the plan at your employer* – If you have adequate investment choices and control, if you need additional creditor protection, if you're over age 55 but younger than 59 ½, or if you feel you may need to borrow against the value in the future, you may consider leaving the assets in the plan.

2) *Take a distribution* – If you're younger than age 55 and you don't qualify for any of the exceptions to the 10% penalty, you'll have to pay regular income taxes on the amount you take out PLUS a 10% penalty (a 25% penalty applies to distributions from S.I.M.P.L.E IRA's within the first two years). Refer to our earlier example for a reminder of how this works. If you take receipt of the money, your employer will be required to withhold at least 20% of the amount withdrawn. Your actual tax bill may be higher or lower than that amount.

You can *rollover* any amount paid to you into a Traditional IRA within sixty days of receiving the funds in order to prevent having to pay the taxes and penalties, but you'll only receive credit for the amount you rollover into the IRA. This type of rollover is different from a direct rollover because it's money that you've actually received as a distribution that you would like to put back into a tax-favored account. A direct rollover occurs when the money goes directly from your employer provided retirement plan into an IRA.

For example, let's assume you had $10,000 in your 401(k) and then left the company and told them to send you a check for your account because you thought you were going to need to spend the money. You would only get $8,000 and the company would send $2,000 to the IRS because they withheld 20% of the total amount to go towards your tax bill for that year. If you decided that you didn't need the $8,000 in cash and that you had made a mistake by not leaving it in the 401(k) or by failing to perform a direct rollover to an IRA, you could put $10,000 into an IRA within sixty days and avoid the taxes and penalties. However, the IRS still has the $2,000 that was withheld by your employer when you took the distribution. You won't be able to get that $2,000 back until you file your income taxes and tell the IRS that you didn't actually take the $10,000 out of the 401(k) because you rolled it to an IRA within 60 days. Confusing, isn't it? In short, be sure of what you need to do before you do it. Keep in mind that there is a sixty-day window available to repair any mistakes you may have made, but you may need to have some extra money on hand to replace the withholding amount that was taken out of your distribution and sent to the IRS.

3) *Perform a direct rollover to an IRA or another qualified plan* – For people under the age of 55 who will not need to start receiving income from the money and who need to have the money continue growing, your best option is to perform a direct rollover to an IRA or another qualified plan.

Simply put, go see your financial professional and open a Traditional IRA (sometimes called a Rollover IRA) and notify your old employer who has the 401(k) that you want to perform a direct rollover. You can do this by completing the forms that employers generally send to you about thirty days after you leave the company, or by calling your employer directly. Some companies will allow you to handle the rollover via telephone, but some insist that your instructions be in writing. The benefits to you of performing a direct rollover are that you get to be in complete control of how the money gets invested, you get the professional advice of a financial consultant; you have more investment selections available to you, you get more diversification by not having "all your eggs in one basket" in your company's 401(k), and your beneficiaries may have more income choices available to them if you were to die.

If you so desire, and if a qualified plan is available at your new place of employment, you could roll your old retirement plan over into your new retirement plan without suffering any negative tax consequences. The new retirement plan may not be available to you until you've worked at your new job for quite some time, the investment choices inside the new plan may not be as good or as diverse as those available inside of an IRA, and you won't have a professional advising you on how to invest the funds. However, you would be able to borrow against your balance (if the employer allows) and you would have one less account to maintain. Weigh the pros and cons that apply to your situation, make the best decision you can based upon the facts at hand, and move on to other issues in life.

Other Investment Benefits Provided by Employers

Employee Stock Purchase Plans (ESPP's) – This is a benefit that your employer may offer you that allows you to have money deducted from your pay on an *after-tax* basis. Since this is after-tax money, it is money that you will pay tax on during the year that you earned it, regardless of whether or not you deposit it into an ESPP. This money goes toward purchasing shares in your company's stock. Generally, the company may give you somewhere around a 15% discount on the average value of the stock during the year so that you can purchase it at a price lower than its current value.

For example, if Bill had $100 per month deducted from his pay, he would have $1,200 (12 months x $100 per month) at the end of the year that would be available to buy shares of his company's stock. Hypothetically, if the stock traded between $14 and $10 per share over the year, the company would then allow him to buy the shares at $12 per share minus a 15% discount. This means that he could buy the stock at $10.20 per share. Hopefully, the stock is trading at a higher price at the time his company allows him to buy the shares. Bill could then decide to sell the stock right after he bought it at a 15% discount or hold on to it until a later date. Bill would be very happy if the stock were trading at $14 per share and he was able to buy it at $10.20 per share because the company gave him a 15% discount! If you have this benefit available to you and you took advantage of it like Bill did, I'm sure you'd be happy also.

Employee Stock Option Plans (ESOP's) – This is an account that gives you the *option*, the *right*, or the *choice* to purchase shares in your employer's company stock at a price they designate. This purchase must be completed by an expiration date that is usually several years in the future.

For example, Bill has worked at his company for five years and they give him the option to buy 100 shares of his company's stock at $10 per share. The company gives him a certificate that is called an *option*. Bill has three things he can do with the certificate (and the option it represents):

> Consistency, discipline, and fact-based decision making are the keys to financial success.

1) Bill can turn the certificate in and use it to buy the company's stock at $10 per share and hold onto the stock for a long time in the hopes the stock will go up in price;

2) He could hold the certificate for a while and wait to redeem it to buy the stock; or

3) He could turn in the certificate, buy the stock, and sell the stock immediately.

Bill just needs to choose one of these three selections before the option expires. Once the option expires, he has missed his chance and the option will be worthless.

Continuing with our example, Bill's company stock is currently worth $12 per share, so you can see that Bill could *exercise* his stock option and buy the stock at $10 per share. He would have an automatic profit of $2 per share. Bill would be excited about automatic profits! He would need to have the $1,000 on hand to pay for the stock if he wanted to buy it and hold onto it. If the stock then continues to increase in price by 10% per year, this portion of stock that Bill received an option to buy would be worth approximately $8,072 in twenty years. That's a pretty good return on an investment that originally cost him $1,000! What's even more important to realize is that if Bill receives and exercises stock options each year for the next twenty years until he retires, he would have 2000 shares of stock (100 shares per year times twenty years) that would probably be worth a great deal more than the amount he originally invested. This is a simplified example, but I'm sure you get the point. Consistency, discipline, and fact-based decision making are the keys to financial success.

Instead of exercising his option immediately, he could wait until just before the options expire and then exercise the option. If he waits five years to exercise the option to buy the stock at $10 per share, the stock (at a 10% growth rate) could potentially be worth $19.32 per share. Bill would have an automatic profit of $9.32 per share! Waiting to exercise his option would defer income taxes until he exercises his option and he would not have to tie up $1,000 in buying and holding the stock. He could use that $1,000 to do other things such as fix up his house or buy groceries. He would still have the benefit of possessing the certificate - and the right to own the stock - whenever he chooses to exercise the option.

On the other hand, if Bill needed to have some additional money for home repairs or wanted to purchase an investment that he thought would be better than owning stock in his company, Bill could buy the stock and then turn right around and sell it for $12 and pocket the $2 profit per share ($200 total). He would have to pay income taxes on the transaction, so his financial professional would advise him to talk with his tax advisor so that Bill would know what to expect.

There is a potential downside to stock option plans, as found by employees who worked for companies whose stock price dramatically fell. Let's say you were granted the right to purchase 100 shares of your company's stock at $10 per share, but your company's stock soon was only worth $5 per share. Would you want to exercise your right to buy the shares at $10 per share when you could call your broker and buy the shares at $5 per share? This is an example of a *worthless stock option.* The certificate in your hand would not be worth the paper it was written on because you could buy the shares at a lower price on the open market without exercising the option. In this case, you probably would have wished you had exercised your option when the stock was worth more than $10 per share and immediately sold the stock that the option allowed you to buy. Hindsight is always 20/20, so consult with your financial professional about investment diversification, timing, and tax implications.

Things You Need To Do Now

1. **Make an appointment to speak with a representative from your human resources department about the choices that may be available to you for retirement.** If you work for a small company or a sole proprietorship, schedule a meeting with the owner or manager to see if anything is currently available or if something may be available for you in the near future. You may find after reading this book that you may know more than they do. That's okay as long as they're willing to learn like you are. Suggest they speak with your financial consultant for guidance.
2. **Review any statements you may be getting in the mail from previous employers that reflect retirement savings you might still have with your old employer.** Talk with your financial advisor about the benefits of rolling those funds over to a Traditional IRA.
3. **If you and your financial professional feel that your company has an adequate retirement plan in place, start contributing money to your employer's retirement plan.... today!**

SECTION I - FINANCES

Chapter Six

Personal Ways to Invest for Retirement

The government has recently passed laws that allow you to save more for retirement in a tax-favored manner. Your employer probably offers you some type of retirement plan and hopefully you're taking advantage of their generosity. If your employer doesn't offer a retirement plan, if you don't qualify for their plan for some reason, or if you simply need to save more money for retirement, then you need to know more methods that you can save for retirement on your own. This chapter will help you better understand your choices and the options available to you.

Personal Retirement Savings Accounts
Not Provided by Employers:

Individual Retirement Account (I.R.A.) – The most common type of account available is an IRA, and there are two types available to individuals. Earlier we talked about the S.E.P. and S.I.M.P.L.E. IRA's, and they are IRA's available through *employers*. IRA's that are available to *individuals* are either Traditional IRA's or Roth IRA's.

Traditional and Roth IRA's are **similar** in that:

1) The most you can contribute to them in 2004 is the lesser of $3,000 or 100% of your earned income. This means that if you work at a job that pays you $2,000 per year, you can only put $2,000 in an IRA. If you make $3,000 or more at your job, the most you can put in an IRA is $3,000. If you are age 50 or older, an additional $500 can be put into the account each year to help you "catch-up" towards retirement. Please note, you cannot put $3,000 into a Roth AND $3,000 into a Traditional IRA - it is $3,000 maximum between the two accounts. The maximum contribution amount is increasing to $4,000 in 2005. The catch-up provision is increasing in 2006 from the additional $500 to $1,000.

2) You need to be age 59 ½ or older to remove money from these accounts without paying regular income taxes PLUS a 10% tax penalty. This rule is subject to some exceptions such as death; disability; as part of a stream of annuitized payments; to help cover medical expenses that are paid during the year that exceed 7.5% of your adjusted gross income; to cover the cost of health insurance premiums if you receive unemployment compensation for more than twelve weeks; to pay for qualified higher education expenses; and to use toward a first-time home purchase (up to $10,000 maximum lifetime limit) without having to pay the 10% income tax penalty.[1]

3) As the accounts grow, you don't have to pay income tax on the growth each year as long as it stays in the account. This is called tax-deferral or tax-deferred growth. This is a very important aspect of saving for retirement, because instead of having to send a portion of what you earned that year to the IRS, the money gets to stay inside the account (and thus, in your pocket) and compound. More money that is left in your account each year and not sent to the IRS (or to anyone) means that you have more money working for you. More money working for you over a long period of time means more money for retirement! The growth potential and investment choices are the same for both Roth and Traditional IRA's. You can make the same investments inside of Roth and Traditional IRA's.

4) You have until April 15th of the following year to make a contribution to your Roth or Traditional IRA account. This gives you time to see what your income in the previous tax year was and to find extra cash to actually make the contribution.

> With the Traditional IRA, the IRS is simply saying, "Don't pay us tax on the money now, pay us later when you take it out of the account."

Traditional and Roth IRA's are **different** in the following respects:

1) Contributions to a Traditional IRA can potentially be deducted from your income in the year you make the contribution so that you can save income taxes that year. For example, if you make $50,000 per year and you put $3,000 into a Traditional IRA (and you don't have a retirement plan at work), then you can deduct $3,000 from your income that you report to the IRS. Subsequently, you only have to pay income tax on $47,000 and not the full $50,000 you actually earned. This means that the $3,000 contribution is *tax deductible*. If you are in the 25% tax bracket, you would save $750 in income taxes plus you would have $3,000 saved for retirement. With the Traditional IRA, the IRS is simply saying, "Don't pay us tax on the money now, pay us later when you take it out of the account." There are some limitations as to how much you might be able to deduct when you make a deposit to a Traditional IRA, so check with your financial professional. Your income and your participation in a retirement plan at your work must be taken into consideration to determine whether or not your contribution is deductible.

> With the Roth IRA, the IRS is saying "go ahead and pay the income tax on the money today and we won't make you pay any taxes later."

2) Contributions to a Roth IRA are never tax deductible. However, withdrawals taken after you turn age 59 ½ or after you've had the account open for five years (whichever is longer) are not taxed at all! With the Roth IRA, the IRS is saying "go ahead and pay the income tax on the money today and we won't make you pay any taxes later." This situation is great if you don't expect your income to be lower after you retire. If your income is going to be fairly close to your pre-retirement income, you'll appreciate every bit of tax-free income you can get!

3) Withdrawals from a Traditional IRA prior to age 59 ½ (unless you are eligible for one of the exceptions mentioned earlier) are subject to regular income tax PLUS a 10% penalty on the entire amount of the withdrawal. For example, if Bill Smith had a Traditional IRA that he deposited $3,000 into last year, and if he got a tax deduction for that contribution (which saved him from having to pay taxes on the amount of the money deposited into the account), he would have to pay regular income taxes PLUS a 10% penalty because he didn't hold up his end of the deal with the IRS of not touching it until he was at least 59 ½ years old. Bill would have to pay regular income taxes of $750 (in the 25% tax bracket, this means $3,000 x .25 = $750) PLUS a 10% penalty of $300 ($3,000 x .10 = $300). In order to get his $3,000 out of his Traditional IRA, he would have to pay a total of $1,050 in income taxes. Another way to say this is that he would only get 65% of his money back in his pocket, because 35% went to the IRS. In dollars, this means that $1,050 goes to the IRS and $1,950 goes to Bill. That's a pretty expensive withdrawal, isn't it? This is why it is very important to be sure that you have enough emergency money and savings set aside so that you won't have to touch these accounts once you set them up.

4) The Roth IRA offers more withdrawal flexibility before you turn age 59 ½ by allowing you to remove your principal at any time without having to pay any income taxes and without a 10% tax penalty. The IRS will let you have your contribution amounts (your *principal*) back at any time because you've already paid taxes on this money and you didn't get a tax deduction for putting money in the account. The 10% penalty does apply to withdrawals of earnings from Roth IRA's if you aren't at least 59 ½ years old or if you haven't had the Roth IRA for more than five years, whichever is greater.

For example, if you're under 59 ½ and you deposited $3,000 into a Roth IRA last year, and it grew by 10% to be $3,300, you could take out up to $3,000 (the amount of your principal) and not have to pay any income taxes or penalties because you've already paid taxes on that money before you put it into the Roth IRA. Believe it or not, the IRS doesn't want to tax you twice on the same money. If you took out any part of the $300 of growth over and above principal amount of $3,000, you'd have to pay taxes PLUS a 10% penalty on the $300. You'd have to pay the taxes and the penalty because you didn't hold up your end of the deal with the IRS to keep the money in the account until you're 59 ½ or until the Roth IRA had existed for five years, whichever was greater.

To give you a specific example, if Bill Smith took out the full $3,300, he wouldn't pay any taxes or penalties on the first $3,000 because that was his principal contribution. However, he would pay income taxes based upon his tax bracket (25% of $300 = $75) PLUS a 10% penalty (10% of $300 = $30) on any amount he took out after he had taken out his $3,000 of principal. Bill would have a total tax bill of $105.

5) The Traditional IRA, because the money in the account has never had income tax paid on the principal or the earnings, must begin a schedule of partial withdrawals once the account owner turns age 70 ½. The IRS is basically saying, "Mr. Smith, you've never paid tax on that money, and we would like you to start taking some money out each year so that you can pay taxes on it before you die." The account does not have to be closed out when you turn 70 ½; you simply have to start taking withdrawals based on a calculation that takes your age, your spouse's age, and the previous year end account balances of all of your IRA's into consideration. Some people mistakenly decide to close out their IRA's in order to go ahead and get the tax paid so that they don't have to worry about the distribution every year. This is generally a very serious mistake and should be avoided! For example, if you have $100,000 in a Traditional IRA and you decide to close it out in one year, all of that $100,000 gets included as income in that year. You probably will

> You should leave money in the IRA's as long as you can unless you have an estate planning or income tax strategy in place.

have to pay income tax based upon being in a higher marginal tax bracket, and you will be left with a smaller amount of money that you'll then need to reinvest in an account that you'll have to report and pay tax on the earnings every year going forward. In the end, you get less money, more taxes, and more headaches! Generally speaking, you should leave money in the IRA's as long as you can unless you have an estate planning or income tax strategy in place.

6) The Roth IRA never has to start a schedule of required minimum distributions because the IRS has already gotten you to pay income taxes on the amount of your principal deposit into the account. As a result, a Roth IRA is a great place to keep money if you think you'll never need to spend it. Your beneficiaries (other than your spouse) will have to take some money out each year after you die, but that money will be completely tax-free. A Roth IRA is a great tool to help you accumulate wealth and to pass wealth to your heirs in a tax-efficient manner.

The decision of whether to put money into a Traditional IRA, a Roth IRA, or a combination of both is a fairly complex decision that your financial professional can help you understand. Sometimes, the decision simply boils down to the need to get a tax deduction to reduce income taxes in a certain year. Sometimes your income level makes the decision easy because you may not be able to make a contribution to either one of the accounts. The decisions about when and how much to take out of these accounts are very complex, so be sure to seek professional advice. The tax laws regarding these savings vehicles are always changing, so keep in touch with your financial professional and a tax adviser.

Taxable Accounts – Generally, once you have maximized the amount you can invest in a tax-favored way (employer plan, IRA's, annuities, etc.), your only realistic option is to invest money in an account that will require you to report your earnings and pay tax on the growth each year. Over time, this is a slower way to have your money grow because each year you have to send the IRS a portion of your profits, but it is certainly better than doing nothing.

Situations in which it would be good for you to have investments in taxable accounts would be:

- If you plan on needing money for a large purchase, second home, college, etc. prior to reaching age 59 ½.
- If you are uncertain about your future cash flow and feel you may need a larger cushion than what your emergency money could afford you.
- If you're not in a high tax bracket and don't pay much tax in the first place.

A taxable account would be an account that isn't offered through your employer, isn't an IRA, and one that you could take money out of or put money into without having to worry about taxes, penalties, and timeframes. A checking account, savings account, or a regular brokerage account could be examples of this.

As you can see, there are many types of accounts available to you to help you reach your financial goals. Your financial professional can help you find the right type of account if you can tell her when you think you may need the money, what you may need it for, how much you might need, and what your income situation may be at that time. Do your homework before you meet with your financial professional and she'll be able to do a better job to help you reach your goals.

Things You Need To Do Now

1. Review any existing IRA's that you might have with your financial professional.

2. If your budget allows, if you qualify based upon income and age considerations, and if your retirement goal requires you to invest more than you currently invest, consider making contributions to a Traditional or Roth IRA.

3. Talk in detail with your financial professional about the right accounts, amounts, and investments.

SECTION I - FINANCES

Chapter Seven

How Much Should You Invest?

The question of how much you should invest for retirement, or any other financial goal, is complicated and has many variables that you and your financial professional will have to address together. For some of you, the answer to this question is based simply on the fact that you may only have a certain amount of money left every month even if you cut your expenses to the bare minimum. If this is your situation, you will simply be trying to get the best retirement you can for the amount of money you can save and invest. You may have to come to the realization that the retirement that you would ideally like to have may not be a realistic option for you. You may have to work longer than you'd like, and you may still have to live on less money than you would like to have available to you. The value of your investments and the size of your nest egg will determine your standard of living in retirement. It is important that you save and invest as much as you can, that you obtain as great a return on your investment as possible, and that you manage taxes and expenses as prudently as possible.

If you have the good fortune to have *disposable income*, you'll need to know whether it's okay to spend that money on goods or services for your enjoyment and consumption today, or if you shouldn't spend that money today so that you can have money available to purchase goods and services after you retire. *Disposable income* is a term used to describe the amount of money left at the end of each month that could be saved or spent in any way you'd like without adversely affecting your ability to purchase the necessities.

In planning for your retirement, you'll need to determine, as best as you can estimate, knowing that dreams, expectations, and circumstances change with time, the following:

- *When you'd like to retire* – When would you like to be able to stop having to worry about going to work in order to ensure that you can live a comfortable lifestyle? Would you be happy retiring at age 50, 60, 65, 70, etc.?
- *How much income you'd like to have in retirement* – For example, if you were to retire today, how much money would you need to live comfortably? Take into account factors such as whether or not you'll have to pay a mortgage or rent; whether or not your children will be on their own by then; the fact that you won't need to save money out of your income anymore for retirement; and what things you'd like to do during retirement that you don't do now (travel, buy a second home, donate to charity, etc.). It's important that you walk through these expenses on paper and get as close as you can. Assumptions you make will change over time, but you need to have a reference point from which to start.
- *What rate of growth you expect your investments to acquire from now until you retire.* Your financial professional can also help with this – 2%, 5%, 8%, 10%, etc.
- *How fast you think costs will go up each year for the rest of your life* – Historical inflation rates are somewhere around 3.5% per year. Your financial professional will factor inflation into your calculations to give you an idea how much you'll need when you retire. For example, if you think you'll need $50,000 per year in income when you retire at age sixty-five, and you are currently thirty-five years old, you'll actually need $136,328 when you are sixty-five years old to be able to buy the same amount of stuff that you can buy today

with $50,000 (based on a 3.5% compounded annual inflation rate). And that $136,328 will continue going up every year because costs are almost always going up. When you turn sixty-six, inflation will require that you now have $141,099, when you're sixty-seven you'll need $146,037, when you're sixty-eight you'll need $151,148, and so on. Each year will probably be higher and higher. Your parents will easily be able to tell you that they used to live comfortably on a lot less money than what they have to have now because postage stamps, milk, cars, etc. all go up in price. Remember, inflation is an evil that you must not fail to take into account! You must stay ahead of inflation.

- *How long you expect to live* – No one knows this for sure, but you can generally expect that *mortality tables* are going to be pretty accurate. *Mortality tables* are mathematical analyses done to see how long a person is expected to live based upon his or her current age. Be sure that you take into account factors in your situation such as a history of longevity in your family, your current health, and the risk levels of your hobbies and interests, etc. It is much better to plan to live longer than you think, as neither you nor your financial professional would like for you to come into his office on your eighty-sixth birthday to pick up your retirement check only to find out that you had planned to live to be eighty-five years old and that all of your retirement money had been spent the year before.
- *What income tax bracket you expect to be in – both before and after you plan to retire* – You'll need to know what your potential income sources will be when you retire (pension, Social Security, etc.) and you'll also need to have some idea of what your income might be up until you retire. Take a copy of your most recent tax return with you to your meeting with your financial professional. If you're self-employed, take a couple of years' tax returns.

Again, there are countless ways to invest for retirement and other financial goals. Let's talk about investments for a moment.

Investments 101

The best investment for you is one that allows you to:

- Sleep at night without excessively worrying about your investments;
- Meet your goal of retiring at a certain age with a certain amount of income;
- Live happily in your current lifestyle while you are working and investing, without having to dramatically cut back on things you like to have or things you like to do.

In short, the best investment is one that historically can get you from your current lifestyle to your retirement lifestyle with as much return and as little risk as possible.

In short, the best investment is one that historically can get you from your current lifestyle to your retirement lifestyle with as much return and as little risk as possible.

In general, the safer an investment is, the lower its rate of return. The more aggressive (or risky) an investment, the greater the potential for a higher return. Investing appropriately means you've analyzed the different options available to you and chosen a mix of investments that will generate a return that will most likely allow you to meet your financial goals. Some people mistakenly think investing is like gambling and use phrases like "play the market," or "roll the dice," but prudent purchases of investments other than bank accounts and placement of monies in places other than mason jars and mattresses is a time-tested and proven way to have your money work most efficiently for you. Michael Maulboussin, chief investment strategist for Credit Suisse First Boston said, "Investing is really the *opposite* of gambling. The longer you gamble, the more assured you are of a loss. The longer you invest, the better your assurance that you'll be up."[1]

Some people, for fear of making a bad decision, choose not to make any decisions about their investments. This book combined with a relationship with a financial professional can dramatically help simplify your decisions. The best intentions never put into action are soon forgotten in the pace of today's lifestyles.

An Example to Help All This Make Sense

Let's talk about Bill Smith again. He's earning $50,000 per year and he thinks he'll need about 75% of that amount when he retires as he expects to have his house paid off; he doesn't think he'll travel a lot as he likes to fish and work in his yard; and he doesn't think he'll have any other major changes in his lifestyle when he retires. Bill doesn't want to factor Social Security into his retirement plan as he doubts that it will be there when he retires. His company does not have a pension plan (a pension, in this case, is a monthly payment Bill could receive after he retires). Bill's further assumptions are as follows:

Current Age	35
Age at Retirement	65
Years until Retirement	30
Current Value of Investments	$10,000
Expected Growth Rate of Investments	8%
Assumed Inflation Rate	3.5%
Desired Retirement Income at 65 (in today's dollars inflated by 3.5%... $37,500 at 3.5% inflation for 30 years)	105,255
Expected Lifespan	to age 100

What this means is that Bill is now thirty-five, enjoys his job, and plans to work until he's sixty-five. That means he has thirty more years to work, save, invest, and pay off his mortgage. He thinks he'll need less income during retirement than he's making today, and 75% of his current salary is $37,500. But, in thirty years (when he's 65) he'll need $105,255 to buy the same amount of stuff he would be able to buy today with $37,500 (remember, he'll need more every year after sixty-five because costs keep going up due to inflation). He wants to *plan* to live to be one hundred years old so that he doesn't run out of money, if he lives as long as his grandmother did (she died at ninety-eight). If he dies before he turns one hundred, he's decided to donate all of his remaining investments that he never got to spend to charity. He thinks his investments will have an average return of 10% per year, but he wants to use an estimate of 8% to play things on the safe side.

The Results for Bill Smith

The nest egg that Bill needs to have accumulated when he turns sixty-five should be approximately $1,833,605. Yes, that is 1.8 million dollars. He'll start taking money out of this nest egg in the month he retires, and he'll keep taking money out every month during his retirement to pay him enough money to afford the lifestyle he's planned for.

An important thing to remember, and Bill fortunately does remember after talking with his financial professional, is that *investing doesn't stop when he retires.* His style of investing may change, and he may invest more conservatively, but he knows that he can't take this nest egg out of the investments on the day he retires and deposit it into his savings account. Bill realizes that he has thirty-five years (from age sixty-five to age one hundred) that he needs his money to continue working for him, and he expects that his investments will continue to average 8% per year. If he averages less than 8% per year, he runs the risk of depleting his nest egg before he reaches age one hundred because it isn't growing fast enough to stay ahead of the amount he is withdrawing.

In order to accumulate this nest egg of $1,833,605 by the time he's sixty-five years old, we'll look at the following assumptions. The $10,000 he already has in his 401(k) should grow to be around $100,627. So that means that he'll need to save money every month to make up the $1.7 million difference ($1,833,603 needed minus the $100,627 that his existing investments should grow to), and the amount that he needs to invest is $1,163 per month. He needs to put this money into accounts that can obtain an overall average of 8%. It does not mean that he can put that amount per month into a 1% savings account and believe that his money will grow into the required nest egg. Bill fortunately knows that he can't just put $1,163 per month into a no risk account and expect it to average 8% per year. He knows he has to take some risk to attain his retirement goal.

The harder your money works for you (the higher return it gets), the less you have to invest every month. The slower your money works (the less return it gets), the greater the amount you must contribute to your nest egg. Basically, you can either have your money working hard for you, or you can work hard for a longer period of time. The ideal situation is for you to work for a short period of time by having your money work hard for you. Which situation would you prefer?

To summarize, here are Bill's results:

Desired Retirement Income per Year (today's dollars)	$37,500
Nest Egg Required at age sixty-five	$1,833,605
Growth of Existing Investments	$100,627
Remaining Nest Egg to Accumulate	$1,732,978
Return on Investments	8%
Monthly Investment Needed	$1,163

Let's look at a couple of scenarios for Bill's financial plan – one in which Bill gets scared of taking risk and wants to assume a lower return on his investments, and one in which Bill gets more aggressive and wants to try and obtain a greater return on his investments.

What If Bill Gets Scared?

If Bill one day said, "I'm scared of the stock market because I've lost some money and I've seen other people lose a great deal. I just want to play it safe." Bill could then maybe average about 4% per year. If he only got 4% per year (instead of 8% that he potentially could average in the stock market), he would need to have a $3.3 million nest egg (versus $1.8 million) and would have to invest $4,784 per month to get there (versus $1,163). Do you see why these numbers change so dramatically? If your money is paying you a lot less (paying you 4% instead of 8%), then you have to have a lot more of it to get the bills paid. In order to get a lot more money in a nest egg, especially when the nest egg is only earning 4%, you need to invest more money. For those of you that do a lot of cooking, in order to make a larger cake (the nest egg), you need to increase the quantities of the ingredients. The recipe for retirement when you use a lower rate of return requires you to add more ingredients, and the main ingredient (for your retirement nest egg) is money! Again, you can choose to work hard if you'd like, or you can let your money work hard for you.

If Bill stands firm in his decision to not take much (if any) risk, his choices at this point, in order to maintain his plan to retire at sixty-five and live on $37,500 per year, are

- *He'll need to invest $4,784 per month* -Knowing that Bill's current income per month is $4,166, he would realize that there is no way he can invest that amount per month because it's more than he actually makes.
- *Work longer* – At 4% growth on his investments, Bill would need to work until he was over ninety years old to meet his goal for retirement income. This is not realistic, as Bill would never have enough years to enjoy a retirement.
- *Reduce the amount of income he'd like to have in retirement* - If Bill decided that he could save the $1,163 per month that was shown when he thought he would like to obtain an 8% return per year and retire at age sixty-five, he would have to reduce his retirement income goal from $37,500 to $9,500 per year. This decrease is a 75% pay-cut, and it comes as a result of getting 50% less return on his investments. Bill knows there is no way he could live, much less live happily, on $9,500 per year.

What should Bill do? Bill has looked at his choices, and he's decided that he needs to take the time to learn more from his financial professional about investing so that he can feel comfortable about taking more risk. The math has proven that taking less risk means that he has to work until he's too old to enjoy retirement or he has to live on an amount that is far below even his lowest expectations and his worst financial nightmare. He has decided that there are more drawbacks to taking less risk than there are drawbacks to taking more risk. He's realized that his conservative stance will *guar-*

antee him an *unsatisfactory* retirement. He decides that taking more risk is definitely worth it for him. Bill meets with his financial professional, and together they set up a plan in which Bill is investing $1,200 per month as that is simply the most he feels he can squeeze out of his budget. Bill decides that he could live on $30,000 per year in retirement (instead of $37,500), and so he'll need to try to obtain an average return of about 7.25% per year (instead of 8%).

The $1,200 per month will be invested in a diversified investment portfolio that historically has returned about 7.25% per year. There are some investments that take more risk and have gotten an average return greater than 7.25%, and there are some investments that are less risky that have averaged less than 7.25%, but the average over all the investments is about 7.25%. Bill's financial professional tells him that based upon historical statistics the portfolio could go down as much as 10% in one year. Bill is willing to assume that risk in the hopes of averaging 7.25% per year. He also tells Bill that the portfolio could have a great year of up to 22%. Bill appreciates his honesty, ability to present both the good and the bad, and the time he spent educating him about the alternatives available to Bill.

To summarize, here are Bill's results after he's changed his mind regarding how much risk he feels comfortable taking:

Desired Retirement Income Per Year (in today's dollars)	$30,000
Nest Egg Required at age sixty-five	$1,621,915
Growth of Existing Investments	$81,643
Remaining Nest Egg to Accumulate	$1,540,272
Expected Return on Investments	7.25%
Monthly Investment Needed	$1,200

Knowing the issues prior to retirement is extremely important, and Bill is glad he talked about these issues at age thirty-five, instead of waiting until it's too late (a time when there is not enough money being earned through his job and not enough time left to save enough for retirement).

Be sure that you do not wait until it's too late to become educated about the issues, to talk with your financial professional, to decide what your financial goals are, and to decide what assumptions you want to use to create those goals (such as the age when you would like to retire, the amount of income you'll need, and the rate of return you think is reasonable based on your risk tolerance).

What If Bill Gets More Aggressive?

Let's assume that Bill feels that the stock market is the place to be for the next thirty years, and that he puts all of his money (except for his emergency money) in stocks and growth investments that invest in a wide range of companies (large, medium, small, international, etc.). Let's assume that he earned an average of 10% per year instead of getting the 8% that he was hoping to obtain. Bill's alternatives under this more aggressive example are much better than the alternatives he had if he only obtained a 4% return.

Let's review the math that Bill and his financial professional used to put together his original financial plan....

Desired Retirement Income Per Year (in today's dollars)	$37,500
Nest Egg Required at age sixty-five	$1,833,605
Growth of Existing Investments	$100,627
Remaining Nest Egg to Accumulate	$1,732,978
Return on Investments (Expected)	8%
Monthly Investment Needed	$1,163

If Bill obtained a 10% return and invested $1,163 per month for thirty years until he was sixty-five, his numbers would actually look like this:

Retirement Income Available Per Year (and have investments last until Bill's age one hundred)	$59,000
Amount of Nest Egg at age sixty-five	$2,248,787

If Bill were able to obtain a 10% return on his money instead of the 8% he had planned to obtain, he would have the following options:

- *Retire early* – Bill could retire when he turns fifty-nine, as he would have accumulated a nest egg big enough to pay him $37,500 per year (in today's dollars) until he turns one hundred. Bill's example shows that you should try and be a person that is able to retire ahead of schedule, versus a person that is always a "day late and a dollar short." You can pursue this by creating and sticking to your investment plan, by following professional advice, and by having the faith to trust that the law of long-term averages will prove itself true.
- *Continue with his plan to retire at sixty-five and have a larger nest egg available to pay him a larger monthly amount after he retired* – If Bill continued making his monthly investments and kept working until he was age sixty-five because he enjoyed his job, he would have a nest egg worth approximately $2,248,787. This amount is over a half million dollars more than what he had expected to have when he estimated the growth rate of his investments at 8%. This larger nest egg would allow him to withdraw the equivalent of $59,000 per year in today's dollars throughout his retirement. These calculations factor in inflation, and Bill's first year withdrawal from his investments would actually be $165,601 due to costs increasing 3.5% per year, but he would have enough money in his nest egg to have it last until he turned 100 years old. A 10% return on his $2,248,787 nest egg in his first year of retirement would be $224,878, and if he only needed to spend $165,601 in his first year of retirement (equal to $59,000 today), he would still see his investments grow by almost $60,000! These dollar amounts are attainable if you set goals early, approach them systematically and with discipline, achieve adequate investment returns, and make prudent changes when necessary after discussion with your financial professional.
- *Reduce or stop his monthly investments as he nears retirement* - When Bill (after talking with his financial professional) sees

> that the value of the investments will meet his goal even if he reduces or stops his monthly investment, he could decrease or stop his monthly investment as he gets closer to retirement. This would give him more money to spend and enjoy before he retires instead of having to stick to his goal of saving $1,163 per month. I'm sure you'd like it if your financial professional told you, "It looks like things are going to be fine for your retirement. Why don't we cut back on the amount you're investing? You can take a vacation instead." Based on a 10% return, Bill could stop investing $1,163 per month as early as when he turns age forty-three because the value of his existing investments plus the monthly investments he had made between the ages of thirty-five and forty-three would grow enough (by themselves) to be an adequate nest egg. However, it would be prudent for Bill to continue some savings schedule in order to provide a cushion for retirement in case he doesn't average 10% per year after he turns age forty-three, as he would still have another twenty-two years until he retired. A lot of things can change over twenty-two years – both good and bad. During that time, Bill could also change his mind and desire less risk, want more income in retirement, or want to retire sooner. He could also lose his job, have a reduction in earnings, or have family emergencies that take money away from his nest egg. In any of these situations, Bill would wish that he had continued investing even when the road looked like it was paved with gold. It is always better to err on the side of caution, to plan for the worst case, and to under-promise but over-deliver.

In summary, consult with your financial professional and invest as much as you can as early as you can. She will help you decide which type of account would be best for you, what investments would be the best for you to own inside of those accounts, and what amount you need to invest. She will also keep you aware of the risks that you are taking, how you could reduce risk without sacrificing any return, and of other potential investments.

Things You Need To Do Now

1. **Consult with your financial professional about risk, return, account structure, goals, amounts, tax considerations, growth assumptions, inflation assumptions, historical returns, asset allocation.** Use your common sense and this book to help guide you.
2. **Go back to the start of this chapter and write your answers to the assumptions that you need to make in the margin so that you'll put yourself through the paces of actually thinking about these issues before you meet with your financial professional.** Until ideas and thoughts are written down, they are still ideas and thoughts. Write down the information you need to help you create goals, and then write down the goals. Put it in writing!

SECTION I - FINANCES

Chapter Eight

Financial Issues for Younger People

Investing for retirement is not the only financial issue that you will have to deal with in your life. The purpose of the next two chapters is to try to give you a brief discussion of many of the remaining topics you may encounter. This chapter will discuss issues that need to be addressed early in life, issues for investors who are just getting started, young families, those rebuilding wealth after divorce or financial disaster, etc. The next chapter will discuss issues relevant to middle-aged to older people – those who already have some financial framework started, those who are quickly approaching retirement, those in retirement, and those who are trying to protect what they have for themselves or their family members. I urge you to read both chapters, regardless of your age or situation, so that you can be aware of the issues that other family members and coworkers may need to address and so that you can be sure you know what you need to do in order to ensure your financial well-being. As we've previously discussed, your financial professional should be able to help you understand what your options are regarding these issues and to help you make a decision that is best for you.

Now that you've determined how much you're worth, where you are currently spending your money, what your ideal budget should look like, developed a game plan to obtain an adequate amount in savings, and gotten a good general understanding of the options available to you to help you towards retirement, your next prudent step would be to make sure you have adequate insurance.

Health Insurance

Health Insurance is vitally important to the financial well being of people in America today. Most people have some sort of health insurance coverage available through their employers, called *group health insurance*. Typically, the employer pays some, or all, of the cost of the policy for the employee as a perk to help attract and retain employees. If you have *pre-existing conditions* (medical issues that you have dealt with in the past that could need continued treatment), a group health insurance plan through an employer may be your only option to obtain coverage, as they have to accept most individuals. If you are in great health and you are in a group health insurance plan, you are paying a higher premium than you would if you purchased a policy on your own because your premium is helping pick up the cost of the less healthy people (unless your employer has negotiated a great deal with an insurance company). When evaluating health insurance, you need to consider the following issues:

- *Covered items* – What exactly does the insurance policy pay for? Does it pay for annual physicals, extended hospital stays, allergy shots, psychiatric counseling, emergency room visits, prescriptions, and pregnancy issues? Look at your life, family history, and your habits and determine what issues you feel are likely to crop up, and try and make sure they're covered.
- *Deductible* – This is the amount that you must pay out of your pocket before the insurance company has to start paying for your expenses. The higher the deductible, the more you have to pay, the less the insurance company has to pay, and thus your premium is generally lower.
- *Copay* – This is the amount that you must pay each time you

have an occurrence and can be a flat dollar amount ($20 per visit) or a percentage of the cost (the insurance company pays 80% and you pay 20%) or a combination of both.

- *Out of pocket maximum* – This is the amount that is the most you will pay in a single year for covered expenses. Once you exceed that amount, the insurance company pays all of the expenses until the amount paid reaches the policy maximums.

Life Insurance

Life insurance is vitally important to the continued financial stability of your family once you pass away. Life insurance pays a death benefit to a beneficiary (or beneficiaries) and is used for two primary reasons:

1) *Income Replacement* - To replace the income your family depends upon that you would have made if you were still living and
2) *Estate Planning* - To help pass your estate most effectively to your heirs.

Let's talk about each reason in more detail.

1) Income replacement – Let's talk about Bill Smith, and assume that he's married to Mary Smith and they have two children, ages three and one. Bill makes $50,000 per year, and Mary stays at home with the kids. If Bill were to die, how would Mary pay the bills?

We learned earlier in the section about Social Security that there might be some monthly benefit available to each child while they're under age eighteen and at home, and that there may be a benefit available to Mary while she has children under the age of sixteen. Let's assume that Social Security is able to provide monthly benefits of $2,000 ($24,000 per year). If Mary needs $50,000 to live on, she needs an additional $26,000.

Bill and Mary would need to talk to their financial professional to determine the right amount of coverage on each of their lives. Factors they need to discuss are:

- *Working situation of surviving spouse* – Would Bill want Mary to have to go back to work or would he like her to be able to stay at home? If Mary were to die, would Bill need to hire a nanny or put the kids in daycare, or would he like to be able to quit his job and stay with the kids himself?
- *Payment of debts* – Would Bill want to have all the debts paid off such as car loans, credit cards, mortgages, personal loans, funeral expenses, etc.? If these debts were paid off, how much would Mary then need to live on since the monthly expenses would be lower?
- *Planning for college* – Would Bill want to have an amount paid from life insurance set aside to be invested for future college expenses? If so, how much?

Hypothetically, let's say that Bill would want Mary to be able to stay at home with the kids so that she wouldn't have to go to work if he died. He knows that she'll have her hands full with the kids and he doesn't want her to have to worry about making ends meet while at the same time having to deal with the death of her husband and helping the kids deal with the loss of their father. Bill would want all the debts paid off, but he would want to keep her annual income at $50,000 even though her monthly expenses are lower so that she can have some cushion in her budget. He also would like to have an amount set aside from the life insurance to be earmarked for college for each of the kids.

The estimate for the appropriate amount of life insurance is as follows:

Debts to be paid off (mortgage, car loan, credit cards)	$200,000
Lump sum investment for college for two kids	$70,000
Funeral	$10,000
Total Lump Sum Debts and College	**$280,000**
Additional income needed ($50,000 desired less $24,000 from Social Security)	$26,000

Interest rate expected to obtain on life insurance proceeds to generate income	5%
Lump sum needed to generate required income (26,000 ÷ .05)	**$520,000**

(This means that $520,000 invested at a 5% return will provide an income of $26,000.)

Total Life Insurance Needed on Bill's life ($280,000 + $520,000)	**$800,000**

If Mary were to die, Bill would like to have all the debts paid off, have money set aside for college, and be able to hire an in-home nanny at a cost of $20,000 per year. Evaluating those needs in the same format reveals that Mary needs $680,000 life insurance on her life.

Now that they know how much life insurance they need, they need to decide *what type* of life insurance is best for their situation. In general, there are two types of life insurance – term and permanent.

Term insurance provides a death benefit if the insured dies during the term of insurance – ten years, fifteen years, twenty years, etc. During that period of time the policy provides coverage, the amount you pay for insurance does not change and is guaranteed by the insurance company to stay the same. Most young couples generally buy term insurance because it is inexpensive in the short term compared to permanent insurance.

If Bill is thirty-five years old, does not use tobacco products, and is in great health, he may have an annual premium for a 20-year level term policy of $500. Mary, who is also thirty-five years old, a non-tobacco user, and in great health, might have a premium of around $350 per year for a 20-year level term policy. Regardless of changes in their health condition for the next twenty years, Bill and Mary would pay their set annual premiums and be guaranteed to have life insurance. At the end of the twenty years, Bill and Mary can cancel their insurance policies (they could also cancel the insurance before the end of the twenty years) or they could ask the insurance company to cover them for a longer period of time. At that time, the insurance company would be able to charge them a rate based upon their current ages and health status – and it would certainly be more expensive because Bill and Mary would be fifty-five years old.

Insurance rates vary depending upon the state that governs your policy. Your health, your age, your habits (scuba diving, racing, private pilot, etc.), and the additional features you choose (waiver of premium, child riders, accidental death benefits, etc.) will also affect your rate, so get your financial professional to get you a few quotes, be sure you tell him what he needs to know, and get the insurance *before* something happens to you!

Permanent insurance is also known as *cash value life insurance*, and this type of insurance has two parts – the first is the death benefit that is paid when you die, the other is the cash value that accumulates inside the policy. When you make a premium payment for term insurance, all of your payment is going towards paying the insurance company for the cost of insuring your life. When you make a premium payment in cash value life insurance, some of the payment goes towards the cost of insurance, and some goes into the cash value in the hopes that it will increase in value over time.

The benefit of having cash value life insurance is that the amount growing inside the policy is protected from income taxes and can be used in future years to pay the costs of life insurance or can be drawn out of the policy to be used for any purpose. The cash value can grow at a fixed rate that's paid by the insurance company (whole life or universal life) or it can change in value based on the performance of investments inside the policy (universal life and/or variable life). The cash value builds up over time, and it is hoped that at some point in the future you won't have to make any more payments because the policy can pay for itself. Another benefit of having cash value is that the cash value can be borrowed against without having to pay income taxes to help fund your lifestyle in later years. Many business owners and wealthy people use cash value life insurance to shelter money from taxes while it grows inside the policy (you don't generally get a deduction for putting money in a cash value life insurance policy) and to provide them with some tax–free cash flow in later years.

It can be argued that one should buy cash value life insurance while you are young because the costs are far cheaper than they will be in later years, and that over your lifetime you'll pay less in premiums for cash value life insurance than you will for term insurance even though the annual premiums are higher at first. Check with your financial professional for the best course of action for you and your family.

2) Estate planning – Life insurance can be used very effectively in the estate planning process because life insurance proceeds are paid directly to a beneficiary (or beneficiaries) without having to go through probate *and* the proceeds are not taxable as regular income to the recipient. Life insurance is important for you to have if you want your beneficiaries to have money on hand to help settle your affairs versus having to sell real estate (or other assets) that you would prefer kept in the family. This provides the estate with enough *liquidity* – cash on hand to pay expenses.

There are three parties to a life insurance contract:

a) The *owner* is the person or entity that has control over the policy
b) The *insured* is the person whose life is being insured
c) The *beneficiary* is the person or entity that receives the death benefits.

It is very important to be sure the owner is the right person or entity (such as a trust or corporation) to make sure that *estate taxes* are minimized or avoided. *Estate taxes* are the taxes payable to the IRS if a person's estate – including life insurance owned by that person – exceeds the *estate tax applicable exclusion* of $1,500,000 in 2004-2005; $2,000,000 in 2006-2008; $3,500,000 in 2009; and an unlimited amount in 2010. In the year 2011, the estate tax applicable exclusion reverts back to the amounts applicable for 2003. Due to the current estate tax situation, it sometimes makes sense to have other family members or an *irrevocable life insurance trust* own the insurance policies on your life so that the death benefit can be paid to the beneficiaries without any income tax (as is the case with any life insurance death benefit) and without being included in the calculation of estate value for estate taxes. Estate taxes can be as high as 49% of the amount over $2,000,000! How would you like to see 49% of your $500,000 life insurance policy that you paid for over the years go to the IRS?

A large number of retired people have the good fortune of having large accounts that probably won't need to be used for living expenses in their lifetime, and they would like for other family members (children and grandchildren) be the ones to really benefit from their situation. Oftentimes, people with large tax-deferred retirement accounts can start making withdrawals from these accounts in order to use that money to purchase a life insurance policy before *required minimum distributions* must begin at age 70 ½. This policy will allow the beneficiaries to receive money that is not subject to income taxes (as high as 35%) or estate taxes (as high as 50%). Basically, these people are easing money out of retirement accounts that they weren't going to spend anyway, paying the taxes on the money when it's withdrawn, and using it to create more money to be given to beneficiaries that won't be subject to as much as 85% in taxes.

For example, if Bill had an IRA worth $1,000,000 that he and his financial professional felt he really wouldn't ever need to support his lifestyle, he might consider taking $30,000 out of the IRA each year. He would pay income taxes on that $30,000 at his regular tax rate (about $10,000 tax) and use the remaining after-tax money (approximately $20,000) to pay an annual premium towards a life insurance policy. Depending upon his age and health, he might be able to have a policy that would pay a $1 million tax-free death benefit to his beneficiaries. In short, if he died in the first year that he took $30,000 out of the IRA to pay for the life insurance, he would have turned $30,000 into $1,000,000. That's a pretty good return, isn't it?! And - no taxes would be due on the $1,000,000!

Ask your financial professional about using your IRA to

fund a life insurance policy inside a trust. She'll help you, along with your accountant and attorney, to decide if this strategy is appropriate for your situation. Conversations with your financial professional should include the topics of insurance, estate valuations, estate taxes, proper ownership and beneficiary designations, acceptable rates from reputable insurance companies, etc.

College Education Planning

Planning for adequate funding for college for children and grandchildren is becoming a tremendous priority in people's' lives as the cost of college is increasing at a rate faster than inflation. The average cost for all expenses (tuition, fees, room, board, books, supplies, transportation, miscellaneous expenses) associated with attending an average in-state public college or university in the 2001-02 academic year was $11,976; out-of-state (nonresident) public four-year colleges and universities $17,740; private four-year colleges and universities $26,070.[1]

If college costs are increasing at an average rate of 7.7% per year on average,[2] it means that in ten years the average four-year public college or university will have an annual cost of $25,145; thus, four years of school will cost over $100,000! If you were able to start saving money for your eight year-old child in order to have enough money in ten years to pay for college, you'd need to invest $546 per month assuming an 8% growth rate.

> Keep in mind that if you don't start saving today, you have to save more tomorrow to make up for what you didn't do today.

Now that you know that college is very expensive (I'm sure you already know this) and that college is very necessary (I'm sure you know this, too), let's talk about how you could most prudently accumulate enough money to pay for your child's college education. Keep in mind that if you don't start saving today, you have to save more tomorrow to make up for what you didn't do today. If you never save any (or enough) money, you'll end up paying for college out of your cash flow. If you don't have any spare cash flow now to invest for college, you probably won't have any spare cash flow to pay for college in a few years – unless you have a plan in place. As a result, your child may have to borrow money (if they qualify) to attend school, or they may not be able to attend an adequate school, if at all.

A *Coverdell Education Savings Account* is an account in which you can place up to $2,000 per year until the child turns eighteen. The money can be invested in a diversified investment portfolio and the money grows tax-deferred (like your IRA) until the money is withdrawn from the account. You do not get an *income tax deduction* for making contributions, but the *growth* of the money receives preferential treatment from the IRS. If you make too much money (over $160,000 in 2004), you may not be able to contribute to one of these accounts, so check with your financial professional. You do not have to have earned income to open an account for a child beneficiary, and anyone can open an account for any beneficiary. However, the maximum amount that can be deposited each year for any beneficiary is $2,000. For example, this means that cach grandmother would not be able to open a $2,000 account each for one grandchild, because that would mean that $4,000 would be placed in an education account in that year, and the total amount for the child cannot exceed $2,000.

As long as the money is used for qualified educational expenses (tuition, fees, room, board, books, supplies, equipment, transportation, miscellaneous expenses), no income taxes are due on the withdrawal. If you do not use the money for college expenses, you (or your child) would have to pay regular income taxes on the increase in value that you withdrew PLUS a 10% penalty. The money has to be used for college by the time the child turns thirty years old or it can be rolled into the Education Savings account of another family member. A really good feature that makes this account flexible relates to the fact that money distributed from this type of account can also be used for qualified elementary and secondary school education expenses such as tutoring, computer equipment, room and board, uniforms, special needs services, and extended day program costs.[3]

A *529 College Savings Plan* is an account that allows you to make large contributions to an educational account that grow tax-deferred and can be drawn out free of income taxation if used for qualified education expenses. These plans are becoming increasingly popular because of the investment flexibility inside the account, tax benefits at withdrawal, and the fact that there are no income, state residency, or age restrictions regarding contributions.

Basically, a 529 Plan is sponsored by a specific state, and that state gets an investment company to handle the investments. Depending upon which state you live in, you may be able to obtain a state income tax (not federal income tax) deduction for amounts deposited into 529 Plans. You can use the benefits from any state plan for any college and you are not restricted to your state's schools. A *donor*, such as the parent, opens an account for a *beneficiary*, and the donor remains in control of the money as long as he desires. This is different from the Coverdell Education Savings Account in which the beneficiary must always receive the benefit of the funds withdrawn from the account and, depending upon the rules of the Coverdell Education Savings Account where you opened the account, the beneficiary gets control of the money in that account when he or she turns legal age (eighteen or twenty-one, depending upon your state). If money is drawn out and not used for college, regular income taxes PLUS the 10% penalty are payable by the person who got the benefit of the money (either the donor - if the donor just wanted to take the money out for himself or to close out the account - OR the beneficiary - if the donor let the beneficiary take money out to use for himself).

If you are able to contribute more than $2,000 per year towards investing for college, and you're reasonably sure that the child or some other member of the family will use the money for college education purposes, then a 529 Plan would probably be a good fit for you. You can make contributions to the Education Savings Account and the 529 Plan in the same year. If you can't invest more than $2,000 per year for your child, you should probably use the Coverdell Educations Savings Account.

An added benefit that a 529 Plan brings is that one donor can contribute up to $55,000 in one year without reducing the amount that the IRS will let them pass to their heirs at their death free of estate taxes. This is an excellent feature for grandparents with sizeable estates who would like to help family members pay for college while staying in control of the money, having that money grow protected from tax, having the option to change beneficiaries or draw the money out, and not having the value included in their estate tax calculation. Currently, the IRS will let a person give $11,000 per year to anyone without triggering any gift tax reporting. The 529 Plan allows someone to deposit five years worth of gifts of $11,000 into the account in one year (5 years x $11,000 per year = $55,000). Additional gifts to that person in that five-year period would be subject to gift tax since the exclusion amount was used up in the first year. For example, grandpa can deposit five years worth of $11,000 gifts in the first year for his grandson, and grandma can do the same thing (into the same account if desired). This means that grandpa can deposit $55,000, grandma can deposit $55,000, and so very quickly $110,000 has been placed into an education account that grows tax-favored; grandpa and grandma still stay in control of the money (they determine who uses it and for what purposes); the $110,000 is not included in their estate (the amount is pro-rated if they die before the five-year gift period has passed); and they can feel good knowing they're helping the family with college education expenses. If the first grandchild does not use all the money, the grandparents can change the beneficiary to another grandchild, and on it goes. If grandpa and grandma die, the person they named to take their place in control of the money takes over. Talk to your parents about helping pay for college for your children – everyone benefits from open communication and 529 Plans.

If you'd like to have money saved for a child for college or other uses, a *custodial account* may be of use to you. You can gift money to the account, and the money is the child's money as soon as it is deposited, but because the child is a minor there has to be a *custodian* in charge of the money. You may be the custodian, and you have a legal responsibility to manage the child's money prudently. Once the child reaches legal age for custodial accounts (legal age varies from state to state), he can use the money for whatever purpose he would like or he can leave it in the account - and it's totally up to him - not you. While it's a good idea to have money saved for the child, it may be even more important to train the child and to be ready and able to prudently use and manage the money.

Another method that is used to help accumulate money for college is to invest money in *taxable accounts* in the name of the parents or grandparents. The investments can be gifted to the children when they're ready for college. Although taxes may need to be paid each year because the money is not in a tax-favored account, once the investments are in the child's name, you can sell the assets and the taxes due are based on the *child's tax bracket*, which is probably lower than the parents' or grandparents' bracket. If the child doesn't need the money for college, the investments can be used by the parents or grandparents in any way they see fit because they haven't obligated themselves to a specific use of the money in order to receive beneficial tax treatment nor have they given the control of the money to anyone else. This situation is best for people who aren't sure if college is a reality for a child.

Business Retirement Plans

If you own a business, you have a lot of opportunities available to you to help you save income taxes <u>and</u> save money for retirement. You should do everything you can to take advantage of every legal deduction and benefit that the government will allow you.

As a business owner, whether you are a sole proprietor, a partnership, or incorporated, you can set up a retirement plan that allows you to get an income tax deduction from money you normally would have to pay income taxes on when you deposit that money into a retirement account. Just as we talked in an earlier chapter about ways that employees can save for retirement through their employers, business owners have the opportunity to set up those very same types of plans to help themselves and their employees. Some retirement plans currently allow people to deduct and defer up to $41,000 in 2004. This amount is scheduled to increase through the coming years.

If you have employees, you have a responsibility to offer your employees the same benefits that you have available to you once they've been with your business a certain amount of time and make a certain minimum amount of income. In some retirement plans like profit sharing and pension plans, the employer has to make contributions for the employee each year in which a contribution is made to the owner's account. In plans like 401(k)'s or S.I.M.P.L.E. IRA's, matching contributions to employee accounts are made only if the employee makes contributions to the account out of their pay. If the employee's budget or financial situation does not allow him to put money into a retirement account, the employer does not have to make contributions to the employee's account. This is good for the employer because he has lower expenses and thus more profits.

A business retirement plan can help you, the owner, hopefully reach retirement faster with lower income taxes each year. The retirement plan will also help you attract and retain some quality people through the years – people who will be loyal to your operation and appreciate your willingness to help them towards retirement. In addition to being able to set up a retirement plan through your business, you still potentially have the opportunity to save and invest money in personal retirement accounts (like Traditional and Roth IRA's). The rules regarding retirement planning and income taxation change constantly, so work closely with your financial professional and accountant to allow them to find the best plan for you now and to keep you aware of new and better plans for you to take advantage of as your business changes along with regulations.

Real Estate

We've talked a great deal about budgeting, retirement, and investing, but real estate is also a great way to accumulate wealth. Successful high net worth people typically have some portion of their net worth in real estate (in addition to their home). As with anything, it is prudent to diversify among types of investments. Just like you shouldn't have all your money in small-cap stocks, you shouldn't have all your money tied up in real estate.

The good things about real estate are that it can potentially generate income through rents collected; you do not have to pay income taxes each year on the amount the property increases in value; you can potentially have some tax write-off's from depreciation; and you can potentially defer the taxes due on the sale of investment property by reinvesting the proceeds from the sale of the property into another similar piece of property. This is called a *1031 exchange*. Talk to your accountant before you accept a contract to sell your property if you think you'd like to perform a 1031 exchange as there are several rules you must abide by in order to receive the full tax benefit.

> Current tax law allows you to sell your primary residence and pay no tax on the profits if you've lived in the home for two of the previous five years.

The bad things about real estate are that you might have to wait a long time before you can get your money out of a piece of property; you never really know what it's worth until you find someone willing to write a check and buy it from you; property taxes will increase as the value increases; expenses can suddenly appear for repairs, increased insurance costs, and marketing; and if someone gets hurt on your property you could be liable.

Current tax law allows you to sell your primary residence and pay no tax on the profits if you've lived in the home for two of the previous five years. Single persons can have up to $250,000 in profits exempted from tax, couples can have up to $500,000. For example, if you and your spouse have lived in your home for the last four years, you can sell your home and not have to pay any taxes on the increase in value up to $500,000. If you bought your home for $150,000 and sold it for $200,000, you do not have to pay any tax on the $50,000 profit. You can then use the money for anything you'd like – you can buy another home, travel, invest, etc. You do not have to roll the profits into another primary residence.

Asset Allocation

Asset allocation is a term used to say "don't put all your eggs in one basket" or "make sure you're diversified." You should have proper asset allocation inside of your investments; you should have proper asset allocation of types of investments (real estate, insurance, etc.); and you should have proper asset allocation between personal investments (your home, cars, etc.), your investments, and business investments.

With regards to proper asset allocation in your investments, you should generally operate under the principle that younger people can take more risk because they have more time to make up any downturns in their investments and that older people should be more conservative because they don't have as much time to recoup any losses. This does not mean that all thirty year-olds should all be invested exactly alike because you have to take into account factors such as income, risk tolerance, amount being invested, investment experience, and net worth. Proper asset allocation means that you have the right amount of money for your situation in investments that are appropriate for your age, risk tolerance, net worth, investing experience, financial goals, etc. Your financial professional can help you determine the right amount that you should have in each category that is appropriate for you.

The next chapter will discuss some other issues you'll more than likely encounter sometime in your life.

Things You Need To Do Now

1. **Compare your situation to some of the examples in this chapter by using actual numbers from your financial picture.**
2. **Read the next chapter.** (That was easy, wasn't it?)

SECTION I - FINANCES

Chapter Nine

Financial Issues For Everyone

This chapter will benefit people who already have done some financial planning and who have assets to manage. Usually, this situation applies to people who are middle-aged or older. I know that you're thinking, "At what age does one become 'middle-aged,' and when is someone defined as 'older'?" I don't know the answer to that question either. As a result, it makes sense for you to read this chapter regardless of your age. I say this because you can benefit from the information or you know someone that can benefit from the knowledge and awareness. In some cases, younger people who have inherited money or have high-paying jobs may have a need for knowledge about some of the topics in this chapter.

Long-Term Care Insurance

Also known as *nursing home insurance*, long-term care insurance is becoming an extremely popular way for today's baby boomers to protect their savings and investments from being spent on in-home or nursing home coverage. Approximately seventy-five companies sell a long-term care insurance product, and sales of individual long-term care policies increased 13% per year from 1995 to 2000.[1]

When people become sick, disabled, mentally impaired, or in need of continuing care, they have a need for ongoing attention to help assist in *activities of daily living. ADL's* are six activities that are used to determine a person's ability to care for himself. They are bathing, dressing, eating, continence, toileting, and transferring. Most policies require a person be unable to do two of the six ADL's listed above or be cognitively impaired (deterioration or loss in intellectual capacity) before the insurance company will consider paying a claim.

The national average annual cost for a nursing home stay is about $136 per day, or over $50,000 per year.[2] Costs in your area of the U.S. may be higher or lower, and they could range from $40,000 to $100,000. Unfortunately, almost seventy-two percent of people ages sixty-five and older are expected to use some form of home health care. That's almost three-quarters of that age group![3] Almost half of the people age sixty-five and older may spend time in a nursing home. Less than ten percent of older adults (age sixty-four and older) and even fewer near-older adults (those aged fifty-five to sixty-four) have purchased long-term care insurance.[4] This equates into the following statistics:

- An estimated sixty percent of disabled older adults living in communities rely exclusively on their families and other unpaid sources for their care.[5]
- The number of *working caregivers* (family members who have other jobs that are taking care of those needing care) is expected to increase over the next ten years to one in every ten employees. Those working caregivers currently spend an average of twenty-two hours per week providing elder care, and care giving responsibilities can last as long as eight to ten years. These working caregivers lose an average of $650,000 over their lifetimes in lost wages, lost Social Security benefits, and forfeited pension contributions.[6]

These statistics point towards the fact that there is a pretty good chance that you could use the benefits available in a long-term care insurance policy sometime in your life and that if you don't have insurance, a family member is going to have to take care of you. This care given by a family member will cost them time, money, and potentially their health. Have you seen a spouse work herself sick from taking care of the other spouse? The need for long-term care insurance is growing every day.

If you don't care about protecting your assets so that your surviving spouse or your family can have a comfortable lifestyle; if you don't care about the well being of your spouse or other family member who will probably turn into your unpaid caregiver; or if you simply cannot afford the premium for the insurance, don't purchase the coverage. However, if you can afford premiums that range from $1,500 to $10,000 per year; if you do want to make life as easy and enjoyable for your healthy family members; if you do want to protect your assets from being spent on nursing home costs; and if you do want the peace of mind associated with obtaining prudent insurance coverage (do you have insurance on your car and your house?), then talk with your financial professional or find a reputable long-term care insurance agent in your area.

When searching for a policy, you will need to make a determination concerning the following issues:

- *Rating and history of insurance company* - Is it a quality company that has been around for a long time? Does it have a history of stable rates or have they been increasing their rates? Is there an unusual history of complaints against the company or the agent?
- *Maximum daily benefit* – How much do you want the insurance company to pay per day of care that you need? The national average is about $135 per day, and that cost is increasing every year. If you purchase a policy that covers $120 per day, and the nursing home costs $135 per day, your family will need to pay $15 per day out of their (or your) pocket.
- *Elimination period* – How many days must you need home health care or nursing home care before the insurance company starts paying a benefit? Generally, Medicare has benefits for the first ninety days of nursing home stays. You can

generally choose an elimination period from fifty to one hundred days.

- *Maximum lifetime benefit* – What is the total amount that the policy will pay in your lifetime? If you purchase enough insurance to cover three years and you stay four years in a nursing home, the policy only pays for three years. You're on your own from that point forward.
- *Inflation protection* – Will the amount the policy pays for your daily benefit increase over time to try and keep up with the rising costs of nursing home coverage? At a five percent inflation rate, a nursing home that charges $130 per day will charge $211 per day in ten years. If you had a policy that did not allow for increases each year, you would be paying $81 per day out of your own pocket. $81 per day times thirty days equals $2,430 per month.

Insurance companies will evaluate your medical history, your age, and the benefits you select to determine how much your premium will be. If you have certain medical conditions, you may not be able to obtain coverage at a reasonable premium, if at all.

I need to mention a *Medicaid spend-down strategy* that people sometimes ask me about. The theory behind this strategy is to spend-down or give away assets so that the cost of in-home care or nursing home care will be paid for by Medicaid benefits. Medicaid benefits are available to people who do not have a certain amount of assets or a certain minimum amount of income. If you create a situation where you don't have either of these minimums, you have created a situation you spent your whole life (and reading this book) trying to avoid. You would have given away everything, spent everything, and lost complete control of everything in order to accomplish this goal. If you don't ever need continual care, you'll certainly wish you still had control of your assets and your financial life won't be very enjoyable. If you do need continual care, the good news is that you won't be paying for your nursing home care – the government will. The bad news is that you generally don't get to pick your location, you probably won't be feeling well enough to really care, and you won't be receiving the quality care that you could have gotten if you had purchased adequate insurance. It is illegal to willfully hide, retitle, or give away assets in attempt to qualify for Medicaid. The government can look back at your previous three years for attempts to knowingly defraud the system. Your financial professional can help you see whether or not you can afford long-term care insurance. Odds are that most people will find out that they can't afford to NOT have long term care insurance.

Retirement Income Planning

We live most of our lives working towards building a nest egg and our investments so that we will be able to retire. If we retire at age sixty-five, and we live to be ninety years old, that means we spent two-thirds of our life accumulating money and we'll spend one-third of our life dispensing what we've accumulated.

Because retirement is so important to people today and the actual targeted retirement date is such a focus, a lot of people lose sight of the fact that investing and managing money doesn't stop when you reach that magic retirement date. A great many people think that on your retirement date you take all of your money out of your IRA's and retirement accounts, deposit it into your checking account or certificates of deposit, and hope that the money lasts long enough. Someone that is sixty years old and planning to retire at age sixty-five typically thinks that they only have five more years left to invest, but they actually have the rest of their lives!

> Dipping into your principal that you've saved is okay, as long as the bucket that you're dipping the money out of is big enough to last you the rest of your life.

Since people are living longer, you have to make sure that you don't outlive your money. Costs go up every year (we talked about inflation earlier), and if costs go up faster than the rate that your pension and Social Security increase, in ten years you may have to be dramatically dipping into your investments to help make ends meet. Dipping into your principal that you've saved is okay, as long as the bucket that you're dipping the money out of is big enough to last you the rest of your life. The best way to ensure that your bucket is big enough is to make investments in assets that can consistently go up in value faster than the combined negative effect that taxes and inflation have on your money.

Although some people have pensions that pay them far more than they actually spend, or they have accumulated a nest egg so large that they could spend twice their normal amount during retirement even if they earned 2% on their money and never run out of money, most people need to take steps to make sure their money is still working hard enough and smart enough for them after retirement. If inflation is 3.5% per year, and your pension goes up at 3% per year, you're losing .5% per year. If you have unexpected expenses to repair your home, help a family member financially, or pay for uncovered medical expenses, what you thought was a good balanced budget in retirement changes dramatically. As we discussed earlier about the types of investments available, you have to take risk in order to get a higher return. As you get older, you want to take less risk because you're in more of the *protect mode* versus the *growth mode*. However, if you put all your investments in the safest investments available, you've subsequently made the decision to put them in the lowest returning investments. If these lowest returning investments don't keep up with inflation and taxes, you've guaranteed that you'll be in the *lose mode*. Most people would like the chance for gain versus a guaranteed loss. A chance for gain for most retirees is found in a diversified mix of conservative investments.

Your financial professional can set up a plan where you are sent a certain amount of money out of your account each month, each quarter, or once per year. You can also get money out of your accounts whenever you need some money. Investments that you spent years sending money to can be set up to send you money every month during retirement. Interest from investments can be paid to you whenever it is paid or it can be used to purchase more shares of your investments.

Your financial professional can also help you plan your income throughout your retirement so that you'll be able to roughly anticipate when you'll be dipping into principal (if ever) and whether or not that's okay for your situation. Investing does not stop when you retire; it stops when you stop living. Your *style* of investing will change over the years to a more conservative style. Investments do not have to entirely be liquidated in order for you to take an income from them – they can be sold little by little to fund your retirement lifestyle – this keeps your investments working efficiently and prudently in your best interests.

Investing does not stop when you retire; it stops when you stop living.

Income Taxes & Required Minimum Distributions

"There are only two certain things in life - death and taxes." We've all heard that saying, but one thing is also certain – there are ways to lower your tax bill. You should take advantage of every legal alternative available.

In the interests of brevity, consult with your financial professional and your CPA (or other tax advisor) about the best ways to lower your taxes based upon your individual situation. Some of the best ways to do that are for you to contribute as much as you can to the retirement plans offered by your employer (if available); make deposits to IRA's each year that you're eligible (even if you don't get a deduction when you put money in a Roth IRA, you are laying a foundation for having lower taxes at retirement); itemize deductions; invest in rental real estate so that you can have the depreciation write-off; spread the withdrawals from your retirement accounts over two or three tax years so that you aren't pushed into a higher marginal tax bracket due to lump-sum withdrawals in one year; meet regularly with your tax advisor to stay abreast of tax code changes; and sell investments when appropriate to *capture losses* to use against your existing capital gains or to reduce your income taxed at regular income tax rates. I would like to discuss this final point in a little more detail.

Capturing tax-losses - I hear a lot of people say, "I'm not going to sell any investment at a loss," or "I can't sell it now, it's below what I paid for it." People say these things for a couple of reasons. The first reason is usually because their pride won't allow them to admit that they might have made a bad investment decision or that they watched the investment go too far down in value without selling it. The other reason is that they want to stick to the common theory that says that if you hold onto an investment long enough, it will eventually come back. I need to make it clear that there are times when you need to sell an investment at a loss.

There are times when you need to sell an investment at a loss.

Investments are purchased so that they can hopefully be sold at a later date for a profit. Investments sitting inside of an account don't do you much good. You actually have to sell the investment and take the money outside of the account to enjoy the increase in value. Investments are bought with the full intention of selling them in the future, hopefully for a profit. But, not every investment is going to turn out to be a winner. A good investment manager knows when to sell his winners. An even better investment manager knows when to sell his losers. A stock that you bought for $10,000 that is now worth $5,000 does you absolutely no good, especially if the chances of that $5,000 going up in value are smaller than the chances of going up in another investment. The analogy I like to use compares an investment to a horse race.

The stock market doesn't care whether you have a profit or a loss, and it has no obligation to help you recover from poor investments.

Some horses start fast, some finish strong, but it's how a horse performs over the entire race that counts. You have the opportunity to change horses in the middle of the race when you see that your horse is fading (or has faded) and you see another horse that looks like it can improve your situation. It does absolutely no good to look back and see what it used to be worth or how fast your horse used to run. What is important is how reliable your horse is in the future. The stock market doesn't care whether you have a profit or a loss, and it has no obligation to help you recover from poor investments. You have to make the best of every situation as you try and look forward into the future. The only thing that matters is that you find the best place for the amount of money you have today, regardless of where it used to be in the past. True, you may hop onto another horse only to see it fade the minute you get on its back, but you have to make decisions based on fact – not emotion – and be willing to live with the ramifications. The benefit of selling a loser is that you can save yourself income taxes and have the chance to see your money perform better in another investment.

The *bear market* (bad market) of 2000-2002 gave us a very strong taste of what it's like to have to deal with losses. That bear market came on the heels of a very good *bull market* (good market) where just about everyone saw their investments increase in value. In a lifetime, people will encounter many years of both types of markets. It is important to be planning for the good times during the bad times, and it is also important to plan for the bad times during the good times.

The IRS has given the American public an economic incentive to capture losses because they allow you to write off up to $3,000 per year against regular income. The IRS also allows you to offset any profits you've made in your investments in taxable accounts (not IRA's, 401(k)'s, etc.) against any losses. For example, if you buy a stock for $10,000 and sell it two years later for $5,000, you have a $5,000 loss. You can deduct up to $3,000 of that loss from your regular income in the first year, and you can deduct the remaining $2,000 in losses next year. If you're in the 25% tax bracket, selling the investment and deducting the $3,000 in losses off of your income will save you about $750 in taxes. As a result, the government has helped you get back $750 of the $5,000 that was lost. Also, if you sold a stock that you owned for ten years at a profit of $10,000, you might have to pay $1,500 in long-term capital gains taxes. If, however, you also sold in that year a stock that you had hoped would rebound for a $5,000 loss, you could deduct the $5,000 from the $10,000 gain and only pay capital gains tax on the remaining $5,000. As a result, you'd only have taxes of about

$750 to pay. Do you see how the timely sale of an investment at a loss can save you tax money and help you move that money to a better investment?

An investment should be sold at a loss if the growth potential for that money you have in the investment is better in another investment of similar style and risk – plus, the actual step of selling the investment, and thus capturing the loss, will help on your taxes. If you have an investment that is less than what you paid for it, you're simply looking at a potential loss. The IRS says you have to actually sell the investment before you can recoup any of the loss through the tax benefits. Be careful when you sell an investment at a loss to not buy or sell that investment within thirty-one days before or after the day you sold it for a loss. If you do this, you violate the *wash-sale rule* and you won't be able to deduct your loss.

In summary, don't get attached to an investment, don't let your pride stop you from making a good investment decision based on current information, and do all you can to take advantage of the benefits available from the IRS to help you on your taxes. Talk to your financial professional about your investments on a regular basis, and if an investment no longer makes sense, sell it, move on, learn from your mistakes (if you made any), and try and find the best investment for the dollars you have available to you. Yesterday's prices don't matter, only tomorrow's.

Withholding - It is also a good idea to adjust your withholding amounts at work if you're consistently getting money back when you file your tax return. Anytime you get money back from the IRS, it means you've let them use your money all year, and the IRS doesn't pay you any interest while they use your money. Wouldn't you agree that it's not very good business to loan money out and not receive any interest on the loan? It would be better for you to have that money coming to you each paycheck and for you to invest it wisely. If you need that tax refund each year to help pick up the slack or tie up loose ends, you probably need to do a better job of creating, analyzing, and sticking to your budget!

Required Minimum Distributions - If you're approaching age 70 ½ and you have retirement accounts like 401(k)'s, Traditional IRA's, profit sharing plans, etc., then you've probably heard about *required minimum distributions - (RMD's).* With RMD's, the IRS is saying, "We've given you a chance to invest money for retirement and we haven't made you pay taxes on that money. Before you die, we want you to at least start taking money out of the account so that we can get some tax revenue off of that money."

In a nutshell, you must start (you do not have to take all the money out at age 70 ½) taking a certain minimum amount out each year. The current IRS rule says you must begin taking money out by April 1st of the year following the year in which you turn 70 ½. The amount that you take out for a certain year is determined by taking the previous year-end value of all your qualified retirement accounts and IRA's and dividing it by a number provided by the IRS that is based upon your age. If you have a spouse who is greater than ten years younger than you and he/she is the beneficiary of the account, the number will be based upon your joint life expectancy. The IRS recently simplified this calculation, but your financial professional and your CPA are the most qualified persons to help with this because there is a 50% penalty if you don't take out enough.

The required minimum distributions can be given to you in the form of a check, and this is good if you intend to spend the money or if the money came from an investment that has a rate of return equal to or less than what you could earn in a bank account. However, if you don't need to spend the money, consider taking an *in-kind distribution.* An *in-kind distribution* allows you to simply pick up an investment, move it out of the retirement account into a taxable account, and your distribution for that year is based on the value of the investment when you moved it out of the account. For example, if your RMD for this year is $5,000, you could move out 100 shares of a stock worth $50 per share, and the brokerage firm would provide you with a 1099 tax report that shows you took out $5000. The benefit to you is that you don't have to sell an investment you would like to keep, you made the IRS happy, and you didn't have to pay any transaction costs. Your brokerage firm can usually accomplish this for you after you sign one or two forms. If you don't need the money to spend, keep the investment by performing an in-kind distribution.

Read the section on "Life Insurance" in the previous chapter to see what else can be done with required minimum distributions from a retirement account if you don't need the money to help pay your expenses.

"Stretch-IRA's"

The IRS recently changed their rules regarding the required distributions from an IRA when the owner of the account died and passed his account to his beneficiaries. In the past, the beneficiaries had to stick to a withdrawal schedule that forced the account to be completely withdrawn (and thus taxed by the IRS) within a very short period of time. The IRS now will allow a beneficiary to take out a minimum amount each year over the remainder of his expected life – and thus "stretch" out the length of time and the amount of money that is taken out of the IRA. Instead of having to take all the money out and pay taxes over a very short time, beneficiaries now have the option to take small amounts over a long period of time. Through the power of compounding, this means that a beneficiary can actually receive a lot more money over his lifetime than he could under the previous rules.

There are important rules regarding this, so be sure you talk with your counselors. The process of setting up a Stretch-IRA is very simple, but it requires you to name your beneficiaries correctly. Be sure you update your beneficiary designations and always name a *contingent beneficiary*! A *contingent beneficiary* is a person (or persons) who would receive the account if your primary beneficiary died before you did. Stretch IRA's are one of the biggest ways that you can help your family after you're gone. Most people today would rather see their children and grandchildren take a little bit out of an account each year versus taking large sums out very quickly as they have seen many people blow through inheritances and having nothing to show for it.

Estate Planning

We've talked a great deal about how to make, spend, save, and invest money, and so it makes sense that we also talk about how to protect your assets for the future benefit of family, friends, and charities. Here is a brief discussion of the issues that relate to planning your estate:

Joint tenancy with rights of survivorship – If you own your home jointly with your spouse, if you have accounts jointly with your spouse, or if you have other assets with someone else's name on them when you die, that person obtains complete ownership of that asset once they prove that you died by providing a death certificate. If you have your name on your mother's checking account and she dies, you can walk into the bank, withdraw the money and do whatever you so desire with that money because, as joint tenant with rights of survivorship, you both have the same amount of rights.

A great number of people think that putting their names on all of their parents' assets is the best way to handle the estate planning process, but there are several negatives to this strategy. The first negative is that if a parent places a child's name on his checking account, it is legally perceived that the checking account now belongs as much to the child as to the parent. If the child has a car accident, is sued (we all know this happens regularly), and has a judgment ruled against him, the courts could potentially seize the money that is in the joint account. When you place someone's name on your asset, you immediately assume his/her liabilities.

The second negative issue regarding joint tenancy with rights of survivorship is the fact that the survivor (and thus the person who owns the asset when the other person dies) inherits the cost basis that pertained to the original purchase date and amount. Under current tax laws, if your mom passed away, you inherited her house through her will, and you were not a joint tenant, you would be allowed a "step-up in cost basis." This means that if your mom bought the house in 1950 for $30,000 and it is worth $150,000 on the date of her death, you could sell the house after you inherit it for $150,000 and pay no capital gains taxes because the IRS allowed you to use the value on the date of her death ($150,000) as the cost basis. $150,000 sales price minus $150,000 cost equals $0 profits. $0 profits means $0 tax! But you get to walk away with $150,000!

If, instead of giving you the property through her will, she put your name on the deed anytime before her death, you would have to pay capital gains taxes on the increase in value. You would potentially have to pay up to 15% taxes on the increase from $30,000 to $150,000 (which is a $120,000 increase). Thus, you could owe about $18,000 in taxes. True, you would not have had to wait on the probate court or pay an attorney for processing the will through the probate process, and you could sell the home very quickly as joint tenant, but is that worth $18,000 in taxes? Every situation is different and state laws vary, but, generally, joint tenancy is less desirable than having the proper estate planning documents created that allow you to remain in control of your assets while you're alive and that allow the assets to pass to the proper people once you die.

Probate – The probate court is responsible for making sure that your debts are paid; for publishing a public notice that allows anyone to contest your will or file a claim against your estate; and for making sure your estate gets in the hands of the people you named in your will or the people that current law says should get your estate if you die without a will. The probate process typically takes about six months but could last several years if there are suits filed against the estate by unhappy people. On average, the legal fees associated with the legal process range from three to five percent of the value of the probated assets. If you own real estate in other states, your estate must go through probate in each of those states also. If you do not have a will, your estate will go through the probate process to determine who gets your assets. If you have a will, your estate goes through the probate process to try to make sure your instructions are carried through (after attorney fees and court costs). Unless you have other estate planning strategies in place, your estate will go through probate whether or not you have a will.

Estate taxes – Estate taxes are the taxes payable to the IRS if a person's estate – including life insurance owned by that person – exceeds $1,500,000 in 2004-2005; $2,000,000 in 2006-2008; $3,500,000 in 2009; and an unlimited amount in 2010. In the year 2011, the *estate tax applicable exclusion* reverts back to the amounts in 2003. We pay income taxes on money we earn, and *our heirs* pay estate taxes on money we give them that is over and above the amounts the IRS allows us to exclude. For example, if your home is worth $500,000, you own an insurance policy that will pay $1,000,000, you have other real estate of $500,000, and you have $500,000 in retirement accounts and investments, your estate is worth $2,500,000. The IRS will allow your estate to pass $1,500,000 to beneficiaries without any estate tax due. Your estate would owe taxes on the $1,000,000 that is over and above the first $1,500,000 - approximately $300,000. For the very wealthy, estate taxes can be as much as 50% of the amount over the exclusion amount. Estate taxes are very expensive but can be reduced by proper planning, gifting, asset titling, and legal work.

Will - This is a legal document that tells the probate court in your county what to do with your assets when you die. If you die without a will, you will be considered to have died *intestate*, and the court decides who gets your assets based upon specific state laws regarding those who die without a will. Even if you verbally tell your son that he's going to get the condo on the beach, the probate court will make its own decision since there is no formal will that expresses your written desires and instructions.

A will names an *executor* or *personal representative* to be the person who handles the affairs of your estate once you're gone. This can be one person, or more than one person. If you have minor children, you need to name a *guardian* for your children inside the will. If you do not name a guardian, the court will choose one for you. If you want your brother and his wife to be the guardians of your children when you die, you need to have this spelled out in a will. The court may decide to award custody to someone entirely different. It is prudent to name other people to serve as *contingent* or *back-up* executors or guardians in case your first choice is unwilling or unable to serve.

A will must be properly drawn up, witnessed, and notarized in order to be valid. The person must be legally competent to be able to make decisions when the will is signed. Most wills are contested on the grounds that the will is not valid due to improper witnesses or accusations of incompetence. There are several ways to draw up a will, ranging from handwritten, to do-it-yourself computer programs, to attorney-prepared documents. In my opinion, the small amount of money spent to have an attorney draw up a will for you is well worth the peace of mind obtained. An attorney generally prepares a will, durable power of attorney, and a living will as an estate-planning package for about $300 - $500. Once your will is created, you need to keep it in a fireproof location that can easily be accessed by your executor if and when the need arises.

Durable Power of Attorney – This document gives someone the legal right to act on your behalf if you're unable to do so. For example, if you're now alive and able, you can take care of your own business. If you die, your will names an executor to take care of your business. The durable power of attorney is a person (or persons) you name to take care of your business if you're still alive but unable to handle things yourself. Examples of this would be if someone were in the hospital after a stroke, in a coma, or with Alzheimer's.

This person you name as your power of attorney would be able to pay your bills, buy and sell property, and basically be able to act on your behalf regarding any issue that is specifically named in the document. You can have this document give a person the authority to act on your behalf while you're alive and able, so that if you were out of town and needed someone to represent you someone could, or you could have the document worded so that no one actually has the power to sign your name until you're unable due to sickness, competence, etc. The important thing, as with any legal document, is to have it filled out *before* you actually need it.

The important thing, as with any legal document, is to have it filled out *before* you actually need it.

Living Will – This is the legal document that tells the doctors and the hospital whether or not you want to be placed on life support. These documents vary by state and offer several alternatives regarding situations requiring life support, withholding of food and water, etc.

Revocable Living Trust – Also called a *self-administered living trust*, this is a document that is created to actually own your assets while still allowing you to stay in control of your assets. The benefit is that when you die, the owner of your assets (the trust) still exists, and thus your assets do not have to go through the time, expense, and public display of the probate process. You can still conduct business as usual, you can buy and sell property, give money away, file the same income tax returns, etc., but because you personally don't have any assets in your name, there are no assets to go through probate.

A revocable living trust is sort of like a company. If the CEO of Wal-Mart dies, does the company have to close up and stop operations? No, the company names a new CEO to take care of business as usual. With a revocable living trust, the attorney creates the entity (the Bill and Mary Smith Revocable Living Trust dated 6/15/2004) and you are the *trustee* of the trust, which means you have the power to do anything you so desire with the assets. You could even completely dissolve the trust, which is why it's called a *revocable* living trust. Your accounts (except for IRA's and retirement accounts) and real estate held in your personal name will then be retitled from your personal name to the name of the trust. If you do not retitle the accounts and property, even after you've had the trust drawn up and signed, the assets will still be in your personal name and you would have wasted time and money - as well as not accomplished your goal of protecting your estate from the probate process and expense.

Inside of the trust document, you name whom you'd like to take your place as trustee when you're gone. If you're married, your spouse will probably continue as trustee alone. If you're the sole trustee, you'll name someone to be the *successor trustee*, and this person is responsible for following the instructions that you've given them inside the trust document. The successor trustee can be a trust company at a bank or brokerage firm if you don't have confidence in any one person to handle the affairs of your estate. The successor trustee would make sure that all of your personal debts are paid, that your taxes are filed and paid, and that the people you want to receive your assets actually get your assets. The important thing to note is that the probate court is not involved in this process, and this saves your estate (and thus your beneficiaries) a lot of time, money, and headache. You could also instruct that the trust manage money over a long period of time and provide income payments to beneficiaries instead of paying them a lump sum inheritance.

Generally, if you want to do all you can to try and make sure your beneficiaries get your assets instead of the attorneys and the probate court; if you have real estate in more than one state; if you can afford the additional cost to have a living trust drawn up (about five times the cost of having a will drawn up); and if you want to try and keep your beneficiaries from spending their inheritance quickly, then it might make sense to check into a revocable living trust.

Your estate planning team should consist of your financial professional, your attorney, and your CPA. That team will help you prudently address estate planning issues of income taxation (before your death and after your death); proper asset titling; wills and trusts; estate tax reduction and avoidance strategies; and legal and administrative cost reduction strategies. Your financial professional acts as the "coach" of the estate planning team instructing the other coaches, you are the owner of the team, and the attorney and CPA are the players on the team following your instructions and playing their positions to the best of their abilities.

Charitable Giving

Charitable giving is one of my favorite areas to work in because it has many creative ways in which money and assets can be given away to help others while providing tax and estate planning benefits to the person making the donation.

If you regularly make donations to your church or other charitable organizations, you might want to consider gifting *appreciated securities* to the organization instead of donating by cash or check. *Appreciated securities* are investments that have increased in value since you bought them, and as long as you've held them for greater than one year after the purchase date, you can donate them to the charity and receive a tax deduction (if you itemize) based on the current market value. For example, if you paid $5,000 for some stock in Wal-Mart and it increased in value over two years to $6,000, you could donate the shares to the charity and receive a deduction for $6,000, even though you only paid $5,000 for the investment. Your financial professional can help you get your investments to the charity that you'd like to contribute to.

If you would like to make charitable donations after you die, one of the best ways to accomplish this goal is to make the charity (or charities) a beneficiary of some (or all) of your retirement accounts. It's probably a good idea to separate any money in a retirement account that you'd like to go to a charity into its own account so that you're not mixing people as beneficiaries with beneficiaries that are not people. Your financial professional can help you get part of your retirement accounts into another retirement account without any tax consequences and more than likely without you having to sell any investments. If you're sure that your family is taken care of and you know an amount that you'd like to donate to charity, donations from a retirement account (401(k), IRA, annuity, etc.) will help your family and help the charity. Your family is helped because they will receive their inheritance from other assets that won't be taxed at regular income tax rates when they make withdrawals (retirement accounts are taxed at regular income when withdrawn, and this is in addition to estate taxes if your estate exceeds the maximum exclusion amounts). The charity can receive the money and, since it's a charity, it does not have to pay taxes when it receives the money. As a result, more money gets used by the people and the charity that you selected because less goes to the IRS. Less to the IRS means more for someone else!

Widows and Widowers

In her book *Sudden Money*, CERTIFIED FINANCIAL PLANNER certificant Susan Bradley talks about a *DFZ*. This is the *decision-free zone*, and it lasts about one year after losing a spouse. She says that no major decisions or changes should be made during that time. I agree with her completely. The loss of a spouse is one of the most traumatic experiences that any person can endure, and many people don't wake up from the fog associated with that period of trauma until several years later. You should do whatever is needed to protect your assets, but use patience and counsel to forge ahead in making major changes without your spouse by your side. In addition to taking your time in making major changes, widows and widowers should:

- Make sure that each spouse knows where assets are, how much they're worth, where income is coming from, how to change the oil in the car – or at least who to go see about each of these issues – *before* someone dies. Many husbands realize after their wife passes away that they've never had to write a check, balance a checkbook, or cook a meal. Many wives realize that their husbands weren't good money managers while they were living because he only put money in bank certificates of deposit, he never sought financial advice, he didn't have any/enough life insurance, and there isn't going to be enough money for her to live comfortably – alone.
- Find a qualified professional person (not a son, daughter, or neighbor) to help guide you in your financial, tax, and legal decisions. Hopefully you are used to making decisions after talking to another person (usually your spouse), and the old saying "two heads are better than one" is true in normal circumstances. This saying is even more valid when one person has lost a spouse and is left to make major decisions alone.
- Immediately contact Social Security, insurance companies, banks, brokerage firms, etc. and inform them of the death and take appropriate action to secure any benefits.

We covered a lot of material in these last two catch-all chapters. Take your time and go back through the points that apply to you, make notes in the margin, and really use this book to its fullest potential!

Things You Need To Do Now

1. **Conduct a thorough review with your financial professional about how any of the topics in these two chapters could impact your life by confirming amounts, costs, potential problems, and potential solutions.** Putting things down on paper really make the issues come to life. Take the time to bring your situation to life! Make copies of important papers, store the originals in a safe place, and make sure the right people know where to find the necessary information if it's ever needed.
2. **Review and update your beneficiary designations on life insurance policies, retirement accounts, IRA's, etc.** Always name a contingent beneficiary!
3. **Take steps to safeguard your health so that you can qualify for a life insurance policy at their preferred rates.** You'll appreciate the lower cost, and your family will appreciate the benefits. Take the time to inform your family about your plans, take the time to show them how you'd like them to handle things, and take the time to introduce your family members to your financial professional.

SECTION I - FINANCES

Chapter Ten

Putting It All Together

Congratulations! You've now read and become somewhat familiar with information that some people wait their whole lives to try to understand. It is crucial to have a basic understanding early in life regarding topics like budgeting, saving, retirement, investing, and other financial issues. You've learned who you need to talk with concerning your financial well being, and hopefully you've already made your appointments with qualified persons, completed the suggested exercises, and maybe you've already found the right financial professional for you.

I have a degree in economics, I work in the financial industry, I have licenses in insurance and securities, I have had two years additional schooling to become a CERTIFIED FINANCIAL PLANNER certificant, and I have successfully passed a CFP® Board Exam that a great number of people failed, but there are still some financial topics that sometimes cause me to pick up the phone and call someone for guidance or for an objective opinion. Investments, markets, interest rates, taxes, laws, and opportunities are always changing, and you have to be willing <u>and</u> able to continually stay on top of information that pertains to your situation, or you must find someone to do that for you. You are not expected to be the expert in the topics we've discussed, but you should be able to comprehend what a financial professional is saying, you should be able to make objective decisions based on fact (not emotion), and you should be willing to hear about new ideas and opportunities from someone you trust.

In Summary, If You're....

Young and single – Find a financial professional whom you would trust and enjoy working with for many years; keep an adequate amount in savings; invest as much as you can; don't run up any credit card balances; pay off any balances that you owe; secure life insurance before you are too old or too sick; and strive to lay a solid financial foundation to keep you ahead of the game.

Young and married – Love your spouse every minute of every day; find a financial professional whom you would trust and enjoy working with for many years; make sure both of you are aware of your current financial condition and direction; maintain an adequate amount in savings for emergencies; don't run up any credit card debt; pay off any debt balances with unfavorable interest rates; obtain adequate insurance coverage for both of you based on your current and future expected needs; and make sure your beneficiary designations are correct.

Married with children - Love your spouse and children every minute of every day; find a financial professional whom you would trust and enjoy working with for many years; make sure both of you are aware of your current financial condition and direction; maintain an adequate amount in savings for emergencies; don't run up any credit card debt; pay off any balances that you owe; obtain adequate insurance coverage for both of you based on your current and future expected needs; invest an appropriate amount for college expenses; teach your children about money and investing; address your estate plan; and name guardians for your children.

Divorced with children – Love your children every minute of every day; forgive your ex-spouse and don't say bad things about him/her in front of your children; find a financial professional whom you would trust and enjoy working with for many years; maintain an adequate amount in savings; determine your investment priorities if you have to choose to invest in either retirement or college; make sure your will and other estate planning documents are accurate; teach your children about money and investing; and obtain adequate insurance coverage.

Approaching retirement - Find a financial professional whom you would trust and enjoy working with for many years; maintain an adequate amount in savings; reduce any excess cash that you haven't used in the past by investing it appropriately through your financial professional; have your financial professional analyze your projected retirement income to see if you're on track to have a healthy retirement; review insurance policies and beneficiary designations; make sure your Social Security report is accurate; consider consolidating accounts that you may have accumulated through the years; take advantage of any IRS tax benefits that may be available that make sense for you (Roth IRA, cash value life insurance, etc.); make a commitment to have at least an annual physical with your doctor; implement or review your estate plan with your financial professional; remember that investing doesn't stop the day that you retire; and start developing a plan to have a productive and enjoyable retirement.

Retired - Find a financial professional whom you would trust and enjoy working with for many years; have your financial professional analyze your expected retirement income through your age one hundred to see if you appear to be on track for a healthy retirement; *spend your money and enjoy life* if you have adequate income and enough in savings; reduce your expenses and think about the impact of inflation if your financial picture does not look very promising; review your estate plan and beneficiary designations; be sure you meet your annual required minimum distributions from retirement accounts; be sure your spouse knows how to handle the finances if you're not around; consolidate investment and bank accounts to make life simpler; and actively teach those younger than you lessons that you learned in life that can make their lives easier.

In addition to discussing the proper objectives based upon your age and family situation, people can be defined in three major categories:

1) Just Getting By – If you're just getting by, every dollar means a lot to you, so it is very important that you maximize every opportunity you are given. Opportunities can be staring you right in the face in the form of matching contributions from your employer in a retirement plan, financial aid available to your children to help pay for college, available tax deductions or credits due to recent tax law changes, interest savings from refinancing loans and mortgages, potentially better investment returns obtained after following professional advice, and monthly bill reduction by using common sense and a written budget.

2) Comfortable – If you're comfortable, you have money left at the end of each month after your bills are paid and investments funded. The money that is left at the end of each month can be spent, saved, or invested and is called disposable income. Your financial professional can help you determine what the best choice is for those extra dollars in order to help you enjoy life today while still providing for a comfortable lifestyle in the future. A lot of people in this situation get lulled into a feeling of comfort in the present time, but they wake up when they are seventy years old wishing that the money spent on the motor home they never used had been invested in a good investment. Rely on your financial professional to show you the issues that you should be thinking about, to urge you to take action when needed, and to stay on top of your financial condition, expectations, and changes in markets and laws.

3) Wealthy – If you're wealthy, you've either inherited money, worked hard to accumulate what you have, or you've been in the right place at the right time. You have more than enough income each month to meet your needs, and you have more money and investments than you could spend in your lifetime even if your worst-case scenarios came to life because you're adequately insured and debt free. You have the potential to make a financial difference in the lives of your family members or in the lives of people in your community.

A healthy, honest, and trusted relationship with a financial professional can enhance the quality of your life while you are living by giving you perspective on the difference that you can make by taking advantage of estate, investment, and tax planning strategies. If you are wealthy, money may not mean much to you because your mind and heart are free to focus on the bigger picture of what life is really about, but do not let that perspective hinder the benefit that your wealth can have on your desire to make a difference, on your family, and on society. Charitable giving, educating family members on wealth management and prudence, and continued fact-based decision-making should be a priority.

Small percentage differences in rates of return, tax savings, and expenses can have huge actual dollar amount impact for the wealthy. Small changes in your asset allocation, wisely timed withdrawals from investment accounts, and smart tax strategies can mean there could be a lot more wealth to be used by yourself or others.

We must control our finances, and we do that by making fact-based decisions, by listening to trusted advice, and by sticking to the plan unless the plan needs to be changed.

Knowledge about your finances is very, very important, but we can't take our finances with us to heaven, and we can't let our finances rule our lives. We must control our finances, and we do that by making fact-based decisions, by listening to trusted advice, and by sticking to the plan unless the plan needs to be changed. Money can't buy happiness, but healthy dealings with your family and a strong commitment of personal faith can really help you understand the level of importance that money should have in your life.

I hope that you'll use this section on finances as a reference tool to give you a good, solid foundation on the basic issues. Refer to it often, and use it to help educate family members and friends about their finances. You can help educate others about the basics without prying into their personal financial issues by giving them a copy of this book. Hopefully, they will find it as interesting, informative, and easy to understand as I hope that you have.

Now it's time to move on from dealing with our complicated issues regarding our finances to the even more complicated issues encountered when dealing with our family.

Things You Need To Do Now

1. Enjoy your financial life – today and tomorrow. You are in the situation you're in for a reason – make the best of it – for you, your family, your church, your community, and the world.

SECTION II

FAMILY

SECTION II - FAMILY

Chapter Eleven

What Is A Normal Family?

Overview

When you think about it, money can be a lot easier to work with than family members are. Money doesn't talk back; it doesn't get its feelings hurt; it doesn't ask you to help pay off a credit card; it doesn't reveal emotional scars twenty years after the pain was inflicted; it doesn't remember every inappropriate thing you've said or done. Money will always be there if you make the right decisions.

In the introduction to the book, I talked about the impact that losing a Nerf® ball while playing catch with my mother on a Sunday morning had on me. The sacrifices that my mother made at that time, including buying that $3 Nerf® ball, were tremendous, as we didn't have much money at all. My financial savvy developed due to my desire to never have to worry about having enough money. A deeper issue revealed that day was that family relationships are extremely important in forming a healthy self-image and maintaining personal relationships in the future.

My dad wasn't around the day my mother was throwing the ball with me, and statistics show that many children today don't ever have a father there to throw the ball with them. It was a great blessing for me to have a mother that was willing and able to throw the ball with me, and it is unfortunate that so many do not have anyone they can rely on for any stability in life. Take a look at the following statistics from 2002:

- Fatherless homes account for sixty-three percent of youth suicides, ninety percent of homeless/runaway children, eighty-five percent of children with behavior problems, seventy-one percent of high school dropouts, eighty-five percent of youths in prison, and well over fifty percent of teen mothers
- Sixty-nine percent of children under age eighteen lived with two married parents, down from seventy-seven percent in 1980
- About twenty-three percent of children lived with only their mothers
- Five percent lived with only their fathers
- Four percent lived with neither of their parents.[1]

During my childhood, I could have helped support several of the above statistics. Try and follow this history of my movements from house to another: I lived the first eight years of my life with both my mother and father until they divorced. After the divorce, my mother, my sister, and I moved to Jackson, Mississippi, where I lived with them for about six months. Then I went to live with my mother's mother, "Gaga," for four years. I was with her from the fourth to the seventh grades. Jim Langston was our next door neighbor and he was like a father to me. I moved back with my mother and sister for the next four years (from the eighth grade to halfway through my junior year). Half way through my junior year of high school, my mother was offered a teaching job in a small town an hour away, and the Gamblins, a family with children at my high school, asked me if I would like to live with them until I graduated. Their oldest son was president of our school's student council, and I was vice-president. We took the Gamblins up on their offer, and my mother paid them a monthly amount for my room and board. I basically became another member of the family. I learned a great deal about families from my variety of family experiences – normal things – and abnormal things.

Webster's dictionary defines *normal* as "conforming with, adhering to, or constituting a norm, standard, pattern, level, or type; typical; approximately average." The words approximately average would lead us to the conclusion that normal is basically somewhere in the middle - or a blend of highs and lows. If a normal family were described as two married parents with children, we would have seen that seventy-seven percent of families in 1980 were normal. In 2003, we saw that there were about ten percent fewer normal families as only sixty-nine percent of families with children lived with two parents.[2]

If you're evaluating what is normal with regards to children being born in today's society, you would see that nearly two-thirds of women under age twenty-five having their first child were not married. In 2001, thirty-four percent of all births were to unmarried women.[3] Today's children are having children without the presence of a husband in the house.

You would also see that over twenty-five percent of the U.S. population is a single-occupant household, and that number has increased in the last ten years while the percentage of family households has decreased.[4] This could indicate that, in addition to the fact that the American population is getting older and that women generally outlive men, people are choosing to live a life without family members in the house. This could be an attempt to reduce the number of challenging issues in life, such as dealing with family members in a healthy way. Sadly, a great number of people are living by themselves simply because it has less headaches.

The norm for families today is certainly not the ideal. Each one of us should strive to make the ideal the norm by investing more time in our families than we do in our jobs, money, hobbies, and friends. Our family members are the only people who can really know us from the day we were born until the day we die. Our family members are probably going to be the main people who attend our funerals. Our family members are the ones who are most likely to rejoice with us in the good times, reprimand us in the wrong times, and cry with us in the sad times. Family members and family relationships should be treated with the utmost care and devotion in an attempt to make the fruits of those relationships blossom through the character of each person. Traits and qualities such as gentleness, patience, kindness, love, compassion, empathy, passion, sincerity, and hopefulness can be trained and nurtured in a family environment. These qualities and traits can then be passed on to family members, friends, coworkers, neighbors, and classmates.

My family background is extremely varied from my having lived with both of my parents, with my mom and my sister, with stepfamily members, with my grandmother, with friends of the family, by myself, with my wife, and with my wife and children. As a result, I think you'll find at least some morsel from my observations, reservations, victories, and defeats. Hopefully, this insight may help you deal more lovingly with your family. So, I'd like to give you some more detailed background on my life; the influences I've had in life from situations and from people; and my outlook on the future as a son, a father, stepson, grandson, son-in-law, and a husband.

I Never Saw Them Hug Each Other

My father was born in 1931, right around the time of the Great Depression, in Meridian, Mississippi. My grandfather was in his sixties when my dad was born, and he lost his eyesight when my dad was young. My grandfather was married and had children prior to marrying my dad's mother, and I assume my father learned how to get along with his father's other children, but I've never seen them together. My mother's father died of a heart attack when she was eight years old, and my mother's mother (yes, this is the same Gaga that I lived with for four years) raised my mother and her two younger brothers by herself.

I think it's important to know this background because I feel that these situations and people had a tremendous effect on who my parents were to become - as husband and wife, and as parents. I doubt that my dad ever saw my grandfather give his wife any affection due to the dramatic difference in their ages and due to my grandfather's poor health. As a result, I don't think my dad had a real good example of a loving and outwardly affectionate father to follow and to learn from in his younger years. My grandfather died when my father was a teenager. I know for a fact that my mother didn't have a good example of how a father or a husband should act, because her father died early in her formative years when she was just barely old enough to remember.

Both my mother and father were married once before they married each other, and my father had three kids (two boys and a girl) from his first marriage. Here are some interesting statistics about divorce and children:

- In 1998, four million children under the age of eighteen lived with their grandparents (six percent of the population). I was part of this group.
- The average drop in the standard of living after divorce for a female was forty-five percent in 1998 – I can attest to this statistic.
- Fifty percent of women with children prior to marriage were divorced within ten years.[5]

I'm sure that my parents were affectionate towards each other when they dated and in their early years together, and I'm living proof that they did have some sort of physical contact (as you are proof of your parents' contact!). I do have some recollection of a Sunday afternoon or two before my parents divorced when they had their bedroom door shut and locked because they were "taking a nap." Regardless of whether or not they were sleeping, the fact remains that I don't have a visual memory of ever seeing them hug each other, hold hands, or express any affection. Children learn how to act, not necessarily by doing what they're told, but more by imitating what they see. I'm fortunate that I had other family influences in my life that taught me some appropriate ways to handle people and situations, even though my actions don't always show that I recall these appropriate ways. I have to be honest and say that my parents did not teach me how to

Children Learn how to act, not necessarily by doing what they're told, but more by imitating what they see.

express affection for family members. Do you recall seeing your parents look at each other like they truly cared for each other? Did you see them holding hands, having an extended embrace, or maybe even kissing? Did your parents spend time just to themselves or did they go on dates or vacations just to be with each other? Are your children seeing you do any of these things? If the answer is yes to any, several, or all of these questions, you were (and are) very fortunate!

We humans learn from watching other people – babies learn very early in life how to mimic facial expressions, how to blow bubbles, and how to carry ourselves in posture and tone. We also learn *what to do* by having other people show us *what not to do.*

But I Do Remember...

I don't ever remember seeing my parents hug each other, but my earliest recollections as a child are extremely vivid.

When my oldest daughter, Whitney, was three years old, she was in the habit of waking up at 3:30 AM. I don't know why it was usually around that time, but she would come and crawl into bed with my wife and me. We were recently given a king-sized bed, and she was able to get in bed with us sometimes and we didn't even know it until morning because there was so much extra room in the bed. When the bed was smaller, we certainly knew when anyone moved on the bed because there wasn't any room for anyone else. A few times, she'd come into our room and I'd hear her Pull-Ups crinkling as she walked, and before she started climbing into bed, I'd say to her quietly (in the hopes of not waking up my wife, Wendy), "Sweetie, it's too early to come in here. Go back to your bed until it's time to wake up." Most of the time, she'd sleepily say, "Okay, Daddy," and she'd return to her bed to continue sleeping.

Whitney knows exactly what she's going to see when she comes into our room. She knows that Mommy and Daddy both will be there; she knows that we love her very much; she knows that God and Jesus love her; and she knows that we will always be there for her. Almost every night that she has gone to bed in her short life, she's had Mommy or Daddy say prayers with her on her knees "like the little children" she saw in a book, tuck her into bed next to her two stuffed dogs, Cody and Scrapper, read or tell her a story, turn on her ceiling fan, leave the hall light on so that she has a little light coming in to her room, turn on her radio because she loves to hear country and Christian music, and tell her, "Night, night." She usually goes to bed about 8:30, but she's now getting old enough to ask if she can stay up later. She usually wakes up right at 7:00 AM.

Before Wendy gave birth to Whitney, she and I both read a book called *Becoming Baby Wise* by Gary Ezzo and Robert Bucknam, M.D. That book absolutely saved our lives! Neither Wendy nor I had ever spent any time with small children, much less infants who relied upon us for their every meal, diaper change, and loving contact. When Whitney was born, she was the first infant that I had ever held in my life. I had never held anyone else's child! *Baby Wise* helped us know what to expect, and it has helped us tremendously by teaching us how to create a safe, predictable, and loving environment for our children.

The premise behind *Baby Wise* is a theory called *parent directed feeding*. If we had not read that book, we would have probably tried to feed her every time she cried, or we would have not fed her at times when we thought she was simply crying because she was a baby when she actually needed to be fed. Parent directed feeding revolves around a baby's natural need to eat every 2 ½ to 3 hours, and it teaches parents the value of having a schedule based on this desire. The further premise is that an infant's pattern of life should be "feed, wake, sleep." This is different than what we would have done had we not read the book. We probably would have fed her and let her fall asleep after eating like many people do, and like many parents and grandparents told us to do. However, we learned that we should feed Whitney, then play and interact with her, and *then* put her down for a nap. The benefits are that we got to interact with her while she was full and happy, we were able to take her to her crib and put her down for a nap when she was aware of what we were doing versus having her fall asleep in our laps and then try and sneak her into her crib without waking her, and then wake her up at her next feeding time (if she wasn't already awake) to eat. There were times when we had to stray from the schedule if Whitney was going through a normal growth spurt when she needed to eat every hour, when we were on a trip and out of her usual surroundings, or when she was sick. Whitney started sleeping through the night at seven weeks old. If your child slept through the night that soon, you know how great a blessing that is. If your child didn't sleep through the night that soon, you probably can even more adamantly attest to how great a blessing that is! Have you read *Baby Wise*? It is a great book and a great method. My wife and I recommend it to all new parents who can read the book and balance its facts with a good dose of teamwork, love, and common sense. We've given some young parents a copy of the book, and the parents who receive great results are those who can:

- Listen to, and follow, advice from experts (just like you should do with your finances),
- Make decisions based on facts (Does she have a dirty diaper? Is she sick? What time is it? etc.),
- Put emotion on the back burner (I can't stand this screaming. I sure would like to sleep late myself. I can't believe she just threw up on my second clean shirt today. I haven't slept or eaten in what seems like days.), and
- Use common sense

Parents who think they are the exception to the statistics for one reason or another, parents who aren't able to stay home long with the baby due to working outside the home, and parents who let family members get in the way with their words of wisdom (I use the word wisdom loosely) find their children not sleeping through the night, being fussy, staying in diapers longer than they should, and not feeling comfortable with their surroundings or family members.

The reason that Whitney was able to sleep through the night so soon was because her environment was predictable, safe, and constant. When she was four months old, you could almost set your watch to her sleeping cycle. She would literally open her eyes just as the time for her next meal arrived. Wendy and I knew this because a time or two we'd be standing there looking at our miracle from God when she woke up. Whitney has never heard Wendy and me yelling at each other, and we even try not to raise our voices to each other even when the kids aren't around. However, Whitney can tell when we're trying to make a point with each other by the tones of our voices. Whitney will tell us to be nice when, in our opinion, we are simply having a healthy, direct discussion. Whitney even put me in my place recently when she told me to quit talking to Mommy the same way that I talk to Ashley, our one year old, when she's in trouble. That certainly was an eye opener for me, and a humorous relief for Wendy! The point that Wendy and I take away from this is that children know when the loving environment is being compromised by anger, frustration, or disappointment - anything other than love. Children are born unable to speak, but very early on in life they are able to interpret body language, tone, and eye contact.

My earliest childhood memories, on the other hand, are not quite as nurturing and predictable as my daughter's memories. The house that we lived in when I was about six years old had paneled walls that didn't have much (if any) insulation inside of them, so if you tried to nail a picture in the wall where there wasn't a stud behind it for support, you'd drive the nail all the way through. When you made contact with an area that didn't have the wood bracing behind it, it made a hollow sound that, even as an adult, I can identify from miles away. The hollow sound that emanated from the wood grained paneling woke me up from a deep childhood sleep several times, and that sound was accompanied by a great deal of yelling and harsh words. I don't think my parents knew that I was awake the first few times it happened; but I heard every word, felt every contact that objects or my parents made on that paneling, and I quietly learned what marriage was not supposed to be.

I've learned in doing research for this book that children are often the silent victims of domestic violence. I've seen in my in my personal experience that most children know about the violence. Studies also show that school-age children who witness violence exhibit a range of problem behaviors including depression, anxiety, and violence toward peers. Adolescents who have grown up in violent homes are at risk for recreating the abusive relationships they have seen.[7]

> Adolescents who have grown up in violent homes are at risk for recreating the abusive relationships they have seen..

I remember lying in bed, trying to go back to sleep the first few times I heard their arguments and things hitting those paneled walls. At times, things got so bad I felt like I had to get them to stop before someone got hurt. It is very hard for a child who wants to love, respect, admire, and obey his parents to simply go back to bed and go to sleep when he's been told to do so. The words that were spoken by my parents floated down the hallway into my bedroom and pierced my young ears; they made a huge, permanent impact on me. Does this situation sound familiar to you and your family situation?

The Family Violence Project reports common red flags which indicate that children are witnessing domestic abuse are

- Constant anxiety, feelings of powerlessness
- Depression, flashbacks, acting nervous and fearful
- Angry or destructive behaviors
- Very low sense of self-worth, feeling emotionally abandoned
- Attachment problems, issues with personal boundaries[8]

The Violence Prevention Center of Southwestern Illinois reports that seventy percent of men in court-ordered treatment for domestic violence witnessed it as a child and that eight percent of runaways come from homes where domestic violence occurs. Oftentimes I wonder why I didn't turn into an abusive, incarcerated, angry, depressed, manic, addictive, or violent person. I believe the answer to that question lies in my faith in God and in His desire to take my negative situations and turn them into positive situations. Also, I believe that I may be the exception to the statistics about domestic violence because:

- These instances were not very frequent compared to what a lot of children have to endure

- Instead of being exposed to these situations for my complete childhood as some children unfortunately are, I witnessed them for about five years. My parents divorced when I was eight years old
- Neither I nor my sister were ever an object of any physical or sexual abuse
- I had other families, such as the Langstons and the Gamblins, show me how families *should* interact
- I received unofficial counseling from my Young Life leader, John Evans, who met with me for breakfast once a week in high school
- I was blessed with a decent amount of intelligence and common sense.

I am living proof that good things can come from less than ideal circumstances, but the quality of life that my children obtain will be the true scorecard for me to analyze when I am older to see just how well I was able to overcome my upbringing. I had to grow up a great deal faster than a lot of people my age, and I missed out on a lot of potentially positive childhood memories. It wasn't until Whitney was born that I truly learned what childhood is supposed to be like by seeing life through her young and innocent eyes.

In my picture of the world, a normal family is one in which both husband and wife treat each other with respect and love. If there are children in the family, then all members are treated with respect and love. A normal family has members who communicate openly about their hopes and their fears, their victories and their defeats, their appreciation and their disappointment. A normal family has boundaries that define each family member's role of father/husband, mother/wife, and child.

A normal family can look at an abnormal family and see areas where they should be thankful. Normal families should acknowledge and appreciate not having situations in which the children tell their parents what to do; where a husband verbally abuses his wife and/or kids; when someone has bruises, cuts, or broken bones more than other people do; or where families never seem to talk or enjoy each others' company. These situations should seem strange to someone in a normal family. Normal families do not say, "I hate you" or "you'll never amount to anything" or "you're ugly" or "you're stupid." If you're hearing these words or seeing these situations, go find help, and find it fast! If you're causing these situations, go find help, and find it fast! You owe it to yourself, and you owe it to your family. If you, or someone in your family, has trouble with authority, is frequently getting into trouble, or exhibits some of the red flags outlined earlier, then help needs to be found.

If you feel that something isn't right in your family, go talk to a professional. Many times in life I've had to deal with the phrase "perception is reality." If you perceive that something isn't right, then you have to follow your gut instincts and act on that feeling to find out what it is that doesn't feel right and why it doesn't feel right. Your perception of something not being normal is your reality, regardless of what others in your family think. Take some steps to see what an objective person says. If you're willing to go talk to a financial professional about your finances and your investments, one of the best investments that you can make is one in yourself and in your family by going to talk to a professional. I was fortunate to have my Young Life (a Christian organization similar to Fellowship of Christian Athletes or Campus Crusade) leader take an interest in me. As I mentioned earlier, he and I met every week on Tuesday mornings for almost three years when I was in high school. In these meetings, he asked me questions like, "How does that make you feel?" and "What do you think about that?" He was objective, trustworthy, supportive, loving, and patient with me. If you do not have someone in your life that has those qualities, you do not have a normal family. You should seek out someone who can help. That person may be your pastor, a teacher, a coworker, or a professional counselor or psychiatrist.

What are your childhood memories? Do you have a memory more like Whitney's, or do you have a memory more like mine? What kind of memory will your children have of their childhood? What steps are you taking to improve the effects that those memories have on you and your family. Invest in yourself.... go talk to someone that can help!

Things You Need To Do Now

1. **Tell your family members that you love them.** I hope that you mean it when you say it. If you don't mean it when you say that, do everything you can to let your heart be molded into one that loves and cares for your family. Tell yourself that you love them over and over again. The power of positive thinking can work miracles in changing how you feel about someone.

2. **If you're in a violent situation, seek help immediately!** If you've been hurt more than once and you think that the person hurting you will change, that the violence is your fault, or that things will be different tomorrow/next week/next month after he or she gets through this tough time – statistics say you're wrong. Go find professional help. Wouldn't you rather err on the safe side by seeking help first? Airline flight attendants always instruct parents to put the oxygen masks on themselves before they put a mask on their child so that they won't pass out and render themselves helpless. Your situation is similar. You can't help someone else until you are protected. Take steps to heal yourself first!

3. **No matter who you are, go talk to a professional or your pastor to gain some insight into who you are, why you are who you are, and what you can do to help yourself and your family in the future.** If you consider yourself a pretty bright person or if you think no one can really understand you or your situation, put this book down and go make an appointment right now because your intelligence is isolating you from help! Truly intelligent people realize how much they really don't know versus knowing everything. Exhibit some real intelligence and go talk to someone. Yes, I'm probably talking to YOU. I'm sorry I have to be so blunt. I had to learn the hard way, and I hope my experiences can help save you from losing years of your life to an unhealthy situation.

SECTION II - FAMILY

Chapter Twelve

A Complicated Life

Now that we've talked about a *normal* family, I'd like to spend some more time talking about the unique features that are involved in my family so that you can have something to evaluate where you are and where your family ranks on the normal scale.

After my parents divorced when I was eight years old, my sister, my mother, and I moved ninety miles north from Hattiesburg, Mississippi, to Jackson, Mississippi. Mom had been commuting to Jackson to take care of things, but we moved to Jackson to get a fresh start and to get her closer to the business that she owned. We enrolled in a public school about a mile away, and my straight A's and perfect attendance before the divorce were replaced with D's on my report cards, fighting at school, and fights at home resulting from my unwillingness to obey my mother. We were all in very uncomfortable places in our lives.

Stress Upon Stress

Instead of talking about *my* complicated life, I'd like to talk about my mother's complicated life for a moment. I was eight years old, mad at my mother for moving us away from Hattiesburg, mad at my father for not being the husband and father he could have been, mad at my sister for wanting everything I ever got (my mother always got her the same thing she got me so that my sister wouldn't be jealous), and just plain mad at the world. But my problems were selfish and small compared to those that my mother had to deal with.

To give you an idea as to how stressful my mother's life was at that time, we need to briefly talk about the Holmes-Rahe Social Readjustment Scale. Life has many stressful events, and the Holmes-Rahe Social Readjustment Scale strives to attribute a point value to a life event. The points for each life event are added up (you can have more than one life event going on at the same time), and the resulting final score gives a probability that a stress-related illness will appear. Stress-related illnesses include: hypertension; panic attacks/anxiety; asthma; insomnia; chronic fatigue; addictions; allergies; memory and concentration difficulties; ulcerative colitis; ulcers; overeating. The probabilities revealed by the scale are as follows:

Life Change Units	Chance of Developing a Stress-Related Illness or Accident Within Two Years
Less than 150 units	30% chance
150 – 299 units	50% chance
Over 300 units	80% chance

The stresses and their respective point values that my mother was under at that point in her life were:

Divorce	73
Business Readjustment (she was also selling her store in Hattiesburg, MS)	39

Change in Financial State (Dad was no longer around to potentially help with the bills and she was not receiving any alimony or child support)	38
Total	**150 units**

With these issues in life, she had a thirty percent chance of developing a stress-related illness. That's a pretty high number, and I wouldn't wish a thirty percent chance of illness on anyone. But my mother had even more of a burden to carry because she also had the following events in her life:

Change in frequency of arguments (this change can be good or bad, but is still stressful)	35
Major Mortgage (she bought a house by herself)	32
Outstanding Personal Achievement (her franchise was doing well and she was recognized for that success)	28
Change in Residence	20
Change in Schools	20
Additional Stress Total	**135 units**
Complete Total	**285 units**

Based upon this study, it's easy to see that my mother's stress level was high and that her life had a fifty percent chance of developing a stress-related illness or accident within two years. Within the previous twelve months, she had separated from her husband, divorced, moved to a new town, bought a house and acquired a mortgage, given up any network of friends that she had while married to my father, changed schools for my sister and me, run a business, solely cared for two children who were suffering greatly from the divorce, and not been able to have exercise or recreation for herself. I can't imagine going through all those life changes, let alone going through those changes without my wife at my side!

Do you know anyone who's been through similar situations, all of these changes, more than these changes, or even just one of these changes? Are you going through some similar issues in your life? My mother did not even have the time to identify the amount of stress that she was under, much less take any steps to reduce the stress even - if she had a way to ease the burden. If you have stress in your life, take the time to realize it and take the time to reduce it. Your life, and the lives of those around you, will suffer if you do not take the time to invest in yourself. When we don't take the time to help ourselves, our bodies start taking the steps for us. We get sick easier when we're stressed, we tire more easily and frequently, and we do things that we wouldn't do if we were free from stress.

My father started drinking in his mid-twenties, and he is the type of drinker that can function no matter how much he's had to drink. Daily, he'd wake up and have coffee, then a bloody Mary, and then he'd have his first beer around 10 A.M. Around mid-afternoon, he'd start drinking hard liquor. To my knowledge, he never had a car accident, never passed out from drinking, and never failed to meet a commitment due to his drinking. He's what I would call a functional drinker.

Dad would probably say that he was always under tremendous stress because he never knew when he would be called away to work, as he worked primarily when major weather catastrophes occurred such as hurricanes, floods, hail storms, and earthquakes. He would be called away to work all over the U.S., and he would work hard while work was available because he never knew where or when his next paycheck would be coming. Then he would come home and wait for the next disaster. Sometimes his wait was short, and sometimes his wait was long. Immediately before the divorce, his wait was over two years, and that lack of work weighed heavily on their minds and their marriage.

Some people are able to handle stress a lot better than others, and it seemed that he was able to handle the stress associated with the divorce better than my mother. Maybe it was because he was able to stay in his hometown; he kept his job; he had a girlfriend quickly after the separation whom he soon married as his third wife; he had been divorced with children once before already; he wasn't responsible for the daily commitment of raising children; and he was not financially burdened with alimony or child support. In hindsight, my father's stress level probably greatly decreased, but my mother was not so fortunate, and I thank her willingness to keep on moving forward under such heavy burdens.

My father drank because that's what he did, and that's how he had always operated. Work in the morning, golf course in the afternoon, playing cards with friends at the club in the evening, and then home when he felt like it. Their marriage had deteriorated badly at this point in time, and Dad was probably not coming home because he honestly did not want to be there. I always make a point to be home at the time I told my wife that I would be home because my mother never knew when my dad was going to walk in the door. How do you feel when someone tells you they'll be home at six o'clock and they show up after ten? How do you feel if it happens again, and again, and again?

> My father drank out of habit; my mother drank with a purpose.

While my dad functioned quite well when drinking, my mother drank to forget and to get away. My father drank out of habit; my mother drank with a purpose. How about your situation? *Only you can be honest with yourself.*

Home Should Be Safe, Predictable, and Consistent

I love the fact that I can walk into my house after work knowing that Whitney will be playing on the floor with her sister and that Wendy will be the same Wendy I married, the same Wendy who gave birth to our kids, and the same Wendy I left early that morning. Our children will always be able to bring friends over, and their friends will be welcomed into a healthy, consistent, and predictable household.

One of my first memories of the negative effect that my mother's drinking had on me could have ended much worse than it actually did. I was in Cub Scouts in the third grade, and I had on my blue uniform along with the others in my pack. Our parents each took turns making the refreshments that we would have at the scout meeting, and that day was the day my mother was supposed to bring the refreshments, pick us all up from school in her station wagon, and take us to another scout's house to have our meeting. I'll never forget the smell when I opened the passenger door to get in with my friends; it was a mixture of Kool-Aid, fresh chocolate chip cookies ….. and vodka.

She was wearing a very thin robe with her nightgown on underneath, and she smiled at my friends and me. But I knew something was very, very wrong. She was "moody"; a term that my sister and I used as a code word to mean drunk. I don't know if my friends realized her condition, but I was humiliated. Some parents regularly embarrass their children by how they dress, what they say, or the way they act, but I was humiliated by this event; and the entire scout pack was in danger from riding in a car with an intoxicated driver. She said, "I made you boys some fresh cookies!" I looked at the cookies, and they were completely submerged in Kool-Aid that she had accidentally spilled into the container. The cookies were ruined, the Kool-Aid was gone, she smelled horrible, and we were in danger. We made it safely to our destination, but I don't ever remember car-pooling with any of my scout friends ever again.

The level of stress in her life was very high at that time as she had a failing marriage, no real friends, two young children, and ownership of two businesses. But the level of stress in my life as a third-grader was tremendous. In hindsight, I was fortunate that I was not physically abused by anyone, that I had a place to live and food to eat, and that my mother had times when she was the best mom in the world. She was a mom that would cook a great meal, dance in the living room, or throw a Nerf® ball in the yard with her son. But I learned that day that my mother, at that particular time in her life, was a person that I could not trust.

In their book, *Children of Alcoholism – A Survivor's Manual*, authors Judith S. Seixas and Geraldine Youcha titled Part

I "Living in Chaos." Chapter One is named "The Terrible Family Secret," and I know exactly why both of those titles are appropriate. They state, "These children (of alcoholics) see alcoholism not as an illness but as a weakness, an embarrassment – and as a shame that accumulates as time goes on and the alcoholic gets sicker."[1] My sister and I were scared to bring friends into the house when we came home from school if Mom was home because we didn't know which "Mom" would be waiting for us. We didn't know if it would be the busy, loving, competent mom or the angry, bitter, sad, and moody mom. We didn't know if the house was going to be neat or a complete wreck, if there would be food or not, if she would be awake or passed out on the floor, or that we were unconditionally loved. My mother was under tremendous stress, had no outlet for help, and her illness that resulted from her stress was alcoholism and hypertension. All of our lives were spiraling downward in what seemed to be an unstoppable cycle.

Have you had similar situations in your life? Are you creating similar situations in your life, and in the life of others? If so, go find help! Reading this book is a great start, and there are people, books, and processes that can help you in the same ways that could have helped my single, working mother under tremendous personal, chemical, financial, and emotional stress.

Seixas and Youcha further explain that there are four myths working behind the scenes in the lives of most children of alcoholics. If you are a child of someone that drinks too much on somewhat of a regular basis or if you are in constant contact with some sort of disease, addiction, or harmful personality trait (anger, violence, sexual abuse), four common myths and my comments to you are

- Myth #1 - "I caused the alcoholism and I should do something about it" – It is not your fault!
- Myth #2 - "I'm not like anyone else" – You are not alone, and the authors stated that there were twenty-two million adults in the U.S. who lived with an alcoholic parent.
- Myth #3 - "I have to be in control of myself and everything else or my world will fall apart" – This is my biggest charac-

ter flaw, and I deal with it every single day of my life. I have to remind myself daily that others can be trusted to accomplish tasks in their own way, on their own time schedule, and according to their own level of quality.

- Myth #4 - "Someone will come along or something will happen that will change all of this" – Only the person with a drinking problem can change himself, so please don't take it upon yourself to try and change that person. If you try to change another person, you will end up making that person angry and add to your frustration. Take the time to realize that the only person that you can fix is you![2]

Seixas and Youcha explain that children of alcoholics develop some interesting character traits in an attempt to simply survive in an unpredictable environment. They state that children of alcoholics are often unable to trust others; angry; have feelings of guilt, embarrassment, shame, sadness, and mourning; are often controlling, addictive, attention-seeking, over-achieving, compulsive, lonely, and abusive. These character traits and qualities are revealed through the following roles commonly found in children who grew up in homes where alcohol had a negative effect:[3]

- *The "Family Hero"* – This is the child on whom the family counts to take over when other things flounder. When there's no food in the house, this person goes to the grocery store on a bicycle, in a car even before he has his driver's license, or on foot. He strives to receive praise from others and excels at school or at work by doing his best. He often is placed in positions of leadership and finds himself often taking care of others. His striving for success can have very negative effects on his health due to stress, and it can cause his own children to resort to alcoholism if they can't live up to their parents' measures of success. The Family Hero often has trouble feeling good no matter how successful he becomes.
- *The "Scapegoat"* – This person is the one who is always in trouble and who gets attention by doing things he shouldn't. He's labeled as the family troublemaker or the misfit. He's

often the second child, and Seixas and Youcha state that he's the most likely to end up in jail, be addicted to alcohol or drugs, or die an early death due to suicide or accident.

- *The "Lost Child or Quiet One"* – This person is often referred to as "the angel" because he flies below the radar screen and stays out of trouble. He's quiet, passive, and finds inward ways to make himself comfortable.
- *The "Mascot"* – Tense, anxious, and often overactive, this person uses humor to help get himself out of tough situations and moments. The authors state that he rarely has deep, meaningful relationships because he is so flighty.

I can see that I have parts of all four roles in my personality, but I can mostly identify with the Family Hero and the Mascot. My younger sister was definitely the Scapegoat. Do you see yourself in any of those roles? Please read the books that are referenced in this area if you'd like to know more about your situation. Remember, the best investment that you can make is an investment in yourself! That investment will reap dividends for you and for those around you at home, at work, and at school.

Blended Families

An earlier statistic showed that fifty percent of women who already have children when they get married end up getting divorced within ten years. I personally believe the same probably holds true for men. Regardless of the national average, it was true with my family.

"Here's the story, of a lovely lady, who was bringing up three very lovely girls...." I'm sure you could finish the song! It's from the TV show, "The Brady Bunch." When I was growing up, "The Brady Bunch" was a big hit with people my age. The Brady family was unique in that day and time because they were a *blended family*, which means that there were children present that weren't all from the same mother and father. Mr. and Mrs. Brady were both in their second marriages, they each had three children, and they were a novelty at that time because you really didn't see many blended families. Today, a great deal of families have some type of blended family feature – the presence of a step-parent, half-brothers and sisters, step-brothers and sisters, etc. I was fortunate enough to have all of those blended features.

My father is twice divorced and has been married to his third wife for quite some time. When I was in high school and college, he gave me a gas card to pay for my gasoline, and he occasionally would give me money to help out. The checks he would write would be from an account labeled "special account." I often wondered when I received those checks how many times he had written checks out of that account to his other children. He has three children from the first marriage, two from the second to my mother, and two from his third marriage that she already had from her first marriage. I still wonder today how he keeps everything straight in his head. He's practically managing a small corporation with all of his children, stepchildren, grandchildren, and great-grandchildren.

Family get-togethers at my father's house were always stressful, and I'm sure they're stressful for the normal families. With such a large family, there was always a good chance that somebody was mad at somebody at any family event. I think that many family members were always subconsciously looking for something to make themselves feel better, to make a point about something said or done in the past, or to simply redeem themselves from previous altercations and disagreements. I'm sure that several people just wanted to say as little as possible in the hopes of not making someone angry or hurting someone's feelings. Blended families almost always bring a lot of feelings of favoritism and jealousy to the table. I'm finally learning that the best thing I can do is live my life as best I know how and trust that others will replicate the good things they see in my life or learn from my mistakes. I'm finally learning that it's not my job to try and fix everyone, even though that's what the Family Hero usually tries to do. Remember, the only person you can change is yourself!

Financial Struggles

In 1997, eighty percent of divorces ended due to irreconcilable differences. Statistics show that only four percent of divorces in that year were due to economic problems.[4] I believe that economic problems were a huge dividing factor in a large percentage of the divorces that fell under the catch-all phrase "irreconcilable differences." My dad didn't have any substantial amount of work or earned income in the two years leading up to my parents' divorce. My mother worked hard at the candle store she owned, and I know that money was a constant topic of conversation for them. Looking back, I think my mother was angry at a situation that she perceived as unfair. In her mind he wasn't working; in his mind he was stressfully waiting for the next lucrative natural disaster to occur. In her mind he was spending a lot of time playing golf; he probably thought he needed to keep running with the same crowd so that no one would know that finances were tight. As with any disagreement, there are usually two sides to the story. Regardless of who was right or wrong, the unhappiness and the divorce were extremely tough on my sister and me because we, like most children involved in divorced families, inevitably believe that both sides of the story pointed to us.

Dad was able to stay afloat during the two years of waiting for work by borrowing money from banks and friends to maintain his lifestyle of going to the office in the morning and spending the afternoon and evening at the country club. There are many fathers and husbands today who don't enjoy the situation waiting for them at home, so they simply choose to not come home. I'm fortunate to have realized that my family that lives in my home is the most important group of people I'll ever know.

While dad was playing golf and cards at the club, mom was working hard at her businesses. She would then come home and cook dinner for my sister and me. After the divorce, those same responsibilities continued for her, but there was no longer any chance of financial assistance from anyone else. She sold her candle store business and bought a retail business that sold brass. A few years later, a large brass wholesaler moved into town and completely destroyed her business. We lost our home to foreclosure and moved to a townhouse that we leased. My mother, struggling to stay afloat financially, worked at flea markets to make ends meet. As a teenager, I spent almost every weekend at the flea market, and I made some money by setting up the tables that all the booths used to display their goods. I always had trouble finding people who were willing to help me because the work was very hard, but I knew that we had to have some money coming in to help put food on the table.

Mom soon realized that the flea markets weren't generating enough income, and she took a job as a hostess at PoFolks. We look back now and laugh about how a former successful business owner, Ms. Shaw High, the Mississippi state sprint record holder, and holder of a Masters Degree in Home Economics would appreciate having a job simply showing people where to sit in a restaurant. She worked as a manager of a gas station, and she also got a job at a restaurant after I heard the manager say he needed to find an assistant manager. Mom did everything that she could to keep us clothed, fed, and housed safely.

I've been fired from two jobs in my life, one because I told the business owners about drug use on their property by a group of people that happened to include their daughter and son-in-law; the other when the grocery store manager took the time to read my job application a week after I had already started working and found out that I was too young to be able to work for them. I worked during the summer cleaning the grounds for an outdoor mall, I worked nights at a family restaurant, I had a paper route, and I worked in the maintenance crew at our high school. The financial struggles were hard to endure, but our endurance helped to fertilize the seeds of financial wisdom and prudence that were planted in me at a young age.

You can see that my family had plenty of financial struggles, and I know we're not the only family that struggled with money. These struggles made my parents do and say things that they probably should not have. I'm sure that if they could turn the clock back thirty or forty years they would have done some things differently, as we all probably would. Are you, a family member, or a friend struggling with any commitments at work, school, or church because of a habit that can't seem to be broken? Help yourself before it's too late – before you've lost your job or business (and a way to pay the bills), before you drop out or get kicked out of school, and before you lose relationships with people that could really be a positive influence in your life.

Summary

The important observations that you could take with you from this discussion are

- I've spent time trying to understand why my parents did what they did.
- I've spent time trying to understand why they didn't do what I thought they should have.
- I've received professional counseling that has helped me understand that it was not my fault.
- I've had substantial contact with people in my life whom I could count on.

What issues in your life do you need to take the time to deal with to help yourself? Do you realize that if you help yourself, you will be helping your family? At work, have you ever heard the saying that bad things and tough responsibilities always roll down hill? The same is true at home. If you aren't happy, the odds reveal that your family probably isn't happy either. Change starts with you, and you should strive to set the emotional tone in your household. However, please remember, you are not responsible for changing others. Author John Maxwell once said, "I teach what I know, but I reproduce what I am." Are you saying or teaching things to your family, but you're finding that you're not getting the results you hoped for? If so, you may be reproducing what you are even though you're trying to teach what you know. Ask someone who knows you and your family well enough and cares about you enough to tell you things that you might not want to hear if you practice what you preach. You may be surprised at the answer. We're all human and humans are going to make mistakes. One of the best examples you can set is that you are a person who has the strength to recognize your shortcomings, the desire to change your behavior, and the dedication to make a change into a habit.

Things You Need To Do Now

1. **Review the questions asked in this chapter.** Really spend some time thinking about your situation. When you think you've spent enough time, try to spend a little more time. Then spend some more time. You deserve a better understanding of what makes you tick. It just takes time, knowledge, and perspective. Hopefully, this book has helped with the knowledge and perspective. You're the only one who can spend the time.

SECTION II - FAMILY

Chapter Thirteen

Family Solutions

There are many, many books that will help you address issues in your life, deal with issues that currently exist in your family, and gain perspective on how to find healthy, realistic, and positive solutions to problems or discomforts. This chapter should help give you some good ideas that are based on my studies of various self-help, psychological, faith-based, and family-centered books I have encountered while trying to deal with issues in my life. I know that you'll find a great deal of similarities between your life and mine, and I hope that you'll find one thing that you can put to use.

Love Them From a Distance

I heard a psychologist on Christian radio one day answering a call from someone who asked for advice. She said she had done all that she could to help someone, but that person repeatedly inflicted harm on them due to his habits, addictions, and personality. The caller was torn over whether or not she should continue to show unconditional love and endure the pain and suffering that she knew would come in the future or if she needed to protect herself. The psychologist said, "There is nothing wrong with leaving that person to fend for himself if you are repeatedly harmed in the relationship. You can still love that person just as much as you do now; you should just love that person from a distance."

This conversation had a tremendous effect on how I felt I should deal with two family members in my life at that time. I felt that I had repeatedly taken the high road by showing support, love, and trust when their actions showed they didn't deserve the support and trust I was providing. (Please note that I did not say that they didn't deserve the *love*, as everyone deserves love.) I was constantly bending over backwards to accommodate an aggressive personality, lack of mutual respect, harsh words spoken to inflict pain, and their insincere desires to try to change. I slowly began to distance myself from these people so that I could simply survive.

Have you ever noticed that lifeboats attached to big ships are not permanently affixed to the side of the boat? The lifeboats can be lowered and untied so that they can be free to move towards safety and not go down with the big ship. The lifeboats, and the people inside them, are much safer while attached to the big boat out in the expanse of the oceans; but the lifeboats are designed to float on their own if necessary. Loving someone from a distance is similar to this in that sometimes you've got to do all you can to save the ship, but once it can't be helped anymore, you've got to break free and save yourself. Very few people are strong enough to handle their own problems. Even fewer are strong enough to handle their own problems, the problems that others have, and the pain associated with the dynamics of the relationship.

A specific example in my life was a recent interaction with one of these family members. I asked her an honest question with good intentions and she took it as a personal attack on certain people in the family with whom she felt a special bond. I was disappointed to be reminded that even after twenty years, she still viewed and treated certain family members differently from others. Looking back, I probably should have known better than to even have a conversation with her because it was late in the evening and I believe she had been drinking all day. She immediately launched a cruel and hurtful attack against my values, my mother, my lifestyle, my childhood, and me. Every word said was aimed at causing harm, not at finding a solution, just as it had been done many, many times in the past to every member of the family and to every close friend of the family's. I apologized for my question and tried to explain, but the best solution was for me to keep my mouth closed and simply to get away from the situation.

The next day, I walked into the house and she was on the phone with someone. I later found out that the "someone" on the phone was my pregnant wife, Wendy. She had called Wendy to give her an earful of what she thought about me. Several times in the past, she had picked up the phone and called my mother, my grandmother, or my wife's parents in order to vent her frustration. I'm an adult, and I'm fully responsible for my actions. No one else is more responsible for me than I am to myself. But she wanted to drag everyone she could possibly contact into the issues. She was trying to take all the lifeboats down with the main ship.

Have you ever seen a spitting cobra in person or on TV? I don't like seeing snakes on TV, I don't like seeing them in person, and I really don't like ones that can hurt you without even touching you – snakes like the spitting cobra. In addition to being able to bite people, spitting cobras spit venom at their victims who are within reach in an attempt to blind and immobilize them. I think of my bitter family member's personality and reactions as much like that of a spitting cobra. A major difference that makes her potentially more dangerous than a cobra is that she is able to reach people through phone lines to make her attacks. I can deal with her, as I've done for many years. I've forgiven her many times, I'm sure I'll forgive her for future situations, and I hope she has forgiven me for the things she feels I've done wrong. But, who in their right mind would put his innocent children in the path of someone who has a history of saying and doing things simply out of anger, a desire for revenge, or a lack of self-control? In order to protect my family, I've had to make a decision to keep them out of the range of the verbal abuse that might come out of her at any time.

This distance makes a relationship with my father a little more complicated because I won't bring my family to any family functions, I won't stay in the same house with her, nor will I willingly put her in the same room with my family. I am not mad at her, I have forgiven her, I pray for her, and I honestly do love her for the good things that she's done for my dad and for me. At times, she is the most loving, hardest working, and highly intelligent person you could hope to have in your family. Spitting cobras are also good to have because they kill rats; however, I don't want to be around a spitting cobra. She is a time bomb waiting to explode, and no one ever knows what words, actions, or lack of either could set that time bomb off. Loving someone from a distance does not mean that you've given up on him or her, but it does mean that your first obligation is to protect yourself and your immediate family so that you can live a healthy and positive life. Her verbal abuse has existed from the time I first met her over twenty years ago, and her tongue is very, very sharp. Years of behaving similarly and her evident lack of desire to make a permanent change show me that I'm dealing with a person who needs to be loved from a distance. Pastor Rick Warren, in his book *The Purpose Driven Life*, says, "If someone hurts you repeatedly, you are commanded by God to forgive them instantly, but you are not expected to trust them immediately, and you are not expected to continue allowing them to hurt you. They must prove they have changed over time."[1] I've hoped and prayed almost every day that she would change. Since I now have children to protect, I will wait until I know of absolute proof that she has changed before I bring our children near her again.

They must prove they have changed over time.

I gave you all of this detail because I'm pretty sure you have someone in your life and situations that are pretty similar to mine. Do you know anyone like this? Maybe even more importantly, are you a person that others may want to love from a distance? Does your family situation or interactions with each other agree with your answer, or does it prove otherwise? If you aren't sure, ask those around you. Ask them to be honest, and deal with the answer as positively as possible.

Please note that I am not saying that you should turn and run for the hills at the first instance of dissatisfaction in a relationship with a family member, a friend, a coworker, church member, or business partner. You need to exhaust every possible opportunity available to you to love, trust, support, and forgive that person. But, once you see that there is an obvious imbalance between the effort that you've made and the evidence of a desire to change on the part of the other person, you probably need to make the decision to love them from a distance. You've heard the saying, "Absence makes the heart grow fonder" and "If you set him free and he returns to you, he's truly yours." Lower the lifeboats down into the water and turn loose of the main ship. Set yourself free from the chains of trying to make another person respond to you in a better way. Set them free from the burden of having to deal with you also. Freedom can bring perspective, and perspective can bring about a change of heart.

A deeper note:

You might not be as fortunate as I am to have the person you need to distance yourself from live in a town that is several hours away. Your spitting cobra may live in the same town, or maybe even in your home with you. Some people choose to remain in dangerous and unhealthy situations because their fear of the unknown is greater than their fear of staying. Certain family members continue trying to have a close relationship with her even though they know the family suffers from her rage and wrath. I assume they choose to do this because they also know that when things are okay with her, she treats them very well. Their actions, or lack of actions, show that in their minds, the benefits still outweigh the costs. If you are having trouble deciding if the costs of staying with someone are greater than the benefits, go talk to a professional. If you are being physically harmed or threatened, get out now before the spitting cobra's venom damages you beyond repair.

Work Together and Stay Busy

My wife and I owned a horseback riding business in southeastern Tennessee during the first two years of our marriage. We had a lot of issues in our lives at that time. We were newly married, we had just moved from the big city of Nashville, my wife had left a great job working in the country music business, our farmhouse also served as our place of business, we lived seventeen miles from any real semblance of a major town, and our business partner lived in the same farmhouse with us. There's a great example from which to talk about Holmes-Rahe life change units – we were stressed all the time!

In addition to learning a great deal about marriage, my family background, and myself, I learned a great deal from the horses themselves. We had about twenty horses, ranging from a small 850-pound Arabian named Ripley to a huge draft horse named Big Mama. We took groups of people out riding in the 600,000-acre national forest that was literally our back yard, and it always seemed like we were dealing with two sets of infants who were always getting in trouble – the riders and the horses!

The important thing that I learned about keeping the riders and horses out of trouble was that I needed to keep them busy and focused on a task. While the horses were tied up and waiting for their next ride, we kept them a safe distance from each other so that they wouldn't be tempted to kick or bite (sounds like preschoolers, doesn't it?). We tried to give them some hay to nibble on in order to keep their minds off of trying to bite their neighbors or chewing on their stalls. While the riders were mounted and waiting for the group to leave the corral, I had them walk their horses to and from different points in the corral. Inevitably, some rider would not follow instructions and allow his horse to get too close to another horse and trouble would start. On the trail, we always kept the groups moving. If we did stop, one horse would wander off the trail in search of something to eat, mainly because the riders didn't know how to keep them in line. That rider would be scratched and stung by small, wispy tree branches as the horse slowly plodded towards its hopeful morsel of food. The horse behind that horse would then follow along, and then the horse behind that one, and so on. Needless to say, we always tried to keep moving because the riders couldn't control what their animals were doing. I learned the best way to stay out of trouble when dealing with horses and inexperienced riders is simply to stay constructively busy, and I think that's a great principal in life also.

Some of the funniest times that my mother, my sister, and I had together were the times when we worked as a team on a newspaper delivery route. The paper route was a great opportunity for us to learn responsibility, commitment, dedication, and consistency. We had to get up very, very early in the morning on days when it was cold, rainy, and dreary. I had to deliver the papers one Saturday morning before I was to take the A.C.T. college aptitude exam. I had played in a football game in which I sustained a concussion the night before against our in-town rival. My mother had to help me with the paper route a few times when she was still not feeling well from the night before. My sister is probably the only person I know that can successfully drive a car through an entire paper route while sleeping! We were so tired and underpaid from working that route, we didn't have time to disagree, argue, pick on each other, or get into as much trouble as we would have if we had free time on our hands.

Years before, when I lived with my mom and sister, Mom would work long hours at her store and leave my sister and me at home with long hours of unstructured time. Leaving my sister and me at home together was like leaving two hungry horses alone in a small stall with one bucket of oats on the floor between them. We did nothing but aggravate each other because we were simply bored to death. She'd get mad at me and lock me out of the house. I would monopolize the television. We'd reach a stalemate and pick up the phone and call Mom at work and absolutely worry her to death.

> If you are financially and logistically able, I urge you to create some structured recreational time with your family.

Wendy and I have made a commitment to have Whitney and Ashley take music lessons, participate in any sport they would like, and engage in family recreational activities like swimming and boating. My mother did not have the blessing of staying at home with her children in the same way that Wendy is able to stay home with our children, nor did she have the financial resources or another way to get us from one place to another while she was working. If you are financially and logistically able, I urge you to create some *structured* recreational time with your family.

During the summers that passed between my high school years, I would often spend several weeks with my dad. When I lived with my grandmother, he would drive four hours on Friday to pick me up and turn right around and drive four hours back home. Then on Sunday he'd make the same trip again. On these trips to see each other, we would have fun in the car talking about football and listening to the radio, but once we got to his house, the boredom set in because his attention was focused elsewhere. He did make a very strong effort to take us fishing in his boat, and we usually had a swimming pool that we could swim in, but the thing I now know I longed for when I was young was to be close to someone that I respected, loved, and trusted. I wanted to have meaningful conversations, I wanted to be asked questions, I wanted to be taught, and I wanted to obtain acceptance and approval – especially from my father. Pastor Rick Warren said, "The most desired gift of love is not diamonds or roses or chocolate. It is focused attention. Love concentrates so intently on another that you forget yourself at that moment. Attention says, 'I value you enough to give you my most precious asset – my time.' Whenever you give your time, you are making a sacrifice, and sacrifice is the essence of love.... You can give without loving, but you cannot love without giving."[2]

> The most desired gift of love is not diamonds or roses or chocolate. It is focused attention.

My dad has always valued his golf games, and I remember several times that he'd drop me off at their house after picking me up and head straight for the golf course. I was left to spend time with his wife and my stepbrother and stepsister - not exactly the reason I came to see my dad! I enjoyed going to the course with him for a while, but as an eight year old, I tired of the waiting, beer drinking, pre-shot cigarette flips, and the lack of attention on me. Now, as a parent, I know there are times when Whitney is dying for me to read a book to her, and I can use my amazing skills of perception to decipher what she really means when she says, "Daddy, will you read me a book?" She wants me to read her a book! Every adult needs time to himself, time to do nothing, time to not have any responsibilities. But, more importantly, every child needs to know that he is unconditionally loved, that his parents enjoy his company, and that he's very important to them.

While I don't think that any parent should completely abandon the things they enjoy doing in order to please their children, I do know that I didn't need to tag along and watch someone else live his life. He would play four hours of golf and I would sit in the cart, sometimes drive the cart, or run behind the cart. He would finish playing golf and then go play cards in the locker room where kids weren't allowed, and I would spend a couple of hours practicing on the putting green, swimming in the pool, or sitting outside the locker room wishing we could leave. I know there are millions of kids who aren't fortunate enough to have a father around at all and even more who can't spend time at a country club. But all I wanted was to have his attention focused on me.

I think my father felt he was doing his duty if I was safe, had food to eat, a place to sleep, wasn't being physically abused, had clothes on my back, and had recreational opportunities like swimming or golf available to me. I'm willing to bet that his dad treated him the same way. My dad was forty-one when I was born, so we have a fairly significant age-gap. But the age-gap was not quite as dramatic as the one between his father and him. The last thing that I wanted to do when I was going to visit my dad was to be stuck at his house with his wife and her kids or to sit outside at the country club waiting to go home to a house I didn't enjoy. I think that any child, once he's grown up and has children of his own, would agree that he would have traded in all the activities he could have done for just one meaningful relationship that was based on love and trust.

I didn't start playing the guitar until I was twenty years old, and I often wish that I could have had music lessons when I was young. Those music lessons could have planted a seed, whether I wanted a seed planted at that time in my life or not. That seed could have blossomed a lot earlier in life and I could have spent a lot less time with girlfriends I'll never see again or sitting in front of the television. It is very unfortunate, but the television has become today's most inexpensive and ever-present babysitter. Videotapes and DVD's are constantly playing in homes and vehicles across America in an attempt by parents to keep their children busy and out of trouble. Keeping children busy and out of trouble is important, but teaching children useful skills and helping them develop their God-given talents is an even better objective. I can just about quote every word from movies like *Grease*, *Airplane*, and *Caddyshack*, and I laugh every time I talk about those movies with someone. But, honestly, I would like to be able to play the piano or the guitar better, I would like to know more about the Bible, I would like to have spent my time doing something more productive with my time, and I surely would have liked healthier relationships with family members.

How about you? What activities do you have your children doing? Are you simply keeping them busy, or are you encouraging them to be more fulfilled persons with skills and talents that can be used and appreciated for the rest of their lives? What did your parents do for you? Were you kept busy or were you put in situations where you could improve yourself? If you were simply kept busy, you still have time to put yourself in situations that will make you a better, more complete person… don't give up on yourself or think it's too late!

Encourage Support From Others

If you can't be a part of the solution, encourage your family members to spend time with people who can help – professional counselors; honest, loving, supportive, trustworthy people; pastors; or church members. We've all heard that sometimes it is a lot easier to talk to a stranger than it is to talk to someone you know. The important thing is to make sure that the opportunity to talk and listen is given to those in need.

John Evans was my Young Life leader from my eighth-grade year until I graduated high school. Young Life is a lot like FCA or Campus Crusade, and John was responsible for helping bring me into a life of meaning, focus, and assurance. I accepted Christ at a Young Life camp in North Carolina in the summer before my junior year of high school.

John saw that I was a young man who was very hurt and in need of something. He and I met for breakfast almost every Tuesday morning during our relationship. He had just received his degree in counseling, and I certainly benefited from his education without having to pay him a dime. He was continually asking me questions that pulled me out of my angry and bitter shell. He asked me how I felt about things that happened in my life. He rarely, if ever, asked me what I thought. There's a big difference between feelings and thoughts. Feelings reflect the state of one's heart; thoughts reflect the state of one's mind. He wanted to get to the heart of the issues, and I needed someone willing to help me fight through the walls of defense I had created in order to protect me from pain and disappointment.

John was present at school, school events, and Young Life events. He called me on the phone; he met me when he said he'd meet me. He kept his word. He was the trustworthy, professional, qualified, and good-hearted person and mentor who helped me find out why I am who I am. He loaned us his car for weeks so that we could complete our daily paper route after our vehicle was repossessed. He helped introduce me to Vanderbilt University. He's kept in contact with me through the years. He's still doing the same thing for other people in Jackson, Mississippi.

Is there anyone in your life, or in your family member's life who can fill the same role that John Evans played for me? If there isn't, find someone. If you have to pay someone for professional counsel, write the check with a smile on your face as that is the best investment you will ever make. Don't worry about not having the money in your pocket anymore. Focus your eyes on what is unseen; focus your eyes on the hearts of those around you. Even though it may not seem to be true in the short term, everyone will benefit in the long run.

Forgive and Forget

Forgiving someone is sometimes a very difficult thing to do. Forgetting is even harder. We have very long memories, and the world has trained us to always be on the defensive. One of the best ways for you to be at peace with yourself is to forgive and forget what others have said or done to you. Buddy Hackett, a famous actor and comedian, said, "Don't carry a grudge. While you're carrying the grudge the other guy's out dancing."

> Forgiving someone is sometimes a very difficult thing to do. Forgetting is even harder.

More often than not, if you haven't forgiven and/or forgotten something, you're suffering more than the person who offended you. That doesn't seem fair, does it? You can't step into his brain or heart and fix him, so the next best thing you can do is take care of yourself. Often, the simple act of taking care of yourself sets a good enough example for the other person to see the error of his ways. The person may come to you and ask for forgiveness, or he may simply not repeat the act that troubled you. Forgiveness and the desire to forget can many times set both parties free from the burden of anger, disgust, disappointment, and bitterness. This doesn't always happen, but it may. Here's an example from my life that may help you.

My mother's retail brass business was ruined when a brass wholesaler moved into our hometown of Jackson, Mississippi, around 1985. Her business simply could not compete with the lower prices. My mother drew unemployment for a while until she got a job as a hostess at Po Folks, and then I helped her get a job as an assistant manager at a local steakhouse where I was working as the dishwasher. We didn't have much food to eat at home, no car, and no money to do anything other than go to school, work, and endure the tough times together. Mom was still coping with the stress in life by binge drinking, and one day she got a job offer that would allow her to make plenty of money for us. We were all very excited that the tough times were over!

After her first week, Mom told me that she didn't have a good feeling about the job because the two prior managers were there only a few months. This uneasy feeling and fear of losing her job added to her stress of providing for us while maintaining her sanity. She wanted to keep this great paying job so that my sister and I would have food to eat, a car to drive, and a place to live. Mom wasn't working for herself; she was working for us. This additional stress of not wanting to lose what she had gained made her drink a little more than usual; and it got harder for me to wake her up, get her to cook meals, remind her that she had to work the next day, and get her to be the mother we wanted – and the mother she wanted to be. She had already endured more stress in life than any person deserves, but she hoped that job was what God had provided as the answer to her prayers. She thought there was light at the end of the tunnel. Then she had to deal with the realization that the fight wasn't over yet.

I didn't know, as a fourteen year old, that alcoholism is an addictive disease. All I could see was the fact that Mom was having a hard time keeping herself ready and able to go to work and to take care of us. I didn't want to go back to not having any money. I thought she was just selfishly drinking to avoid her problems and get away, so one day I told her, "If you lose this job because of your drinking, I will never forgive you." Those were big words from a fourteen year old, but at that time, I was the parent and she was the child. She was under tremendous stress to provide for us, and one day about four months later I came home from school to find that our nightmare had come true.

I walked up to the apartment door, turned the handle, and found the door was locked. This was strange because we always left the door unlocked, as there wasn't much in the apartment anyone would want to steal anyway. I knew my sister was at school, and so that meant Mom had come home before us. But she wasn't supposed to get off from work for another two hours. I knew something was wrong. I knocked on the door and waited…. and waited…. and finally the door opened. There stood my mother in her robe, she had been drinking, and I will never forget the look on her face. She looked at me in the same way that a young child who knows he's done wrong looks at his father when he walks in the front door after work. My threat I had made to her months prior had echoed in her mind every single day as she trudged to and from work trying to please the business owners who could not be pleased and to provide for my sister and me. She was thinking that she let my sister and me down, and I'm sure she envisioned a tirade by her fourteen year old threat-maker that would last the rest of her life. She dreaded the consequences, and she dreaded the reality.

I angrily asked her, "Did you lose your job?!" She looked down at her feet as I stood in the doorway and quietly said to me, "Yes." She ducked her head and waited for me to really let her have it for failing to keep that job, for failing to continue being a provider, for failing to live up to her promise to us.

But… the threat I had made to her was never enforced. At that very moment I was given the ability to forgive. Instead of yelling, screaming, blaming, and accusing, I was able to quietly say to my broken mother, "That's okay. We'll be alright."

I could visibly see that the weight of the entire world had been lifted from her shoulders when I said those words. She was freed from her mental anguish and torment. And I was freed to grow into a young man. Forgiveness brings freedom, and freedom brings peace. I think about the course of events in this story often in my life, and it is a significant point of reference where I showed someone a tiny bit of the grace and mercy that I had been given by God so many times in my life. God forgave me, even though I don't deserve forgiveness, when he allowed his Son to die for me on the cross. The least I can do, for God and the people in my life, is show others the same type of forgiveness.

She was freed from her mental anguish and torment. And I was freed to grow into a young man.

Forgive the people in your life who have hurt you or let you down. Try to forget what offended you unless you can turn that memory into a positive, uplifting, and beneficial memory. You'll find new horizons for yourself, and you'll feel the weight of the world lifted from your own shoulders!

Don't Try To Fix or Control the Other Person

One of the qualities possessed by children of alcoholics is that most have a desire to be in control of people and situations. People who spend their childhood living in out-of-control situations develop coping mechanisms to make sense out of the chaos. This desire to be in control is one of my biggest strengths, but it is probably also one of my biggest weaknesses.

My desire to be in control is harmful in that it sometimes negatively affects my relationships with other people. Sometimes I don't listen as well as I should because I think I already know the answer; sometimes I override a person's decisions because I feel my way is the best way; and sometimes I say things in such a way that I actually hurt a person's feelings. I can take several steps forward in a relationship and quickly get yanked back many more steps by exhibiting controlling tendencies. I'm working on this problem in my life, and I've recently received a great deal of help.

The help came in the form of a Bible verse I had read many times before. The help came when I was really struggling with a group of people who just couldn't see my point. I think they only had a problem with two things regarding the issue at hand – 1) they didn't like what I said and 2) they didn't like how I said it. That's not very good is it? Woodrow Wilson once said, "If you want to make enemies, try to change something." I learned the truth to that statement the hard way. Even though my heart was in the right place, the ideas were good, and the people were capable of understanding and making a change, my years of internally feeling the need to be in control communicated more strongly to them than the words I was actually saying. They could read between the lines, and they couldn't hear what I was saying because they could see my controlling tendencies inside of me. I could not believe they couldn't see my point and this disbelief and frustration was constantly on my mind. I was not happy with them, but I was even unhappier with myself for letting the issue bother me so much.

Then I read 2 Timothy 2:24–26, which says, *"And the Lord's servant must not quarrel; instead, he must be kind to everyone, able to teach, not resentful. Those who oppose him he must gently instruct, in the hope that God will grant them repentance leading them to a knowledge of the truth, and that they will come to their senses and escape from the trap of the devil, who has taken them captive to do his will."* (NIV)

If you're struggling in a relationship with a family member, a friend, a coworker, a church member, or even the person tailgating you on the freeway, try and have 2 Timothy 2:24-26 ready and waiting on your lips so that you can let go of your desire to show them the way things should be done. God created the whole world and everything in it, and if He wants that person to see the light, He'll show it to them. The best way for you to help make sure that person is looking in the direction of the light is for you to "be kind to everyone, able to teach, not resentful." If you get angry with people, lose your patience, or do anything that does not show the same type of love that Jesus showed to you, then you're not living the way this verse is telling you to live. Your attitude and honest prayers will go a long way towards helping that person see your point of view. The best way for you to be in control of a situation is to let God be in control of you. God deserves it, and you'll be the one to benefit from it.

Go To Church Together

There are many people who go to church on Sunday while another member of the family stays home or chooses to engage in another activity. Many people think that yelling the words "that's what we're supposed to do," or "I look stupid walking in there all by myself," or "you need to go to church more than I do" at the top of their lungs will help sweet-talk the other person into coming to church. Finger-pointing churchgoers get home from church angrier than they were when they left for church, and I'm sure the non-churchgoers are questioning how all the peace, patience, kindness, and gentleness all churchgoers are supposed to receive got lost on the way home. Guilt trips, grudges, and nasty attitudes are used to show the non-attendees that life would be easier on everyone if they would simply go to church on Sundays.

Some people, on the other hand, truly understand the saying, "you can lead a horse to water but you can't make him drink." These devotees get up on Sundays and happily go to church without trying to make others go. The best way to control someone is to show him the benefits of what you're doing through the example in your life versus telling him how he should be living his. People who come home happy and filled with a knowledge and assurance that their prayers will be answered also know that human beings naturally want what others seem to have and enjoy. Going to church is the best thing for everyone, but don't constantly beat others over the head with that information. Simply and earnestly keep on doing the best you can for yourself and trust that someone else can do a better job controlling the others than you can. That someone else is God.

> The best way to control someone is to show him the benefits of what you're doing through the example in your life versus telling him how he should be living his.

I'm sure you've heard the saying, "A family that prays together stays together." I firmly believe this to be true. I didn't go to church for the first two years of my marriage to Wendy, and our marriage almost didn't survive. I was arrogant enough to think that I didn't need God, and I thought that if Wendy would just listen to me and do what I thought was best, we'd be alright. I couldn't understand why she couldn't just say, "Whatever you say, honey," when we needed to make a family decision. I told her that if she would just trust me completely, I could handle things. I now realize that I was saying one thing, but my actions said another. It was not until I finally made the commitment to go to church with her and to trust God to guide me that she felt I was deserving of trust from her. Complete trust in each other is only obtained when you both trust in the same thing. That same thing is God.

If you don't go to church with your family, make an effort to go. The readings, sermons, and discussions at church serve as great ways to build common bonds between family members and are great conversation starting points to teach children the right way to act and think. As long as your children live in your house, they should live under your rules. One of those rules should be that everyone goes to church together. They may not appreciate or enjoy your decision today, but they will be better off years down the road. Pastor Rick Warren said that we, like God, should be more concerned with our children's character than their comfort. Make an investment in your children's character, and in your character, by going to church. They may let you know that they're not comfortable, but your job is to help build their character. Maybe you'll find your character getting uplifted in the process.

Please remember, church is full of people just like you and me – imperfect, searching for something or someone, and from a variety of backgrounds. Make an attempt to focus on the message that you receive at church; try not to focus on the people giving you the message or the people sitting next to you listening to that message. The hypocrisy of churchgoers turned me away from the church for ten years of my life, and my family and I are the only ones who suffered from my disillusionment. Church is not about church; church is not about the people at the church; church is about God. God is always there for you and your family. Focus on God. He won't let you down.

Eat At Regular Times – Together

Back before fast-food restaurants, microwave ovens, and busy schedules, families used to eat every meal together. They all knew when dinner would be ready, and they knew that if they missed dinner they would not get to eat or that they would be eating cold food. Family meals were a great time to communicate, laugh, learn, and love. Nowadays, meals are inconvenient interruptions to our non-stop schedules.

When I was growing up, we ate almost every meal on a TV-tray in front of the TV. We were more concerned with a television show than we were with each other. We'd rather participate in the lives of the families in the make-believe-world of television than participate in our own reality. The only time we would eat at the dinner table was for major holidays. I took that bad habit with me to my grandmother's when I went to live with her. I would sit as an angry young child in front of the TV and she would bring my dinner in on a TV-tray and place it right in front of me. I didn't even show her enough respect and decency to go to the dinner table and eat with her. So, my feelings about these trays are mixed. In one respect, they contributed to the separation in our family; in another way they showed me that someone loved me enough to prepare, deliver, and clean up three meals a day for me.

The turning point in my mother's life came when she was offered a job at a community college one-hour south of Jackson. Just before my sister and I were to leave with her to go live in her new town and attend another school, a family from my high school called and asked if I would like to live with them so that I could finish my junior and senior years of high school in Jackson. Tag and Dot Gamblin, and their four children, invited me into their home for two years. My mother paid them for my room and board, but I can never repay them for the lessons in life and family they taught me through their example.

Mrs. Gamblin was, in my opinion, "Super-Mom." She washed clothes for seven people, made three meals a day for seven people, taught school full-time, helped with homework, read her Bible, attended church, had a great relationship with her children, and was often up until midnight working and then up at five-thirty A.M. to cook breakfast. I remember that we all sat at the table for my first meal at their house, and I thought it was pretty neat that everyone was there together. I appreciated them making a big meal and for being there just for me. I thought they were all there for the special event of having someone new living in the house with them. The next day, I was surprised to see that we were eating a well-balanced meal at the table again. We did the same thing the next day. And the day after that. I was in complete shock that meals were prepared at a certain time, the kids helped set the table, the entire family was there, and they had meaningful conversations without having a television blaring in the background. I loved it!

The Gamblin children knew what to expect when they walked into their homes. They knew when and where to get food.

They knew what behavior was acceptable and what wasn't. They knew their mom and dad were going to ask them about their homework, their friends, their sports, and their lives – and they knew that their parents deserved a respectful response. No member of the family was too busy, too good, or too special not to be at the table at mealtime. In the rare times when someone was not at the meal, you could tell that someone was missing. Fred Astaire said, "The hardest job that kids face today is learning good manners without seeing any." I saw through the Gamblins the way that families are supposed to operate and the way children are supposed to respect their parents. Family members are supposed to be the most consistent, predictable, supportive, respectful, and loving people we know. The Gamblin family showed me that those families still exist. Your family can live that way also – if you really want it to.

The quality of your family's interaction and respect for each other is directly proportional to the amount of time spent eating and talking together. If you're the cook in the house, set a time for meals everyday and ask everyone to be there at that time. If you're too busy to have a set mealtime, your actions are showing that other activities and people are more important than the emotional and relational health of your family. The negative effects of this lost time will reveal themselves for many years to come. If you are supposed to be the captain of your family's relational ship, you should know what its destination should be and be in control of your family's course and heading. If you're supposed to be the captain, put on the captain's hat and act like it. Know what your family's destination should be, determine what course is appropriate, and do all you can to keep the family ship heading in the right direction. Eating together at regular times is a great way to bring your family closer together.

If you are supposed to be the captain of your family's relational ship, you should know what its destination should be and be in control of your family's course and heading.

Have Date Nights Away From the Children

Okay, I have to be honest and tell you that this is where I really have to work hard to practice what I preach. Date nights are great for a couple because you have time to focus on each other and not on the kids. Everyone needs a break, and moms and dads are not exceptions. If you think the kids won't handle being away from you very well, think again. Children do suffer separation anxiety - only because their parents never let go of them. Let go of your kids so that you can maintain a grasp on the relationship with your spouse. Your kids will be fine, so stop making excuses.

Most couples who start having a date night after many years of having children with them all the time find they don't know what to talk about when it's just the two of them. When we first started dating, Wendy and I used to quietly laugh when we saw couples sitting across from each other who didn't say a word to each other the whole meal. Well, it's not too funny anymore because we realize that some people might be laughing if Wendy and I have a silent meal on date night. But,- we both admit that it sure is nice to not be climbed on and sung to for a little while every week.

Your church might offer a "couples' night out" or there may be other programs in town where your kids might receive quality care so that you can enjoy your time away. Wendy and I are fortunate to have both sets of grandparents in the same town with us. If you're not that fortunate, your church family is willing to help. If you don't have a church family, read this chapter again. People are willing to help if they simply know that help is needed.

Read, Study, and Go To Seminars

This book may be the first book you've read regarding family interaction and dynamics. You're doing a great thing by investing your time and mental power by studying how to affect change in your finances, family, and faith. Local churches are always bringing in speakers. These events can give you a great opportunity to hear a great message in a short amount of time. Not only will you benefit from the information, you will benefit from the change in your routine and the opportunity to just slow down and spend some time for yourself.

In football, I played almost every play of every game. I played quarterback, defensive back, returned kicks, snapped on punts and extra points, and was on the kickoff team. I never got a break. I realized recently that I had created a similar situation for myself in real life. As an adult, I've realized that the only person who can take me out of the game to get some rest on the sidelines is me. You are in a similar situation. Schedule some time for a conference a couple of times per year. I made a tremendous amount of headway towards writing this book at a business conference I had in Boston last year because I simply had time to think.

What about yourself could you change or improve if you had the time to just think, read, and pray? Take yourself out of the game so that you'll be a more productive player when you're refreshed, refocused, and injury-free.

If It Ain't Broke, Don't Fix It!

If you find that your family situation doesn't call for any of these potential remedies, you are in the minority and you should celebrate! God has blessed you.

If your family is not suffering from any of the problems that have been mentioned, maybe your family can help be a part of the solution. Is there anyone in your life whom you can mentor; invite over for a weekly dinner; offer a comforting ear; or help hold accountable if they're willing? If my Young Life leader, John Evans; my next-door neighbor at Gaga's, Jim Langston; and the Gamblins in Jackson had not taken their most valuable resource – their time – and spent it with me, I would probably be writing a book from some cold and dark prison. Their lives weren't perfect, but they took the time to make a difference in someone else's life. I thank them, my mother thanks them, and my wife and children thank them. Who could you help in a similar way?

On the other hand, if something is broken, by all means find the owner's manual. This book can be a good start. I'm glad that you're reading it. Try to put some of these principles in motion in your life and give them time to grow. Don't expect miracles overnight. Be patient, and try very hard to be the person you would like to be all. Try and be this person all of the time – twenty-four hours a day, seven days a week. Remember, you can take ten steps forward, but one big step backwards can erase all ten of the forward steps. People are only human, but strive to be the most loving, accepting, and trustworthy person you can be.

Things You Need To Do Now

1. **Try to work things out with your family members.** Love them, forgive them, and respect them. But, remember, you can't control every single aspect of their lives.
2. **Plan at least two times per week when all of your family can be present to eat together at home without any interruptions.** Sacrifice something out of your schedule that shows you're willing to give something up that is important to you for your family. If that doesn't help, sacrifice something else. My mother did that for me; can you do that for your family?
3. **Find a qualified person for yourself or for a family member who can be a good outside influence.** Don't expect results overnight. Commit to giving the relationship at least a six-month try.
4. **Make a family commitment to go to church every Sunday for six months.** It has been said that it takes thirty days of doing something to make it a habit. Go to church every Sunday for six months, and you'll have gone to church for about thirty days. You and your family deserve positive, uplifting, and healthy habits!
5. **If you find your family members are bored, find something that will keep everyone busy and out of trouble.** Start a lawn care business, volunteer somewhere, exercise… just do something that can occupy both the mental and physical aspects of your

life. Family experiences will be remembered forever. It is better to look back on attempts at positive family interactions than to look back and not remember anything. It's dangerous if one horse wanders off the trail in search of something- the whole family may follow.

6. **Schedule a weekly date night with your spouse – away from the kids.** If you take the kids with you, you're missing the whole point. If you don't have much money, your local boys' or girls' club or your church may have a program available that would give your kids a good outlet and you an inexpensive babysitter. If you're a single parent, schedule time away from the kids so that you (and the kids) can be renewed by interactions with other people and be ready to deal with each other more positively the following week. Everyone needs a break sometime!

SECTION III

FAITH

SECTION III - FAITH

Chapter Fourteen

Faith

***We walk by faith, not by sight.*[1]**
***Now faith is the substance of things hoped for, the evidence of things not seen.*[2]**

Knowledge about your finances is vitally important because it allows you to effectively deal with paying bills, saving, investing, and managing money. Knowing how to deal with family is important because they should simply be the most important people in your life. But this section of the book can have the most dramatic impact on your life on this earth… if you let it. Faith can help you deal more effectively with your finances, your family, and yourself.

I had intended to write one-third of this book about finances, one-third about family, and one-third about faith. However, I truly feel that I could have helped you the most if I had written about faith throughout the entire book. I say this because faith brings perspective, faith brings peace, faith brings wisdom, faith brings contentment, and faith brings love; but more importantly, faith in Christ brings the guarantee of eternal life in heaven. Even though only three chapters are spent discussing faith, please know that my heart's desire is that these three chapters will have the greatest impact on your life, your relationships with your family and others, your finances, your desire to read the Bible, and your ability to allow a personal relationship with God guide you in all the different aspects of your life.

What Is *Faith*?

Faith is defined as a "confident belief in the truth, value, or trustworthiness of a person, idea, or thing; the theological virtue defined as secure belief in God and a trusting acceptance of God's will; or a set of principles or beliefs."[3] The Greek meaning for the word *believe* is "to trust in, cling to, and rely upon."[4]

With regard to my finances, I have faith that

- Over time, my investments will perform somewhere near the historical average for that particular investment category.
- My employer will make matching contributions to my retirement plan, pay for their share of my health benefits, and continue to have a job for me.
- My paycheck will arrive on time, in the right amount, and clear the bank without bouncing.
- If I pay my bill on time, our lights will come on in our house when we flip the switch; our phone will work when we pick up the receiver; and we'll have Internet access when we request it on our computer.
- Our bank will keep accurate records of our bank balances or will be willing to remedy any errors.
- Interest paying investments will pay the correct amount of interest at the stated time.
- If I don't manage your finances well, I probably won't have much in the way of finances to manage.
- God will take care of my family and me regardless of how much money He chooses to give us to manage because we try and value a relationship with Him over ownership of money and possessions.

Regarding my family, I have faith that

- We are all human, and we are going to make mistakes, get our feelings hurt, say things we shouldn't, disappoint ourselves and others – but that we're generally born with a desire to be good people.
- My family will have much the same attitude and live in conditions very similar to the conditions they lived in yesterday.
- My car's engine will start when I turn the key to take my family to church, school, work, or a ballgame.
- If I treat my family with love and respect, over time they'll do the same to me.

Regarding my faith, I have faith that

- There is one God who created heaven and earth, the stars and galaxies, the trees and the fields, the air that I breathe, and the water I drink.
- God knows who I am, He loves me, He made me exactly how He wanted, and He has a perfect plan for me that I should always appreciate.
- When I die, I'll be going to heaven to rejoice with the angels and spend eternity in conscious joy.
- The Bible is the inspired Word of God and is completely accurate.
- Jesus will return someday, possibly very soon, to take believers to heaven with Him – and I know my name is on His list.

What Kind of Faith?

Faith in God and in His Son, Jesus, is the specific type of faith that I'm talking about in this book. In order to feel comfortable about having faith in Christ, I think it's important to know some basic facts about the Bible since it's the Good Book that tells us everything we need to know. This basic Biblical understanding will free you to believe even more in the value of having a *personal relationship* with Christ.

We humans are born with an innate desire to communicate with a higher power, an all-knowing being, the Creator of all things. History reveals that many different gods were worshiped by many different cultures. Some cultures worship one god for all aspects of life and afterlife. Some worship specific Gods for specific roles such as the god of beauty, the sea, fertility, or agriculture. All of these cultures speak about *god*, but there is only one true, living God. He is the father of Jesus, the Creator of heaven and earth, the Creator of space and time, the starting point for the beginning and the end of the universe, and the all-knowing and all-seeing God for all aspects of our lives.

All religions worship their god or gods, but the one thing that sets Christianity apart from Buddhism, Islam, and all others is the fact that Jesus was born by a virgin mother; was nailed to a cross and died as a sacrifice for all sinners; rose from the dead three days later; and ascended into heaven to sit at the right hand of His Father. Every human being has the free will and choice to accept or decline the grace that's available to us as a result of Christ dying on the cross for us. We do not have to pray at certain times, we don't have to wear certain clothes, we don't have to take vows of poverty or celibacy, nor do we have to earn our way into heaven by performing deeds or by donating large sums of money or time. God does not pressure us into following Him, and Christians should not pressure other people to believe in God. God is extremely excited when people choose to love and trust in Him. The Bible says that there is "*more rejoicing in heaven over one sinner who repents.*"[5] The angels in heaven are waiting anxiously for you to believe in Jesus if you haven't already made a decision to do so. There's a party waiting to start, a party that's just because of you, if you're still waiting to ask God to forgive you from your sins. The really good thing about this rejoicing for your decision is that the joyousness lasts forever. Why keep them waiting much longer?

Yes, Jesus Loves Me – The Bible Tells Me So!

We all know the song, but do we truly believe it? If the Bible says that Jesus loves us, and we assume that this is true, this means we have faith because we have to believe in something we can't see, touch, or smell. Why should we believe the Bible?

In the preface to this book, I talked about how I have always been looking for the perfect "how-to" guide, the perfect combination of facts with illustrative stories, all put together by the perfect author whom I respect, admire, and want to emulate. I said that my search for this perfect book was over because I had found the perfect book written by the perfect author.

The book is the Bible, and the author is God.

The best how-to book that has ever been written is the Bible. The best author is God.

I realized that the perfect how-to guide and the consummate manual for life was written over two thousand years ago by many different writers who all were directed and told what to write by one source and the ultimate author and editor.... God. When I finally committed to and completed my goal of reading the Bible in one year, I found that my life was irrevocably changed for the better. My treatment of my wife improved, I was able to write Christian songs, I was able to handle situations with other people more effectively, my business prospered, my health improved, and I began to have a taste of the peace, wisdom, and knowledge that could be available to me. I'm sure there's even more of those good things available to me, and I don't mind waiting until I get to heaven to find out what they are.

The Bible is the world's best selling book. Literally more copies of the Bible have been sold than any other book known to man. If you can sit down and read it with the expectation that something good is going to happen, I can guarantee you that it will. You just have to sit down and start reading. Finish this book and go straight to the Bible. You'll never regret the commitment you made.

We've all read books someone recommended to us with the highest of praises. We've all started reading books that had a great beginning, good characters, excitement, suspense, and a great plot.

But then at some point, things in the book got slow, we got sidetracked, and we put the book down and never found the time or the desire to pick up where we left off.

But, what if we had been told that it was a great book, that there were some slower parts in the middle that you have to make it through, but that the ending was life changing? What if the person who recommended the book to you told you that you absolutely had to read the whole thing? What if that person told you that it was a life-changing experience, and you could actually see the changes revealed in the way he lived his life? You'd find a way to start reading or to pick up that book again, wouldn't you? A great example is found in your friend who read a book about weight loss, implemented the plan outlined in the book, lost a great deal of weight, and has been able to keep the weight off ever since. If your goal were to lose weight, you'd probably be willing to follow his recommendation because he'd "been there and done that." You'd be willing to listen because you knew that it had worked for him and could work for you.

Yes, the Bible has some slow parts that are great for helping you go to sleep at night, but once I was given the understanding that the message inside that Book was written just for me, I could not put it down. The Bible is a life-changing literary piece, and the changes in my life are examples of that! The Bible will also feel like it was written just for you when you read it.

The pre-Bible me was a fairly controlling, blunt, fact-based, highly motivated, and goal-oriented person. You now know some of my background and why I might have those qualities. When something needed to be done at work, at home, or at church, I found that it was really easy for me to define the issue being dealt with, determine what the outcome should be, and outline the steps needed to take us from the current situation to the end result. In the process of doing that, I had a unique ability to say things to people in exactly the wrong way. My heart was in the right place, and I didn't have the intentions of hurting anyone's feelings, or of alienating or embarrassing anyone. But my actions sure didn't support that. I couldn't understand why people couldn't just deal with the facts, just like I could, and move on to the task at hand. The problem was that I dealt with things (and people) the way that I thought I should. Two things are wrong with that emphasized phrase… the word *I* and the word *thought*. I should not have relied on myself. I should have trusted in God. I should not have thought. I should have prayed.

If you're just getting started in your walk with Christ, of if you don't have a personal relationship with Him yet, you may be like I was about five years ago. I would hear someone say, "you just need to pray about it" or "I turned it over to God and He worked it out." I would hear people asking others to pray for them about something. I simply could not understand what they meant by pray about it or turn it over to God. Nor could I understand why they were telling other people their problems and asking them to pray for them. I truly thought people were blowing a lot of hot air just to get sympathy or to share their life stories. But then I read the Bible. And I saw all of the stories of people praying to God, asking Him for guidance, trusting Him in how He answered their prayers, and expressing how free they became when they turned control of their lives over to someone else. I began to pray that God would show my wife and me out of $26,000 in loans on our vehicles, $20,000 in unsecured debt, and how to have our monthly income and expenses not worry me so much. I prayed that He would make me more loving and less controlling. And God showed me, in His time, what it's like to have my prayers answered. And He'll do the same for you. He's already taken the first step by having his Son die on the cross for you. Jesus died on the cross in my place for the sins I have committed. I deserved to have the punishment put on my shoulders, but He suffered the penalty for me. And He's done the same thing for you. He's coordinated events and relationships so that you would have this book in your hands. All you have to do is acknowledge His gifts to you, ask Him to forgive you, and believe that He will guide you in your daily decisions from this point forward.

My childhood experiences and the people who influenced my life all mixed together and produced the person I am today.

They will continue to help refine who I will be years down the road. However, the best trainer, teacher, and consultant is God, and His course outline and class notes are all contained in the Bible. His Word is slowly reprogramming the way I think, the way I talk, and the things that I do. The only way I could have ever learned what His Word says was to read it. The powerful thing I found about the Bible is that once I heard His voice whispering in my ear, and I was actually in tune with it and could hear it, the Scripture jumped off of the page to me and showed me what I needed to see. If I spent that same amount of time watching TV or working in my office, I wouldn't have been in the situation for God to speak to me through the Bible.

His Word is slowly reprogramming the way I think, the way I talk, and the things that I do.

No one read the Bible to me when I was a child. As a teenager I had a King James version of the Bible that I simply could not understand, and so I really didn't take the time to read the Bible until I reached adulthood. I believe that God gave me the willingness to read the Bible by putting me in tough situations concerning money, family, and myself. God created the need in me over the years, and I was finally ready, willing, <u>and</u> able to listen to His solution. Again, the solution is the Bible. Maybe you've had a similar background. Maybe you had someone that used the Bible as a weapon against you. Someone may have spitefully told you that you were a fool because you didn't go to church. Or maybe you had the Bible crammed down your throat or you had to memorize verses for punishment for bad behavior. Please let me tell you, the Bible is God's Word and its sole purpose is to allow you to get to know Christ more intimately so that He can help you become the loving person that He wants you to be. His Word is not punishment, it is not busy work, and it is not something that causes you unhealthy discomfort.

God's greatest desire is that we love Him with all of our heart, soul, mind, and strength.[6] If we love Him like that, we will make Him very happy. God created every single detail of the world, He has infinite power, and He sees everything all at the same time.

I cannot begin to fathom the depth of his power and majesty. I'm amazed everyday at the things we have today – the luxuries, the comforts, and the potential to do good things. I'm humbled that God would deem my wife and me worthy of two beautiful and healthy daughters, that He would trust us with large amounts of money, and that He would choose us to lead a ministry. Who is more deserving of my total love, devotion, work, and strength? Certainly not anyone on earth, certainly not my job, certainly not the things I own. Ten years ago I just wanted to have enough money to be financially secure. Now I'm just happy and secure in the knowledge that I'll be going to heaven when I leave this earth. If you truly want to know Christ, you won't have any personal motives to be a certain type of person. You will take joy in being whoever He wants you to be. True fulfillment will be in knowing that you are storing up treasures in heaven that will last for all eternity – not in knowing that you have more money than you could ever spend, that your investment was the #1 performer for the past twelve months, or that you were right and your relative shouldn't have treated you the way she did.

> Ten years ago I just wanted to have enough money to be financially secure.
> Now I'm just happy and secure in the knowledge that I'll be going to heaven when I leave this earth.

2 Timothy 3:16 says, *"All Scripture is God-breathed."* This means that every bit of Scripture originated from God and was conveyed to the different writers of the Bible in His perfect and flawless form. The writers then dutifully recorded the historical accounts, parables, conversations, prayers, songs, and conflicts onto anything that could be written on over two thousand years ago.

John 1:1 says, *"In the beginning was the Word, and the Word was with God, and the Word was God."* 1 John 4:16 tells us that *"God is love."* If God is the Word, and God is love, then the Word must be love. This means that the Bible, God's Word, is love. The Bible is not a weapon for hate, selfishness, pride, confusion, deceit, or anger. Read God's Word and you will feel God's love. If you feel God's love, you won't want anything else. The world will tell you something different, and it will try to make you come back to your old ways. But once you've read the Bible and had its verses enter your very heart, you'll be able to express love to all others because you are being fueled by love of God, the appreciation from Jesus' act of suffering on your behalf, and the continual presence of the Holy Spirit.

Whoa, Slow Down There a Minute!

If you're not a Believer, if you're not sure if you're a Believer, or if you haven't been a Believer very long, these past few pages will seem very intense and hard to understand. That's okay! You've done yourself justice by having read this information. It will take time for you to be able to absorb it and to take it all in. I was there once, and at times I'm still there. The worst thing you can do is get frustrated, put this book or the Bible down, and walk away. Don't make the same ten-year mistake that I did.

One of the things I really appreciate about the perspective that God has given me at this point in my life is that He helps me know how to communicate with non-Christians, new Christians, or educated believers. I heard people use terms like Holy Spirit, Holy Ghost, Trinity, and many others for years before I actually was able to understand what was being said. I do not want this book to talk over anyone's head, so if you're an educated believer, I want to say thank you for reading this section even though it may be a review for you. I would also like to ask you to please be praying for the other readers of this book who are just beginning or are trying to deepen their walk with Christ.

We'll talk in more detail about the Bible later, but here is some information and some terms that help clarify what I wrote in the prior section:

God created everything. He knows everything and sees everything all at the same time. He allowed evil to exist so that through the contrast between good and evil He'd be able to show us what is good. He made me for a purpose – to love Him and to love everyone on earth. He made you for the same reasons. He would have preferred for us to live in the Garden of Eden forever, but Adam and Eve disobeyed His command to stay away from the forbidden fruit. God gets very sad, frustrated, and disappointed when we don't do what He'd like us to do. But He never gives up on us. Nothing makes Him happier than seeing us love Him and others. That's all He wants out of us. Yes, God knew that we would disobey Him, curse Him, turn away from Him, take Him for granted, worship other idols, and hurt Him in the same way that a child hurts his parents.

But He made us anyway. He could have chosen to not make us, but He made us anyway. And all He wants is for us to thank Him, love Him, and focus on living our short life on earth in a way that prepares us for eternity with Him. Our life here on earth is our training ground that prepares us for eternity. Do you have any idea how long eternity lasts compared to our life here on earth? I don't either, but it's a long time.

You can choose to accept Christ in your life at any time – it's totally up to you. I would strongly suggest you choose Christ before He returns to earth (called the *Rapture*) to take all the believers to heaven with Him. If Jesus came back today, I'm sure that He would take me because I truly believe in Him even though I'm not perfect and I sin every day. How about you? Jesus' death and resurrection proved that God, the Creator of everything, also has the power to bring people back to life. If He made everything, don't you think it would be just as easy for Him to blink anyone back to life? Jesus' return is something to be happy about and to look forward to because life in heaven is free of pain, anger, torment, financial troubles, and anything negative. Who wouldn't want to be in that environment?!

All of the non-believers will be left here on earth to endure one thousand years of struggle and pain before Jesus conquers Satan and throws him in a lake of burning sulfur. At that time, everyone will be judged and sent either to hell for an eternity of non-stop hatred, pain, and fire or to heaven for an eternity of peace, love, and perfection. Seriously answer this question out loud as you read… which way do you want to travel for eternity…north.. or south?

God, Jesus, and the Holy Spirit are the three parts of what is called the *Trinity*. I heard this best explained by an unknown person who said

- God MADE it;
- Jesus SHOWED us - by taking human form and living a perfect life here on earth and by being placed in situations just like the ones that you and I have to endure; and
- The Holy Spirit TEACHES us - by whispering in our ears the ways in which we should handle situations, people, and feelings.

All three parts of the One God have a specific role, and we now mostly rely on the Holy Spirit to be the still small voice that helps us understand what the Bible is saying to us, helps us know in our hearts what is right and wrong, and gives us the strength to love God first when life tells us to do otherwise. I used to be really confused about the Trinity. I couldn't understand who I should pray to – God, Jesus, or the Holy Spirit. The short answer to my dilemma was that all three are one in the same. God answers to all three names. Or I can pray to each one for the special duties that each carries out. I can pray and thank God for making things, I can pray and thank Jesus for dying for me, and I can ask the Holy Spirit to help show me how to handle life. The Holy Spirit is our personal trainer – our spiritual trainer – who is always talking to us as He tries to get us in shape to spend eternity in heaven with God and Jesus. How's your spiritual fitness? Have you heard and followed the advice of your spiritual trainer?

The way to get to know who God is, what Jesus did, and how the Holy Spirit can help you truly love God and others from your inner being is by reading the Bible. *"Consequently, faith comes from hearing the message, and the message is heard through the word of Christ."*[7] Can you imagine having so much faith that nothing bothers you? I'm sure you know people in your life who can't be shaken, who are always loving and nice, and who truly seem happy. The way for you to have those same qualities is to trust in God, thank Jesus for giving His life for you so that you could be forgiven of all your sins – regardless of how big or frequent they occurred, and ask the Holy Spirit to show you how to have everything make sense. The Holy Spirit is your interpreter, and He's always trying to show you the right way – God's way. The Bible is your written guide that uncovers the topics the Holy Spirit wants to talk to you about. You just have to actually cover the material to get the conversation going. The Bible is your conversation starter, agenda, homework, and template for your meetings with the Holy Spirit. If you walk through life without reading the material, the Holy Spirit has less of a footing in your heart to truly communicate to you.

Take a break here and ask the Holy Spirit into your heart so that you can better understand why God made you, who God wants you to be, what Jesus did for you, and how to move ahead in this book and in life. Ask the Holy Spirit to give you the ability to understand the role that finances, family, and faith play in your life. Ask the Holy Spirit to give you His fruits of the Spirit – (you like fruit, don't you?) – *love, joy, peace, patience, kindness, goodness, faithfulness, gentleness, and self-control.*[8] While you're at it, ask Him to give you His spiritual gifts such as *wisdom, knowledge, and faith.*[9]

Yeah, But……

So, we now know that the Bible tells us about God, Jesus, and the Holy Spirit (the Trinity); it tells us how to live our lives. More importantly, it tells us how we should feel in our hearts. But some people choose to doubt the content of the Bible. If you doubt the Bible, how can you trust the Holy Spirit to guide you? If you doubt the Bible, how can you trust that God created everything and that He has plans not to harm you, but to prosper you and to give you hope and a future?[10] Do you know people who can hear the most logical argument, agree with every fact presented, but then can turn right around and say, "Yeah, but…"? Some people are just not open to sound reasoning. I don't think you fall into that category because you've taken the time to buy and read this book. The Bible should be taken as the completely trustworthy Word of God so that you can take the word but out of your vocabulary (if by chance it does exist) as it relates the Bible. In order to strengthen your belief in the Bible, here are some reasons why you should believe that every word in the Bible is from God:

- Lee Strobel is a former legal editor of the *Chicago Tribune*, holder of a Master of Studies in Law degree from Yale Law School, and author of the book *A Case for Christ*. In this book, he says, "As someone educated in journalism and law, I was trained to respond to the facts, wherever they lead. For me, the data demonstrated convincingly that Jesus is the Son of God who died as my substitute to pay the penalty I deserved for the wrongdoing I had committed." This statement comes from a man who is evidently extremely intelligent (Yale Law) and trained to research the facts while making sure they're accurate (legal editor). He spent two years researching material for his book, he interviewed "thirteen leading scholars and authorities who have impeccable academic credentials" in searching for the answers to his skeptical questions, and he presented the information in a very fact-based, non-opinionated way.[11]

My pastor, Dr. Douglas Pennington, has said several times that most people who don't believe in God are "intelligent, healthy, and wealthy." As a result, they feel they don't have a need for any god to help them put life and eternity in perspective. Lee Strobel's book can help speak to people who fall into these categories. Or they can just wait until they're no longer healthy or wealthy.

Strobel's study, skepticism, interviews, research, and thought revealed to him that the Bible is a reliable source. He studied in detail whether or not the information provided in the gospels of Matthew, Mark, Luke, and John was recorded and translated accurately for readers of today. His answer was a profound yes! His book can go a long way towards helping you reach your own conclusion about the believability of the Bible. If you're skeptical and can think of several questions, do yourself a favor and read his book.

- The authors of the Bible, under the direction of God, wrote down many predictions of what was going to happen in the future. Predictions about the deaths of certain persons; the fall of certain cities; the end of reign for certain leaders; the length of time that people were to wander, be held captive, or live in exile; or the coming of a Messiah are just a few of the prophesies that actually happened. An entire book could be written on this subject, but my goal is to make you aware of the facts and to tell you where you can find more information. If the meteorologist on one of your local TV stations has been 100% correct in his weather predictions for the past twenty years, if he's never missed a single rainstorm, an expected temperature, or a dew point, you're probably going to rely on his weather prediction versus the prediction of the other weather forecasters in town, aren't you?

ClarifyingChristianity.com makes the following statement on their website:

"One of the strongest arguments for the accuracy of the Bible is its 100% accuracy in predicting the future. These future predictions are called *prophecies*. The Old Testament was written between approximately 1450 BC and 430 BC. During that time, God's prophets recorded many predictions of the future in the Bible. Of the events that were to have taken place by now, every one happened just the way they predicted it would. No other 'sacred writing' has such perfectly accurate predictions of the future."[12]

Lee Strobel's book, *The Case for Christ*, and Paul Little's *Know What You Believe* are two great resources for you if you have any doubt as to the accuracy, reliability, and authority of the Bible. You'll never be able to confirm or deny your doubts until you search for and find the necessary facts to satisfy your mind. For me, the Bible and God's creation were good enough to satisfy my uncertainty. I read the others so that I could understand more and be able to talk intelligently with others. You owe it to yourself to keep searching, reading, and discussing until you're convinced one way or the other that Jesus is the Way and the Bible is the Word.

Summary

This chapter discussed faith, the Bible, the Trinity, and reasons to believe that the Bible is 100% accurate. Before we move forward into the next chapter, use the questions below to help you make some sense of what you've just read. If this information was new to you, it might be a good idea to read the chapter again. If this information was a review for you, this information should go a long way towards helping you make the reasons you believe even stronger.

Things You Need To Do Now

1. **If you don't already have one, go purchase a chronological Bible in a version that communicates most effectively to you.**
2. **Start reading that Bible today. Don't wait until January 1st of next year!** Just make notes in the Bible of what day you actually started and read a section every day. If you get several days or weeks behind, don't quit! One suggestion is to resume reading on the day that you're supposed to be reading and catch up on what you missed by reading one missed day's reading in addition to your scheduled reading. In this way, you'll be reading today's reading and be reaching back and picking up a day that you missed as you go along.
3. **Pray daily that the Holy Spirit will live in your heart and help guide you in every move, every word, and every thought.**
4. **Remember, if you love God and love others like yourself, you are fulfilling God's 1st and 2nd greatest commands.** If you do those things, everything else will fall into place. Above all - love!

SECTION III - FAITH

Chapter Fifteen

Faith, Jesus, and the Bible

The cornerstone of the Christian faith is the belief that Jesus is the Son of God; that He lived a human life on earth free from sin, subject to the same temptations and situations as you and me; that He was crucified, died, and was buried instead of each one of us for our sins; and that He came back to life three days later to rise into heaven to sit next to God the Father.

As I said at the close of the last chapter, if you have any doubts as to the validity of any of those beliefs, you owe it to yourself to convince yourself one way or the other that these statements are (or are not) trustworthy, believable, and worthy of your faith. If you find they're not believable or worthy of your faith, you need to be set free from the doubt that they are true. Either way, spend some time to make a clear decision one way or the other. Now's a good time to get serious and really get to the bottom of things. You owe it to yourself and to your family. I think you'll be happy with your decision. Be passionate, dive in, and give it your all so that you can really live! You are worth the effort!

Talk About Sacrifice!

Earlier in the book, I talked about the stress that my mother endured in divorcing my father, moving to a new town, owning a struggling business, providing and caring for two young children, and struggling with a dependency on alcohol.

I vividly recall a phrase that my mother used to say over and over again when she'd be sitting in her chair on days when she was moody. She would have her glass of vodka and orange juice sitting on the wooden armrest on the right hand side of the chair as it was slightly reclined with the leg rest extended, she would have her left hand resting on top of her head rubbing her hair, she would have her eyes shut, and she would repeatedly say, "I have no life. I have no life. I have no life!" She would start saying that phrase as a whisper, and it would grow to a scream of anger and despair. My sister and I, as nine and ten year olds, would often try to console her. We'd try and assure her that she did have a life, but I now realize that she really didn't. She didn't have the same kind of life that I have at a similar point in my life. She didn't have friends to listen to her; she didn't have friends who enjoyed movies, church events, or sports with her; she couldn't afford a baby sitter to keep my sister and me even if she had things to enjoy strictly for her benefit; and she was constantly trying to bring in an income, raise my sister and me, and recover from her drinking binges that allowed her to escape from the demands of life.

My mother completely dedicated her life to making sure that we had clothes on our back, food on the table, and some sort of presents for birthdays and Christmas. She would often spend her very last dollars to buy us Christmas gifts as a symbol of the love she had for us. We would then quickly show our appreciation by having to leave to go visit our father for the holidays. Mom would be left alone to endure a penniless, friendless, and childless holiday season.

My sister and I always had to split holidays between family members, and I've often read that children of divorced families often dread holidays because they never feel they can make everyone happy on the vacation visitation trips. My sister and I can confirm that feeling. Holidays and vacations were more stressful to us as kids and young adults than other times because we were always on the road and always apologizing for not being able to stay for the entire vacation. We never knew what kind of environment we were going to walk into when we got home to be with our mother, nor did we know what the atmosphere would be like at our father's house.

Mom lived most of the years between 1977 and the year 2000 in a constant battle with her desire to escape from the world by drinking. I firmly believe the burdens she carried those years were so great that it took the full twenty-three years to have the load lightened by time, wisdom, and faith.

As a young adult, I perceived Mom's desire to drink to be greater than her desire to love me and do what was best for me. We've all heard the phrase "two steps forward and one step back." Well, Mom could work all day (for us), come home and cook dinner (for us), shuttle us to practice and ballgames (for us), buy us presents (for us), and do her best to provide (for us). But, all of the good things she had done were erased in our minds if she took just one drink in a two-week period. She could take a million steps forward that could immediately be erased by an episode of drinking and being moody. She would often go a month or two without having any drinking issues, but then we'd come home one day or call her on the phone to find her moody. Her moody times were her times when she was trying to escape from a life that was not her life. She could have easily chosen to give up on the situation she was in – she could have committed suicide. Unfortunately a huge number of people consider and complete this task. She could have sent both my sister and me to live permanently with other family members or she could have just totally given up on life forever, instead of just in spurts of drinking. She could have easily decreased or ended her pain, suffering, and torment. But she didn't. God could easily have done away with the entire world when Adam and Eve so disappointed Him in the Garden of Eden. But He didn't.

The Lord has given my mother great strength and I thank Him that she has not had a sip of alcohol for almost four years. Mom has really enjoyed being able to babysit our daughters, being able to spoil them with gifts purchased without fear of not having enough money to put food on the table, and being able to clearly remember every interaction, every laugh, and every touch.

Have you seen the videotapes when President Reagan was shot in the 1980s? Did you see that the Secret Service agents crowded around him to protect him from the flying bullets? They ran towards the target when the shots were fired. Have you seen war footage that shows a soldier get shot while trying to rescue an injured soldier? Do you know anyone who has totally given every bit of himself or herself so that others could have the opportunity to succeed, to be loved, and to have what he or she never had? Do you know anyone who doesn't have a life of his own or who is constantly giving to others? Maybe it's your mother or father, or your grandmother, an aunt or an uncle… or maybe it's you. All of these stories give us some common reference point regarding the word sacrifice.

Jesus Died Just For You

Whether you know it or not, you and I both have someone in our lives who stepped into our shoes to protect us from harm. Someone who selflessly endured the punishment we deserved. This person could have easily chosen not to take our place, He could have easily snapped His fingers and had the evil rulers removed from power, and He could have made His act of love toward us be free of pain, anguish, and torment.

But He didn't.

He chose to show His love for you by allowing Himself to be crucified so that you could have the opportunity to spend eternity with God in heaven. Our sins were erased when Jesus was placed on the cross as the sacrificial lamb for all sinners who ask for forgiveness.

My mother totally surrendered her life so that my sister and I might live. Because she is human, and not God in the living form like Jesus, she was not able to live a perfect life. But Jesus lived a perfect life, and He died a horrible death that only sinners like you and me deserve. Jesus totally surrendered His life while He was living by following the instructions His Father assigned Him –to live on earth among us, to show us the love that our Father has for us, and to die on the cross as a sacrifice so that our past, present, and future sins might be forgiven.

Jesus endured ridicule, whippings, beatings, a crown of thorns, betrayal, loneliness, and being nailed to a cross so that He could look you in the eyes, tell you that He loves you, and invite you to live in heaven with Him for eternity. All you have to do is tell Him you're sorry for your sins and that you truly believe in Him.

Faith in Christ is the source of all happiness, He's the most loving escape route anyone can take, and He died just for you. As author Paul Little stated, "Jesus came to earth as the Suffering Servant, but He will return as the Reigning King!"[1] If you're using or considering other sources of happiness, I urge you to consider only Him.

He's Coming Back … Soon

Jesus' death and resurrection prove that the body can come to life after death. During his lifetime, Jesus brought life to Lazarus after he had been dead for four days. John 14:3 says, "… *I will come back and take you to be with me that you also may be where I am.*"[2] Don't you want to be where Jesus is? He tells us in that verse that He's coming back for us! Every bit of history and Scripture reveals that we should believe every word He says. The book of Revelation describes in detail the Second Coming of Jesus Christ. The book, written by the apostle John, says that Jesus said, "*Yes, I am coming soon.*"[3]

When Jesus comes back, He will take His people to heaven with Him. We don't know exactly when He's coming, but we do know the negative consequences of not having our spiritual bags packed and of not being ready when He says it's time to go.

When I was fourteen years old and living with my mother and sister, mom arranged for some man (let's call him Jim) she knew to pick me up at our apartment because she was working and we didn't have a car. No car meant that I had no transportation. Keep in mind, I was the Family Hero, the person who strives to make other people happy, who tries to do everything just right, and who can get extremely disappointed when he fails to meet other peoples' expectations. I didn't really know Jim at all, and I was told that he would pick me up at 3:00 PM. One of our apartment doors opened up onto the patio, and the parking lot was six feet from the patio –a total of about four strides from the patio door. I packed my gym bag and placed it by the door, opened the curtain so that I could see him arrive, and sat down in a chair, waiting for him, literally staring out the window for him. I was ready much like a sprinter in the starting blocks. He pulled up a few minutes early. I picked up my bag, immediately walked out the door, and got in the car with this man I barely knew.

When I sat down in the seat next to him, he really let me have it. He didn't hold back even though we barely knew each other. He screamed at me for making him wait and yelled, "I was in the military, son, and you never make transportation wait on you! You should be standing in the parking lot with your bag in your hand and all I should have to do is slow down and let you in! I shouldn't even have to stop this car! I'm wasting my time to come and get you and I've got to sit here and wait?! Never make transportation wait on you!"

I don't remember much of the ride, nor do I know exactly where I had to go, but I do remember exactly what Jim said. I'll never forget his tone and his words, or my shock, horror, and dismay over being chastised when I thought I had done the right thing by being ready and waiting for him.

Jesus is coming to get me and I know I'm ready!

Well, Jesus is coming to get me and I know I'm ready! I also know that Jesus will never treat me the way Jim treated me that day.

Jim was nice enough to give me a ride, but we never asked him again for help, and he never offered. If he's still alive, he's probably still just as mad at me now as he was that day. I've asked Jesus to live in my heart, I've asked Him to forgive my sins, I've been washed clean of all my sins, and I know that Jesus will forgive AND forget. When I walk out to meet Jesus when He comes back, He's going to welcome me with open arms. I have the opportunity to spend eternity in heaven, and I don't even deserve the clothes on my back. Jesus paid my fare by dying on the cross. All I had to do was reach out with my heart and accept the ticket to heaven that His death purchased for me.

I don't believe that Jim knew God, and if he didn't know Him then, and still doesn't know Him now, here's what he has waiting for him for eternity:

- A place or state of everlasting fire.[4]
- A lake of burning sulfur[5] – have you ever smelled or touched burning sulfur?
- A place of eternal torment and punishment.[6]
- The blackest darkness forever.[7]

I've prayed for the strength to forgive Jim, and I hope and pray that I can see him in heaven one day and tell him thanks for helping make me a very punctual person. I didn't agree with his methods, but I can thank him for the end result. Jesus' death on the cross means that Jim can also enter the gates of heaven if he asks Christ into his life and honestly repents of his sins. God, in the form of Jesus, died for me. Jesus died for Jim, and He died for you. No matter how many or how great your sins, Jesus can, and will, forgive you… if you ask Him.

As Paul Little paraphrased, "Heaven is most simply defined as where God is. It is a place of rest (Heb. 4:9), of glory (2 Cor. 4:17), of purity (Rev. 21:27), of worship (Rev. 19:1), of fellowship with others (Heb. 12:23), and of being with God (Rev. 21:3). *'He will wipe every tear from their eyes. There will be no more death or mourning or crying or pain, for the old order of things has passed away'* (Rev. 21:4)." "Everything in heaven will be new: *'The earth and everything in it will be laid bare... But ... we are looking forward to a new heaven and a new earth, the home of righteousness'* (2 Peter 3:10, 13)."[8]

Christians who truly understand the Second Coming of Christ look forward to that time with great hope, expectation and happiness. Committed Christians have a belief that God is in control of all things and for the good of all things. Committed Christians are willing to do whatever God wants us to do because our sole purpose in life is to love Him first and love others as we love ourselves. For some, like my mother, an additional purpose in life may be to set an example of faith and perseverance by escaping from twenty-three years of depressing situations to emerge as a wise, loving grandparent. For some, it may be to write a book, start a ministry, or help people reach their financial goals. For others, it may be to overcome an addiction to drugs, a propensity to react in anger or violence, an inclination to treat their children with love and respect even when they feel like pulling their hair out, or an inability to forgive others as they have been forgiven. What is God's purpose for you in life?

Christ's Second Coming will allow Him to take those who truly love Him back to heaven with Him. Those who don't believe in Christ will have to face an eternity of torment. Those walking closely with God know that eternal life in heaven will be many times happier and more joyous than the happiest and most joyous person on earth – and we're ready. Life on earth is merely a time of preparation for eternity with God. We need to be storing up riches in heaven by loving God, loving others, and by sharing the love of Christ with people who don't know Christ. The only disappointment will be that we didn't help tell enough people about Jesus during the small amount of time we were given to do God's work on earth.

I've used several Bible verses in this chapter, and I'd like to spend some time talking in detail about how the Bible is structured and about some of the main stories. If you're a Bible veteran, please say a prayer for those who are not so that they might have a desire for a deeper, better, more clear understanding of the Bible.

The Bible Basics

The Bible is a collection of books that were written by several different authors. These authors were inspired by God to write exactly what they wrote on ancient scrolls, and thus the Bible is called the "inspired Word of God." I simply look at the Bible as a book that was written by God. He just dictated to several different people what He wanted written, and those people wrote down what He said to them. In a lot of cases, these authors whom God spoke through played a major role in recording history, or they were present to provide eyewitness accounts of what actually happened.

In all, there are sixty-six books of the Bible. The Bible is divided into two parts, called the Old Testament and the New Testament. The Bible was originally written in Hebrew and was translated into Greek around the time Alexander the Great expanded the Greek empire around 331 BC. The books of the Bible are not placed in the Bible in chronological order and some stories are repeated in two or more places by different authors. Some names are hard to pronounce, some people change from one name to another, and some people share the same first name. I still get confused sometimes in my readings. When I get confused, I know to slow down and remind myself of the following facts by asking the following questions:

- *Who's doing the talking or writing?* This person is usually the author of the book or a record of someone else talking. Remember, God is truly the author, and He had people write what He wanted them to write.
- *Who are they talking to?* Who was the Scripture written for? The passage may have been written to a single person, a group of people, or as a historical record.
- *Who are they talking about?* What's the big picture message?
- *When did this happen?* Yes, I know… dealing with BC and AD can get confusing, but take the time to figure out when the events happened. Facts, names, and stories will remain in your brain better if you know when they existed. A great book to read that will help you remember the events in the Bible is

called *Talk Through the Bible* by Bruce Wilkinson and Kenneth Boa.

- *Where were they?* There are usually maps included in most Bibles. This really can be interesting as you can now see photos online or in books of what the land looks like. You can almost put yourself in their sandals!

The best advice I can give you about the Bible is for you to read a version of the Bible that you can understand. You probably remember me telling you that my first Bible was a King James Bible, and that I could not understand most of it. The New International Version (NIV) of the Bible is the version that made the Bible most understandable for me. There are many new versions of the Bible out now that do a good job of putting the stories of the Bible into formats that can easily be understood by young people and new Christians. The Message, The Living Bible, and New Revised Standard, among others, are other versions of the Bible that are now available online or at your local Christian bookstore.

My church offered a Sunday school class that was called the "Bible in a Year" class. The class leaders provided each student with a chronological Bible. This Bible truly opened the doors to the message God had waiting for me inside its covers. I loved that things were presented in the order in which they occurred in history! I like things in order – I guess that's the Family Hero coming out in me. The Bible gave me a specific amount of text to read each day of the year, so it also gave me a measuring stick to keep me on track. I heard someone on the radio recently say that it takes fifty-five hours at an average reading pace to read the Bible from cover to cover. If you read the Bible out loud, it would take an average of seventy-eight hours. This means that you could read the Bible in a year by spending a mere ten minutes per day reading to yourself or you could read it aloud in thirteen minutes per day. How many hours per day do you devote to television, working out, or relaxing? Do you know anyone who thinks he doesn't have time to read the Bible? Any person can find ten minutes in his day to read a life-changing book. Wouldn't you agree?

I encourage you to go find a version of the Bible written in a similar way to how you verbally communicate. If you say "thou" and "thine" when you normally talk to friends and family, then go get a King James version; if you speak the way I have written this book, go get a NIV version; if you communicate in other ways, find a version that can understandably speak to you. Jesus spent a great deal of time with sinners, the poor, and the sick. He talked to them in a language they could understand. He didn't talk over their heads. I believe that if Jesus were to come back today to rural Mississippi or to the ghettos of New York City, He'd speak in a way that all of the people could understand Him. He wants you to understand and He's empowered people to write different Bible translations so that you can know Him better. Any version of the Bible is better than no version of the Bible because it gives God and the Holy Spirit a starting point for conversation with you. It's up to you to listen to the right voice in your head going forward.

> Any person can find ten minutes in his day to read a life-changing book. Wouldn't you agree?

> Any version of the Bible is better than no version of the Bible because it gives God and the Holy Spirit a starting point for conversation with you.

If you already own several versions and you haven't read much of any of them, pick one version and set a goal to read it in one year. Remember, faith comes through hearing God's Word, and God's Word is the Bible. Open the covers of your Bible, and you'll open the doors to who God wants you to become! Trust most any version of the Bible to get you started and ask the Holy Spirit to show you how to understand it. Once you've digested one version of the Bible, you may find that your heart leads you to read and study another version. Trust God and the Holy Spirit to guide you! Now let's talk in more detail about the Bible…

The Old Testament

The Old Testament was written between 1460 BC and 450 BC, and it discusses events that happened between the beginning of time (the book of Genesis) and somewhere around 450 BC (the book of Malachi). The Old Testament has thirty-nine of the sixty-six books of the Bible. These books deal with topics such as law, history, poetry, wisdom and prophecy over its 1,100-year writing period.

The Old Testament gives us some great illustrations about life before Christ through the writings of Moses, David, Solomon, Jeremiah, and others. Yes, some of the names are hard to pronounce and it's hard to have a mental picture of their living conditions and environment, but they were people just like you and me. Their lives are great examples that allow us to learn from their victories and their mistakes. Wouldn't you like to have someone write down how you should respond to every situation so that things always work out? They have; it's in the Bible! These people teach us how to forgive, obey, trust, question, and believe; they also show us what it's like to wonder, doubt, hurt, cry, be angry, and desire revenge; and they experience every emotion and situation imaginable. They may not have had their cars break down on the freeway or keep their children from spending too much time watching MTV, but they struggled with the same internal issues and decisions that all of life ultimately revolves around. Learn from their lives and draw parallels to their situations by reading the Old Testament.

A very brief list of major characters, stories, and events that can be found in the Old Testament is outlined below in an attempt to get you more interested in reading the details directly from the Bible. Remember, ask the Holy Spirit to show you the message He has for you in each story. Don't let Satan throw you off track by getting frustrated or confused!

- *Adam and Eve* – The first two humans were made to enjoy the things God created. Adam and Eve show us that we all have consequences to pay for our disobedience to a God who loves us enough to show us tough love. (Genesis)
- The Devil (Satan, Lucifer) – Led Adam and Eve to disobey

God's command to not eat the fruit of the Garden by communicating with them through a serpent. (Genesis)

- *Noah* – Built a great ark in the middle of a desert where it hadn't rained in years after God told him that He was going to wipe out all living creatures and start new. (Genesis)
- *Abraham* – Name was originally Abram. He showed tremendous faith in God. God rewarded him by giving his wife, Sarah, and him a son when Abraham was 100 years old. God instructed Abraham to sacrifice this son, Isaac, and Abraham faithfully followed the command. God stopped Abraham just before the sacrifice and Isaac's life was spared, but Abraham showed great faith and absolute trust that everyone should possess. (Genesis)
- *Jacob* – Later also called Israel after he physically struggled with an angel prior to confronting his brother, Esau. Some of Jacob's children became the leaders of the different tribes of the nation of Israel. (Genesis)
- *Joseph* – A son of Jacob who was thrown into a well and left for dead by his jealous brothers after he told them about a dream in which he was to be in command of his brothers and his father. Rescued by one of his brothers, Judah, and sold into slavery, Joseph rose to a position of high leadership under the Pharaoh of Egypt, led Egypt through seven years of famine, and forgave his brothers for their actions. Joseph's family stayed in Egypt after being reunited and this began the tremendous growth in population of Israelites in Egypt that in the future led to them being enslaved as a people to prevent them from taking over Egypt. The phrase "coat of many colors" originated from the story that Joseph's brothers proved his death to Jacob by showing Jacob his coat that had been dipped in blood. Joseph's life shows us great examples of suffering, faith, wisdom, forgiveness, and greatness. (Genesis)
- *Passover* – A time of year named for the time when God took the life of every first-born child in Egypt as a result of the Pharaoh's oppression of the Israelites. The Israelites were instructed to sacrifice a lamb and smear its blood above their

doorframes and lintels so that God would "pass over" their homes and spare their first-born children. In the New Testament, Jesus died during Passover, as He was our symbolic sacrificial lamb whose death allows us to have eternal life if we accept his saving grace.

- *Moses* – Chosen by God to lead the Israelites out of Egyptian captivity to the Promised Land. His life shows us the power of faith, how leaders have to trust in God even when their followers do not, and that even the most faithful people have flaws. His life and leadership are some of the most important stories in the Bible. (Exodus)
- *The Israelites* – The nation of people that Moses led from Egypt, through the parted Red Sea, and during a forty-year period of wandering en route to the Promised Land. There are many stories that reveal how quickly these people forgot the promises they had made to God when things were tough. They would pray and make promises to God during the tough times, but when things got better they always went back to their old ways. The nation of Israel later split into two groups, the northern group was called Israel and the southern group was called Judah. (Exodus, Leviticus, Numbers, Deuteronomy, Joshua, Judges, Ruth, I Samuel, II Samuel, I Kings, II Kings, I Chronicles, II Chronicles, Ezra, Nehemiah, Esther)
- *Joshua* – Selected to lead the Israelites into the Promised Land after Moses' death. He led the Israelites in conquests of the natives of the land, including the taking of the great city of Jericho. Instead of directly attacking the city, by God's command the Israelites marched around the city for six days, and on the seventh day, the priests blew their trumpets and all the Israelites shouted as loudly as they could. The city of Jericho fell without any physical confrontation due to God's direction. (Joshua)
- *Job* –The name of a wealthy and successful man of God and the name of a great book of the Bible that illustrates one man's suffering and faith in The Creator. Job went from tremendous monetary and family wealth to nothing and was

restored by God to an even greater level of prosperity after being tempted by the devil. (Job)

- *David* – The young shepherd boy who killed the giant Goliath with a stone and a sling. He became King of Israel after Saul. He wrote most of the book of Psalms, which is a collection of great poems and songs that convey intense worship, love, frustration, fear, anger, personal struggle, and other emotions. David was called "a man after God's own heart." His life reveals the intimate thoughts of a man committed to God who, due to his human imperfection, falls into sin with Bathsheba and has her husband killed by sending him into a battle that could not be won. (I Samuel, II Samuel, I Kings, Psalms)
- *Solomon* – The wise son of David who built a temple for God to house the Ark of the Covenant. When God asked Solomon in a dream what he most would like to be granted, God was very pleased that Solomon requested wisdom and not riches or long life. Solomon's wise sayings are written in Proverbs and in Song of Solomon. (I Kings, II Kings, I Chronicles, II Chronicles, II Samuel, Proverbs, Song of Solomon)
- *Daniel* – A true man of God and the author of a book in the Bible carrying his name. After the Israelites were exiled from the Promised Land to Babylon due to their inability to adhere to God's instructions, Daniel survived being thrown by the leader of the Babylonians into a furnace and being left in a lion's den due to his great faith. (Daniel)

There are many more important characters, locations, terms, dates, themes, messages, prophecies, and words from God in the Old Testament. Take some time to get to know the Old Testament by reading a chronological Bible. I cannot express to you how much of a difference that Bible made in my walk of faith. Maybe God will also speak to you more clearly when you walk through the Bible in the order in which events occurred. Two good things will happen – you'll at least be walking and you'll be walking in the right direction!

The New Testament

The New Testament is made up of the remaining twenty-seven books of the total sixty-six books of the Bible. The books are grouped into the Gospels (Matthew, Mark, Luke, John), Acts, the Epistles (Romans, 1st & 2nd Corinthians, Galatians, Ephesians, Philippians, Colossians, 1st & 2nd Thessalonians, 1st & 2nd Timothy, Titus, Philemon – all written by Paul; Hebrews; James; 1st & 2nd Peter; 1st, 2nd, & 3rd John; Jude), and Revelation. The New Testament was generally written over the one hundred-year period starting from around 37 AD. It is estimated that approximately thirty-two percent of the New Testament – nearly one-third – is made up of Old Testament quotations and allusions.[9]

The significant difference between the Old Testament and the New Testament is that Jesus' death and resurrection repealed the Old Testament requirement that a sacrifice be offered to have sin forgiven. The Old Testament described the strict rules people had to follow to live their lives committed to God and the ramifications of not following His instructions. Old Testament believers had to offer burnt animal sacrifices for their sins, they had to offer their finest and best animals for these offerings, and there were very strict rules to be followed. In fact, there were strict guidelines for almost all aspects of life and worship. Jesus' death wiped away all those rules because He was the perfect sacrificial lamb that covers all past, present, and future sins – both yours and mine. The governing theme throughout the New Testament revolves around the most important command found in Matthew 22:37-39, *"Love the Lord your God with all your heart and with all your soul and with all your mind. This is the first and greatest commandment. And the second is like it: love your neighbor as yourself."*[10]

The New Testament begins with four different people recording their eyewitness accounts of Jesus' work while He was alive, His horrible death, and His triumphant resurrection. Many of the miracles Jesus performed are recorded in the New Testament along with the actual words He spoke. He healed the sick, gave sight to the blind, raised the dead, fed four thousand people from only seven loaves of bread, walked on water, fed five thousand people with five barley loaves and two fish, cast demons from the possessed, and rose from the dead himself.

The *disciples* were a group of twelve men who were the closest companions of Jesus while He performed His ministry on earth. There are great stories that illustrate the varied backgrounds of these people who closely followed Jesus. These stories reveal the flaws in their character – flaws that let us know that Jesus knows that no one is perfect and that He can perform good works through almost anyone with a willing heart and a loving spirit that is focused on doing God's will.

The largest part of the New Testament is made up of the letters that the *apostle* (the word *apostle* can mean "messenger of God") Paul wrote to different churches and people involved in his mission of spreading the Good News. Paul (formerly named Saul) was a former zealous persecutor of Christians who was blinded by a light from heaven while walking. He fell to the earth and heard a voice (Jesus' voice) asking him why he was persecuting Christians. After three days without food, water, or sight, Paul was immediately transformed into a person who, instead of persecuting Christians, was preaching the gospel of Jesus Christ. He went from a murderer of Christians to one of the most dedicated followers of Christ in history. This change reveals the fact that anyone who sincerely repents can step into the love of Christ and that Christ's love can change even the most hardened and violent heart.[11]

Paul wrote a few of the books from prison where he was jailed for preaching and disobeying Roman authority. Even while in prison, Paul's zeal for Christ was clearly evident and is a great example for all persons today who think their situations couldn't get any worse than they currently are. Paul suffered many beatings and much punishment in his work to show the love of Christ to others. It is even thought that Paul might have had some permanent physical damage to his body, but you can't tell from the tone of his writing. He was a man in love with God, appreciative of God for His creation, excited about his role on earth as a missionary for the Gospel, and expectant of his eternal life in heaven.

Revelation is the last book of the Bible, and it states what is yet to come. As Jesus rose into the sky after being resurrected, two men dressed in white told the onlookers that Jesus would return just as He departed. As Paul Little states in his book *Know What You Believe*, "The second coming of Christ is the great expectation of the church. As Christians, we should, with Paul, love to look for that *'blessed hope and the glorious appearing of our great God and our Savior, Jesus Christ'* (Titus 2:13). His coming is an incentive for holy living."[12]

You've probably heard about the *Left Behind* series of books that helps convey the message contained in Revelation through fictional stories. The books have sold millions of copies and have helped educate people in a creative way about some of the basic themes and messages in that book of the Bible. The series does a great job of helping people see that there are some serious consequences for choosing not to make a decision to follow Jesus.

My chronological Bible really did help me understand the New Testament more clearly because the stories that are repeated by several authors are placed together in the form of one narrative, and so I felt I was always moving forward in time through the Bible. I learned about Jesus' birth, His life on earth teaching, healing, and loving, Jesus' death and the impact it had on His followers, the growth of Christianity through the writings and travels of His believers, and the vision for the future given to the writers by God of what is soon to come. The Old Testament predictions all came true, so I certainly have no reason to doubt that the New Testament predictions won't come true. I'm glad that I've made a decision to follow Jesus and that I have my eternal security confirmed through my faith in Him. I'd hate to have to suffer the consequences of doing otherwise. And so would He.

Summary

This chapter discussed faith, Jesus, and the Bible in a way that hopefully whet your appetite to learn more about each. Mel Gibson's movie, *The Passion of Christ*, did a great job showing people how Jesus might have suffered in order to pay the price for our sins. People left movie theaters around the world feeling sad, angry, and disgusted at the horror of Jesus' death. I left the theater with a great sense of appreciation for His selfless act and proud of Jesus for his willingness and ability to finish the job He knew He was put on this earth to do.

I found it extremely moving and symbolic that Jesus would touch the cross He was about to carry to His death in a loving and appreciative way. He did this because He knew it was His mode of transportation to heaven with His Father. He knew the wooden cross was soon going to be the beam that bridged the gap between the world and God. I also was deeply moved by the image of Jesus willingly crawling onto the cross, much unlike the other criminals who had to forcibly be thrown onto their crosses. He was obedient, faithful, and humble. Yet He was strong, courageous, and ultimately victorious over the death brought upon Him by His own people. He could have fought them every step of the way, He could have struck them all down with a sweep of His hand, and He could have chosen to let us suffer the consequences for our own sin.

But He didn't.

Things You Need To Do Now

1. Thank Jesus for dying on the cross for your sins, and tell others about Him.
2. Thank Jesus for dying on the cross for your sins, and tell others about Him.
3. Thank Jesus for dying on the cross for your sins, and tell others about Him.

SECTION III - FAITH

Chapter Sixteen

Faith and You

Clarifying the Reasons

I heard Kirk Cameron, an actor in the television show *Growing Pains* and in the recent *Left Behind* series, speak on television late one night. I awoke about 1:30 AM and couldn't go back to sleep, so I turned on the television and started flipping channels. God woke me up because He wanted me to hear what Kirk had to say. Kirk talked about the reasons why people should believe in Christ, and he made a great analogy that compared asking God for salvation to wearing a parachute in an airplane. The story went something like this:

"Two men boarded a 747 on a flight overseas. After takeoff, the first man sitting in the front of the plane was asked by a stewardess if he'd like to wear a parachute so that he would have a more comfortable, relaxing, enjoyable, and fulfilling flight. The man thought for a moment and decided to put the parachute on his back to give it a try. There was no extra cost for the parachute - all he had to do was say 'yes' and put the parachute pack on his back.

Feeling encouraged by this potential for a more enjoyable flight, he sat happily in his seat waiting for the evidence of a better flight to reveal itself. And he waited.... and waited..... and the pack on his back got heavier and heavier with every passing minute. The weight and size of the pack on his back made him lean forward in his seat, so he wasn't able to sit up straight or recline comfortably. Then he noticed that other people on the flight were laughing at him and making jokes about his obvious discomfort. They were really giving him a hard time. He didn't enjoy the discomfort the pack was causing or the persecution from his fellow travelers at all. He asked the flight attendant when he was going to start seeing some benefits from wearing this heavy and uncomfortable pack and he told her that it wasn't doing much to help make his trip happier and more enjoyable.

After more laughter from the onlookers and increased discomfort, he decided that the parachute pack wasn't doing him any good. In fact, he decided, the pack was making his life even worse than it was when he didn't have the pack. He wanted to go back to the way he had things before – no pack, a comfortable seat, and nobody picking on him. With a mix of anger, disappointment, and dejection, he begrudgingly removed the pack from his back and vowed never to put one on again because it did not bring him the immediate benefits the flight attendant promised him.

At about the same time, a flight attendant approached the second man sitting in the back of the plane with a parachute in her hands. She described the benefits of wearing the parachute a little bit differently than her coworker did. She said, in a nice and professional way, but very matter-of-factly, that everyone on the plane was going to be forced to jump out of the plane at some unknown time somewhere over the ocean. She told him that he could save himself from certain death by putting on the parachute now so that he would be ready when he had to jump at a moment's notice.

The second man thought for a moment. He weighed his choices – certain death versus an opportunity to continue living. It was an easy decision for him to make. With much appreciation, he asked the flight attendant if he could have the parachute pack. She graciously said, "Yes," and he asked her how much the parachute was going to cost him. She told him that someone else had already paid for the parachute just for him and that he didn't owe her a single penny. Looking around the plane for the person who might have paid the cost of the parachute for him, he strapped the parachute onto his back and sat back down in his seat with a great sense of appreciation filling his heart. He sat humbly in amazement wondering why someone chose to pay for his parachute. He was also relieved that he was given the chance to live when everyone else would have to jump to their deaths.

As the flight continued, he began to realize that the pack was fairly heavy and that his back was under some strain from not being able to lean back. He also noticed, like the first man did, that some people were laughing at him. He wondered if they knew that at some point they were going to have to jump out of the airplane. He continued to be very thankful that he was saved from sure death by the generosity of some person, and this appreciation made him more than happy to bear the discomfort, weight, and ridicule associated with wearing the parachute pack. He sat for several hours in his seat, ready for the command to jump, thankfully knowing that his descent would not end in death. He barely noticed the times of turbulence while others became uneasy because he was really focusing on the bigger event that was to come. The plane flew though some thunderstorms that really concerned some of the passengers. But, he knew that even if the plane were to crash, he would be safe."

He sat for several hours in his seat, ready for the command to jump, thankfully knowing that his descent would not end in death.

Kirk used this story to illustrate that people in today's society are being told that a relationship with Jesus Christ that brings eternal salvation will more importantly bring peace, joy, happiness, and fulfillment while alive on earth. He said that people are mistakenly striving to receive the benefits for use in life on earth when they choose to accept salvation. Further, Kirk said that people turn away from Christ when their lives reach times of uncertainty, persecution, and discomfort, much like the first man who took his pack off because it didn't improve the quality of his flight.

Instead, Kirk stated, the Biblical reason we should all be willing to accept salvation is that salvation saves us from sure eternal death and condemnation by assuring us of eternal life with God in heaven. We should accept God's sacrifice of his son, Jesus, for the same reason the second man accepted his parachute – so that we will live past the point in time when others will not. Properly motivated believers will be focused on and appreciative of the gift of life while alive on earth and will happily live life according to God's will for us regardless of the severity of the discomfort and uncertainty the storms of life bring our way. We should all wear the parachute that Christ's death provided us with appreciation, humility, and happiness because we know that we have been saved from sure death! Kirk's prayer, and mine, is that you know Christ, or that you come to know Christ, due to an informed decision to protect your eternal life – not just to improve the quality of life here on earth. We hope that you've decided to have a personal relationship with God to ensure that you have the opportunity to be free from the wrath of Judgment Day, to have your name written in the Book of Life, and to enjoy eternal happiness and joy. If you focus on these things as the true reasons and the gift of Christ's love, then you'll be free to love and appreciate every day, every person, and every situation you encounter while you're here on earth – no matter what circumstance you're in.

Kirk's prayer, and mine, is that you know Christ, or that you come to know Christ, due to an informed decision to protect your eternal life - not just to improve the quality of life here on earth.

Paul stated in Philippians 4:11-13, *"For I have learned to be content in whatever circumstance I am. I know how to get along in humble means, and I also know how to live in prosperity. In any and every circumstance I have learned the secret of being filled and going hungry, both of having abundance and suffering need. I can do all things through Him who strengthens me."*[1]

Paul suffered severe physical beatings, imprisonment, and persecution. He probably walked with a limp and wasn't very pretty to look at. He was an educated man who used to hate and murder Christians. His followers who also believed in Jesus abandoned

Paul. Yet he had the spiritual strength to write those verses. Read them one more time if you'd like. Try and imagine yourself in Paul's shoes writing these verses from a bare, lonely, and painful prison.

I pray that you'll have the kind of faith in Christ that keeps you moving towards the goal of truly desiring to know God, of loving God more than you love anyone or anything, and of trusting God to provide for the very breath that you take. I know I could certainly benefit from the kind of faith Paul exhibited in his writings. Like Paul, I hope that you'll keep your eye on the prize, much like a running back carrying a football towards the end zone. The ball carrier feels the would-be tacklers hitting him, trying to pull him down, and trying to hurt him, but he is so focused on his end goal he couldn't tell you who or how many defensive players tried to stop him. Be so focused on the end zone that life's oppositions and times of turbulence don't slow you down. Through your faith in God, push aside troubles with your finances, hurt feelings among family members, unfair employers, disappointing investment results, and health problems. Trust God to give you the ability to love everyone with the same kind of love that Jesus had for you, regardless of how they treat you. God will have the final say in their reward or punishment. You'd probably much rather let God deal with them since He has a little bit more power than you or me. Give God your heart, ask Him to forgive you of your sins, and read His Word so that you can reserve your place in heaven with Him. Strap on your parachute of salvation that Jesus' death purchased for you and live your life with a daily appreciation of that gift.

If you're wondering if you've ever truly accepted Christ into your heart and asked Him to forgive you of your sins, you can pray this prayer:

"Dear Lord, I know that I've sinned and fallen short of who You want me to be. I know that You sent Your Son, Jesus, to die on the cross for my sins. Thank You for sending Him just for me. I believe that Jesus came back to life, is now with you in heaven, and will come back someday to judge the world. Please forgive me of my

sins, and I honestly promise from this point forward to try and live a life that pleases You. I know that I'll stumble and fall, and I thank You for Your promise to always forgive me when I ask You. I promise to strive to love You with all of my heart, soul, mind, and strength. Send Your Holy Spirit to live in my heart to guide me in Your ways. In Jesus' name. Amen."

If you prayed this prayer, you are now a member of God's family! Your name is in the Book of Life, and your reservation has been made on the first ascension into heaven with Jesus when He returns!

If you've already prayed this in your lifetime, please pray for the others who may be finding Christ for the first time. And remember.....

God has – and will - always love you – no matter who you are or what you've done! His love is a prayer away for anyone.

Things You Need To Do Now

1. **If you don't already have a church home, go find a church that can meet some of your needs.** No church can meet every single need, simply because humans are involved. We are all imperfect, even pastors and church people. If everyone was perfect, there wouldn't be a need for church, would there? Accept other church members' imperfections just as God forgave you of yours. Your church family will help love you, guide you, and challenge you. You may even find that you have something to offer other people.
2. **Get to know your pastor and inform him or her of the status of your walk with Christ.** You may feel led to be baptized after you've prayed to accept Jesus into your heart. Your pastor's wisdom, experience, and prayer can help strengthen your personal relationship with Christ.

SECTION IV

SUMMARY

SECTION IV - SUMMARY

Chapter Seventeen

Perspective

"I will instruct you in the way you should go; I will counsel you and watch over you."[1]
"Leave your simple ways and you will live; walk in the way of understanding."[2]

A Life Gone Astray

When I was a freshman at Vanderbilt, I was involved in a group that trained college students to go to the local high schools to help lead people to Christ. We met in a room on the second floor of a building on Music Row in Nashville. We'd pray, read the Bible, answer questions, sing songs, and talk about God and how we were going to help lead the high school kids. At the end of the second meeting, we were walking down the stairs to leave and I heard several of them talking about where they were going after they left. To my dismay, they all decided they were going to go out to do some hard drinking at one of the local clubs.

I decided right then and there that I didn't want to have anything to do with any religion where people who prayed and acted very religious were hypocritical enough to turn right around and engage in drunken activities. I had been beating myself up as a lonely college freshman anytime I thought things I shouldn't, said things I shouldn't, and did things I shouldn't. I was miserable. My parachute of salvation was heavy, and people were laughing at me! Meanwhile, it seemed like every person that didn't live a life geared towards pleasing God was having the best time of his life. I thought Christians were supposed to have it all and be happy. Somewhere along the way, someone misled me. I felt like I had been had, taken for a ride, and ripped off. I felt like I had pulled the rip cord and nothing happened.

I took that parachute off my back, threw it down on the floor, and turned away from God because I thought that life was too short to live in torment trying to be good while others were having a great time and suffering no ill consequences from their bad behavior. I spent about ten years away from God – I didn't pray, I didn't ask for guidance, and I didn't say thanks. I had a foul mouth, I did completely what I wanted to do, and I was accountable only to myself. I pursued happiness in relationships, I scratched and clawed for every dollar I could make and save regardless of how it affected the other party, I treated my wife in a way that no father would like to see his daughter treated, and I capitalized on the freedom available to me. And, guess what I had to show for it – business debt, credit card debt, a struggling marriage, and bitterness about my situation.

But then one day, the Holy Spirit knocked loud enough on the doors of my heart so that I could hear him. Or maybe He helped create a situation in my life where I happened to be quiet just long enough to hear His soft voice. I had just recently sold the horseback riding business and sold some real estate in Tennessee. I remember thinking that I had been a pretty shrewd and savvy businessman to have those deals fall into place for the right dollar amounts and at just the right time. I was really proud of myself for orchestrating everything perfectly. My people skills were finally being used as finely tuned moneymakers, and things were going to be all right with our move to Florida. We paid off debt, built a home, and settled into well-paying jobs. We had finally made it!

After these victories, I had a spring in my step; I felt invincible. I was proud of what I had done, and I thought people should see how good I was at working with money and people. For years, I just knew that my payoff would be coming soon, and I felt that everyone should listen to me – especially my wife – because I knew what I was doing. Did you notice how many times the word I appeared in this paragraph?

Then one day at the church we had started attending, the Holy Spirit told me, "Walter, I just thought it might help you to know that you didn't have anything to do with how all of this is going right now. I lined it all up for you. And, if you hadn't been so arrogant about everything, I would have given you even more." I heard His voice loud and clear, and I was immediately humbled, mightily crushed, and forever changed for the better.

I heard His voice loud and clear, and I was immediately humbled, mightily crushed, and forever changed for the better.

As I began to reflect on all the things that have happened in my life, both good and bad, I saw the undeniable evidence of God's hand in my life at every turn along the way. He was grooming me through good times and bad, through sad times and happy times, through positive and negative outcomes. And I was foolish enough to think I was in control! I then realized that the word *I* should be replaced by the word *He*.

Words To Live By

Now that I live my life trying to learn and follow His instructions, I've found that I'm truly a lot happier. I no longer try to follow the advice the world gives me. I now know that I don't have to buy a series of DVD's or CD's to help reprogram my mind, I don't have to try and model my life after some mega-rich businessman, nor do I have to "find myself" in relation to who the world thinks I should be. The following verses are the ones that have had the greatest impact in shaping who I am going to be tomorrow. I now know that it's not about me, it's all about Him.

"Whoever can be trusted with very little can also be trusted with much, and whoever is dishonest with very little will also be dishonest with much. So, if you have not been trustworthy in handling worldly wealth, who will trust you with true riches? And if you have not been trustworthy with someone else's property, who will give you property of your own?"[3]

These verses showed me that I hadn't been trustworthy with things that belonged to other people– their trust, their time, and, much less, their hearts. I realized that so much more could have been done with those things over and above what I had done. I know that I am going to heaven because I've accepted Christ as my Savior and I truly see a change in my heart, thoughts, and actions due to the presence of the Holy Spirit. I want God to say to me, *"Well done, good and faithful servant! You have been faithful with a few things; I will put you in charge of many things. Come and share in your master's happiness!"*[4] As the Family Hero who is always searching for approval from someone else, I've finally found that the only approval I truly need is the approval of God. If I can make God happy, then I'm doing all that can be expected of any person. If someone isn't happy with me while I'm making God happy, I can know with confidence that the problem does not lie with me and that I can trust that God will work on helping them see the light just like He did with me.

These verses also showed me what true riches are. To me, true riches are a relationship with Jesus Christ that is founded in love – not rules, regulations, militaristic agendas, punishment, and bitterness. I now truly understand at this point in my life what love and true riches are. *"Love is patient, love is kind. It does not envy, it does not boast, it is not proud. It is not rude, it is not self-seeking, it is not easily angered, it keeps no record of wrongs. Love does not delight in evil but rejoices with the truth. It always protects, always trusts, always hopes, always perseveres."*[5]

Pastor and author Rick Warren said, "Busy-ness is a great enemy of relationships. We become preoccupied with making a living, doing our work, paying bills, and accomplishing goals as if these tasks are the point of life. They are not. The point of life is learning to love – God and people. Life minus love equals zero… Love leaves a legacy. How you treated other people, not your wealth or accomplishments, is the most enduring impact you can leave on earth. As Mother Teresa said, 'It's not what you do, but how much love you put into it that matters.' Love is the secret of a lasting heritage."[6]

As Mother Teresa said, 'It's not what you do, but how much love you put into it that matters.'

True riches are things that you can take to heaven with you: the memories of smiles on the faces of your family members at the birth of your first child; the look of relief on your mother's face when you tell her you've forgiven her; the touch of your spouse's hand in the middle of the night when you roll over in bed; the tears in a military veteran's eyes when you tell him thanks for putting his life on the line for our country; the renewed innocence in the eyes of a teenager at the local juvenile detention facility after you've led her in a prayer of salvation. Our lives here on this earth are infinitesimally small compared to the length of time we have available with which to spend eternity with Christ. And none of the things here on earth are really ours – we're just being trusted with whatever God thinks we're capable of handling until we're proven worthy of more or less.

"Everything in the heavens and earth is yours, O Lord, and this is your kingdom. We adore you as being in control of everything. Riches and honor come from you alone, and you are the Ruler of all mankind; your hand controls power and might, and it is at your discretion that men are made great and given strength."[7]

This verse says it all! This is why I say that you should just give up, let go, and quit. Specifically, you should give up, let go, and quit trying to be in control. God is in control, and this is a good thing!

He is in control, but we still have a definite responsibility to explore every resource and opportunity available to us so that we can be rewarded as good and faithful servants. Have you ever trusted someone to find out the best way for you to fly from point A to point B and found out later that he only checked one airline, one price, and one flight? We have a duty to research things thoroughly and to make good, prudent decisions that are based upon Biblical principles. And once we make a God-focused decision, we then have the assurance that God is in control of everything and that everything He does is done *"to prosper you and not to harm you, ... to give you a hope and a future."*[8] Some people wince or say with a sigh, "I guess God'll take care of it." However, we should say, "God will take care of it!" and trust in His outcome – whatever the outcome. God created the whole earth, and the Bible is full of stories of people just like you and me who have been through the same, similar, or far worse events and situations. Job lost his family, wealth, and his health; Joseph was left for dead by his brothers and then sold into slavery; and Jesus lived a perfect life and died on the cross. We can learn from them so that we can draw closer to God earlier in our lives. The sooner we draw closer, the more time we have available to us to do a better job for Him while we're here on earth. Wouldn't you like to go back to high school or college knowing what you know now? God's presence in your life can give you the wisdom to handle your finances and your family more effectively.

> *"For I have learned to be content whatever the circumstances. I know what it is to be in need, and I know what it is to have plenty. I have learned the secret of being content in any and every situation, whether well-fed or hungry, whether living in plenty or in want. I can do everything through Him who gives me strength."*[9]

If you could snap your fingers and be content with your financial situation, your family interactions, your work environment, and every other aspect of your life, how long would it take you to actually start snapping your fingers? If you understand something, doesn't that understanding give you a level of contentment? If you feel comfortable, if you have peace of mind, if you can let things go, if you can relax, if you can trust – if you can do all these things, doesn't it also mean that you are content to some degree?

I can look back in life and see that I've been hungry (as a child when we didn't have any money), and well fed as an adult. I've had plenty and I've also spent a lot of time in want. I know what it is to need something (transportation) or someone (an absent mother or father), and I also know what it means to have plenty. Wisdom is the character quality that allows people to learn to be content. The word *learn* is important to note – the verse doesn't say "I woke up content" or "all of a sudden I was content." To learn something means you have to study, practice, and be tested. How have you been tested in life? What phases of your life can you plug into this verse like I have?

The verse also says, *"I can do everything through Him who gives me strength."* It is important that you understand that you can do everything because you've been given the strength and ability through Christ. But you shouldn't feel the burden of doing it all by yourself. If you're a single mother with a failing business and a problem with alcohol, take refuge in the fact that you can do everything you need to do through Him who gives you strength. If you're a father who struggles with anger and a desire to be in control of everything and everyone, peacefully realize that you need the strength of *wisdom* to know that you're just not strong enough *all by yourself.* Trust in God for your strength. Call on Him when your tank is low, when you want to take a drink or react in a way you know you shouldn't. Reach out to Him in prayer, through your pastor, through Christian music. Just open up your heart and let Him take your burdens and give you rest. He can fill you up and give you wings to fly higher than you could ever imagine. He can create in you, through your trials, sorrows, embar-

...you need the strength of wisdom to know that you're just not strong enough all by yourself.

rassment, and pride, something that is endlessly wonderful and vibrant. If you're being tested right now (I know for a fact that you are), then you should rejoice, because God has something great in store for you!

> *"Rejoice in the Lord always! I will say it again: Rejoice! Let your gentleness be evident to all. The Lord is near. Do not be anxious about anything, but in everything, by prayer and petition, with thanksgiving, present your requests to God. And the peace of God, which transcends all understanding, will guard your hearts and minds in Christ Jesus."*[10]

When your bank account is overdrawn, when the bill collectors are knocking at your door, when you're considering bankruptcy, when your investments are down twenty percent in one year, when your family seems to be falling apart, when your boss won't give you a spare minute to catch your breath, when no one seems to understand or care about your situation, when you realize how wrong you have been, when your kids are screaming at the top of their lungs and aren't minding you, and when you get a negative doctor's report – "*Rejoice in the Lord always!*" Do not be anxious. With thanksgiving ask God to help you in your situation. And the peace of God, which is deeper, wider, longer, stronger, and more comforting than anything we could ever imagine - multiplied by infinity - will guard your heart and mind. Wouldn't you like that kind of peace? It's pretty huge, isn't it? It's available to you! The only price is that you answer the call to give your life to God as a token of thanks for the gift He gave to you.

The Real C.F.P.

We humans are always seeking balance; we want things to be fair, equal, and evenly divided. Some of us actually want everything in our favor, regardless of its impact on others. However, fair in this situation represents the fact that since God gave Himself for us, we should do the same for Him. We only have ourselves to lose anyway. Through our fears, impatience, unhappiness, confusion, anger, sorrow, and discontent, we are guaranteed to be lost. Why not give God what He deserves – ourselves – and be set free from concern, worry, disappointment, and anxiety that today's pace of life brings? I finally gave in and trusted God with my finances. God brought us out of debt, increased our income tremendously, trained us to manage our expenses well, and gave us more peace than we thought we could ever have. And He has even more in store for us!

As a CFP certificant and a financial consultant, people come to me for answers. My clients trust that I'm going to steer them in the right direction. Some people will only listen to advice from a qualified and educated CERTIFIED FINANCIAL PLANNER certificant, and I'm happy to be that person for them. But, God is truly the ultimate C.F.P. He's our CONTINUALLY FAITHFUL PROVIDER!

Trust God to be your CONTINUALLY FAITHFUL PROVIDER – your real C.F.P. – and let His love set you free from the burden of your finances and your family strains through your faith in Him. Give your heart over to reading His word, to praying to Him, to finding out how He wants you to handle things. Give up on exhausting your methods first and then turning to God. Go to Him first and thus save yourself time and headaches by following His way right from the start. This selfless act will also teach your family how they should handle their affairs. This book gives you some excellent practical advice for your finances, and you should follow the advice found here. God wants you to seek out and listen to counsel. Please notice that it's a two-step process. If you seek out advice but don't listen to it, you've just done a good job of wasting everyone's time. You must seek AND listen.

> Give up on exhausting your methods first and then turning to God. Go to Him first...

Your **<u>CONTINUALLY</u>** FAITHFUL PROVIDER is ever-present, ever-loving, ever-forgiving, and ever-knowing. He will love you continually, teach you continually, and stretch you continually for your own good. As Rick Warren said, "God is more interested in your character than in your comfort." If you're focused on knowing Him better, you'll barely even notice the other issues in life, much like the running back headed for the end zone. Set your eyes on the goalpost of heaven and you won't even realize what yard line you're on or who is trying to bring you down.

Your CONTINUALLY **FAITHFUL** PROVIDER has promised to be faithful in His dealings with you, and the Bible has multiple stories where He proves that He is worthy of our trust and faith. *"For great is his love toward us, and the faithfulness of the Lord endures forever."*[11] Remember, if it's in the Bible, it's true. Step into God's love, and out of your life of worry, concern, and doubt. He is Faithful!

The CONTINUALLY FAITHFUL **PROVIDER** will provide on His level, and we should be happy with whatever level He chooses to give us because we don't deserve a single thing from Him. Prove yourself worthy of managing the small things and He may decide to make you a manager of more. If He chooses not to give you more to manage and you get disappointed, you need to remember that you're evaluating things on an earthly scale. God's measures are altogether different. *"'For my thoughts are not your thoughts, neither are your ways my ways,' declares the Lord. 'As the heavens are higher than the earth, so are my ways higher than your ways and my thoughts than your thoughts.'"*[12] Pray that God's Holy Spirit will show you what His thoughts are for your life, rejoice in every situation, and be a trustworthy manager of whatever He's chosen to allow you to manage.

They Make It Look So Easy

Do you know anyone who seems to continually get rewarded without even having to put forth any effort? Do you know anyone who makes life look so easy that it makes you sick? If she's a Christian, it's probably because she has learned to turn things over to God.

Have you ever been shopping for a car and found THE car, the perfect fit, the perfect color, and the perfect mileage, but the price was just too high? Do you think that the best way to negotiate with the salesperson would be to say, "I absolutely love this car and I'm dying to buy it," while your spouse is giving you the "please, please, please buy it right now before someone else buys it" look? Or, would it be a better negotiation tactic to play it cool and act like you really don't like the car that much but that a lower price might help you like it a little more? The world knows when you want something really, really badly. God knows when you want something really badly, but He also knows WHY you want something. God always knows your thoughts, motives, and reasons, so there's no reason to hide them from Him.

For years, I said, "God, I've done all the right things, stayed out of trouble, and done my best to do what You want me to do. Can you please bless my family and me in our relationships, in our health, in our finances, etc.?" It was not until I had grown enough in Christ and was able to say, "God, if you want me to be broke, I'll be broke. If You want me to work two jobs, I'll work two jobs. Whatever You want me to do, I'll do it, and I'll rejoice in any situation."

Any Christian's goal should be to become more like Christ. While Jesus was praying to God in the Garden of Gethsemane before he was to be captured, beaten, and crucified, He said, *"...yet not my will, but yours be done."*[13] When you can say, "whatever God wants for me is fine with me," I believe that is when God will reward you with what He feels you deserve. It is only when the most important thing in your life is replaced by a relationship with God that is focused on making Him happy are you given what you once wanted. When I replaced my desire for financial security with a desire to know God more intimately, God found me worthy of more responsibility. When I turned my desire to have my wife listen to me and follow my direction into a desire to please God, He showed my wife how she could find a way to trust me more completely. God just had to find out that He could trust me first.

> God just had to find out that He could trust me first.

We used to play football in our neighborhood, and we never picked the kids who were waving their arms saying, "Pick me, pick me!" We knew that their anxiety about being picked was because they simply weren't very good. If you're saying, "Pick me, pick me!" to God, He's probably going to wait until your skills have improved before He picks you. Grow in your relationship with God so that you become very comfortable in your position and in your skills so that when he starts choosing players for His monetary teams or His family management teams, you know that you'll be chosen without having to constantly tell God that you can handle the job. Your actions speak louder than your words. Let God's Holy Spirit change your heart so that your actions can be changed from the inside out. Strive to make your life easy by putting complete trust in God's ability to make good things happen from any situation.

Things You Need To Do Now

1. **Take a step back from your life by writing down some bullet points or an outline of the major events in your life.** You might want to make one list that outlines the events and another list that outlines your character traits or qualities. This will allow you to take a good inventory about who you are. Write them all down, both good and bad, and please be honest with yourself.
2. **Now that you've completed #1, write down an outline of the traits and qualities that you would like to have along with the major events you would like for others to have with you.** Events you'd like others to have with you might include annual family vacations, one-on-one bonding trips with a close friend, leading someone to the Lord, or volunteering for a local charity.

SECTION IV - SUMMARY

Chapter Eighteen

FAITH... Family, and Finances

Since this is the last chapter, this has to give you a great summary of what you just read. This chapter has to put everything in one nice, neat wrapper so that you can easily recall why you read this book about helping make your priorities of finances, family, and faith more understandable. So, here goes.....

Looking back, I guess I'm glad that Mom didn't catch that $3 Nerf® football. Knowing my mom, she probably missed it on purpose because she knew I'd end up writing a book some twenty-five years later about the impact the event had on my life. I'm even more thankful for the perspective that my relationship with Jesus has given me with respect to my finances, family, and faith.

A few years ago, my wife and I enrolled in a Crown Financial Ministries twelve-week small group study that required us to memorize a Bible verse every week, read selected passages from the Bible and study guide, answer a series of questions in writing that pertained to the Bible and money, and ideally read and study a portion of the week's work on a daily basis. The material promoting the twelve-week study said that within a short time after completing the study, graduates increased tithes to their churches from an average of 2% to about 8%. The Bible tells us to tithe 10%, so those graduates took a huge leap towards that guideline. It was also stated that within a short time the average graduate reduced his outstanding debt by $18,000.

I would like to say that my family's finances have faired even better than those statistics. It wasn't because I'm a financial professional. It was because of God's decision to help us turn things around. He has found us trustworthy with the small things, and now He's willing to give us bigger things to manage.

Here's the Secret

Here's the part where I give you the earth-shattering advice from a Certified Financial Planner certificant that completely turns your financial world around and sets it free to fly to new heights... (drum roll, please)… here's where I tell you how to stop losing sleep about your investments and how to stop disagreeing with your spouse about your budget… (keep the drum roll going)… where I tell you the secret to getting yourself on the right road to financial freedom and to growing closer to your family… the way to prove to everyone that you know what you're doing with your money and with your family relationships… the can't miss opportunity of a lifetime… the secret to life and the most important thing you can do is …

Extended drum roll, please…

Here it comes....

The moment you've been waiting for...

Quit trying to find the secret.

Just give up completely. Really, just stop trying.

Throw your hands up in the air and say, "That's it, I've done all I can do."

Was that worth the drum roll? Did it live up to your expectations? Okay, I'll explain myself.

Stop trying to figure out ways around the system. Don't burden yourself with getting more out of your day, becoming more efficient, tracking every penny, calculating and recalculating the amounts required to give you an adequate retirement, comparing your current investment portfolio with every comparable index, transferring balances from one low rate card to another just days before the low rate expires, shopping on the Internet for a cheaper alternative, chatting with your coworker about how to handle your daughter-in-law's shortcomings, arguing with your spouse over which one of you is right about how to address your child's attitude, wondering if your estranged family member will come to you first to apologize, and stressing yourself out about every detail to try and stay one step ahead of the madness. Your burdens are causing you more stress than they're worth.

I can say this because I know that this book has equipped you with the information you need to make good decisions. Now all you have to do is let go. A basketball coach drills his players on shooting, teamwork, passing, defense, and rebounding during practice. They do the same thing over and over again. He does this so that when it comes time to play the game, the players won't have to think. The coach wants things to come to them automatically. Your situation is somewhat similar. You've covered the material, you've answered the questions in each chapter, you've really spent time

> This book has equipped you with the information you need to make good decisions. Now all you have to do is let go.

thinking about your situation, and hopefully you've made or strengthened your commitment to Christ. The next step requires you to stop worrying about things. The next step requires you to put your faith to the test…

I heard a fictitious story about a man who rappelled down into a cave by himself. He descended into this huge, dark cavern when his gear malfunctioned and he fell about one hundred feet before his emergency gear kicked in and stopped his fall, jerking the rope tightly. The sudden jolt of the stop caused the light on his helmet to fail, and he dangled helplessly. Alone. In complete darkness. He screamed and yelled. He tried to climb back up. He tried to lower himself further down. But he couldn't move at all. He waited, and waited, and waited. In total blackness. Two days later he heard a voice say to him, "Cut the rope and let yourself fall, I will take care of you." He heard the voice many times but could never bring himself to cutting himself free from the only source of survival and comfort he knew – the rope he was clinging to in a remote, dark, and lifeless cave.

A few months later some climbers found this man hanging in the cave. No, he wasn't alive. He died in total darkness with his feet dangling about two feet above the cave floor. Had he trusted the voice of the Holy Spirit he heard in his head, he would have cut the rope and fallen to safety where he could have found water or possibly crawled out of the cave. What are you hanging on to in life that you should just let go of and let God handle? Your money, your feelings about a family member, a situation that happened in the past, relationships at work, the death of a loved one? Sometimes the best thing you can do is let go, especially when you know that God is waiting to catch you in His eternally capable, loving, and comforting arms. You never know how far the bottom is below you – until you let go. If you thought you could fix your situation and you haven't been able to, you should open your eyes to the proof – you can't fix it. Let

> You need to let go. It's time. You've tried to do it by yourself long enough. God will catch you. Trust Him.

go of the rope you've been clawing at for years. Seriously, you need to let go. It's time. You've tried to do it by yourself long enough. God will catch you. Trust Him.

You may be thinking, "I've read this whole book and he's telling me what?! How can I give up? Nothing will ever get done! We'll go bankrupt. What if something comes up we haven't planned for? What if the market has another three bad years like it did recently? If I don't keep trying to help her, she'll never be able to take care of herself. How can you possibly just quit trying?!"

Here's why I'm telling you this. I'm a financial consultant and a CERTIFIED FINANCIAL PLANNER practitioner, and I am aware of most financial topics. I've seen almost every type of investment available - every "get rich quick" scheme, every "no money down" scheme, every "all you have to do is sign three people up underneath you and the checks start coming in" scheme. I've also read countless books, spent hours with counselors, and reflected endlessly on interactions with other people to try and find the perfect way to handle other people – particularly family members. And I've also tried to fulfill my commitment to my faith by militaristically following every law, rule, and guideline.

I'm telling you from experience, none of those qualifications and efforts did me much good. And they won't do you much good, until you surrender every portion of your life – your money, your assets, your attitude, your family, your job, your hobbies, your talents, and your liabilities – to God. Just release them from your grasp. You can keep trying it your way for the next ten years and then come to realize you should have surrendered ten years ago – or you can do it now. Which choice do you think is best for you?

Conclusion

While you've been reading this book, have the stories, the facts, and the presence of the Holy Spirit given you a better understanding and a clearer perspective on how to deal with your finances, your family, and your faith? Do you know what a diversified portfolio is or how your company's retirement plan can benefit you? Did any stories from my family background and experiences give you some insight into your family life to help affirm that you're moving in the right direction or reveal an aspect of your family life that needs to change? Do you know God either for the first time or in a deeper, more knowledgeable, heartfelt way? Do you now have a desire to know Him better?

If you completed the tasks presented at the end of each chapter, I want to compliment you on using this book to its greatest potential. If you didn't complete the tasks – either because you think you already know how to handle those issues or because you feel like you don't have the time – you've unfortunately missed one of the main points of this book. In order to simplify your life, you need to actually take the steps that lead to knowledge, not just read or think about them. For your sake, ask God to give you a humble, servant-minded spirit and delete something in your life so that you can find the time to develop clarity, purpose, and simplicity in your faith, your family dealings, and your finances so that you can be the person He wants you to be in all aspects of your life. You would not believe how many people I've had tell me they know exactly how much money they spend and that there's no way they can reduce their expenses anymore – until they sit down and put it down on paper. *Processes* are put in place so that you can *proceed.* I urge you to complete the processes so that you can proceed with a better understanding of your priorities in life.

Did you find that you and I have anything in common with regards to our family backgrounds or the issues we've had in life? If you haven't already encountered some of the issues that I talked about, statistics say that someday you will. I hope and pray that you're prepared for them before they happen because if you're not *prepared*, things will have to be *repaired.* I urge you to take steps toward preventive maintenance so that your repair bill won't be astronomical in terms of dollars, feelings, or more importantly, eternity.

I hope and pray that God's Holy Spirit has spoken clearly to you, as He did to me, and showed you the proper order and importance of the priorities of finances, family, and faith. As a result of my personal growth, I've adopted a simple set of guidelines for determining my priorities in life. I call them "The Three F's." In order of importance, they are

1st Priority - Faith
2nd Priority - Family
3rd Priority - Finances

This order of priorities came about because God simply and wondrously changed my heart. One day I just realized that's how things should be. Sometimes the old me tries to fight his way out – days when I feel like my work comes before playing with my children, or days when I don't read my Bible because I chose to watch television, or days when I was just too busy to slow down and remember that God created me for a reason. That reason is to love Him and to love others. He will take care of the rest. If I love Him completely and am always striving to communicate with Him, I won't be concerned with my financial situation, the stock market, or how badly someone treated me. I strive to do the best I can at work, in writing this book, in treating my family with love and gentleness, in interacting with unfair people, and in every aspect of life because I want to make God proud of me. I want God to say that I'm a good and faithful servant.

Our days are all completely full of things to do, and none of us have time to get absolutely everything done that we should do or would like to do. When I'm faced with a decision about what to do with a certain amount of time I have available, I prioritize it according to the "Three F's".

Issues regarding my *faith* such as prayer time, church, Bible study, and teaching my family about God are always at the top of the list. If I've got to choose between praying with my daughter when she's going to bed or getting back to the computer in my office quickly, I choose to pray with her. If I've got a lot of things to do at home in order to be ready for the next day, I don't skip

Wednesday night Bible study so that I can get things done. Faith comes first.

Commitments to my *family* follow after commitments to my faith, with things such as reading to my children, watching a movie with my wife, or going to the beach with the entire family being good examples. My family knows that my commitment in my life is first to God, and they know that commitment ensures that we'll spend eternity together. They support it completely. My wife puts God first in her life, and we are trying to raise our children to believe the same thing.

Finances come in last behind faith and family. Finances basically means work in my roles as a CERTIFIED FINANCIAL PLANNER practitioner, my role as an author and public speaker, and my efforts in leading a Christian ministry. I do not put making a living first in my life, I do not put earning an income first in my life, and I try not to let the stresses associated with my job or income affect my faith or my family. I take my work and finances very seriously, but my work and finances do not completely monopolize my time, creativity, devotion, or thoughts. I work to live; I don't live to work. How about you? Why do you work?

There are too many people (mostly men) who think about work or money all the time, and their faith and family suffer because of it. There are too many people (mostly women) who give themselves completely to their families and lose sight of their faith, and thus lose sight of themselves.

Focus on your faith in Christ by reading His Word, attending church, and getting involved with a small group. Love your family every minute of every day, tell someone in your family that you're sorry for hurting them, and let your actions prove to them over time that they are the most important people in your life. Learn everything you can about your finances and live your financial life according to God's Word. Take advantage of every legal opportunity to save income taxes, invest money wisely, know the basics regarding all the financial topics

> The key to understanding life's priorities is to place your faith at the top of the list of priorities.

in your life, and work closely with your financial professional.

The key to understanding life's priorities is to place your faith at the top of the list of priorities. You'll then find that everything else will fall into place. If faith comes first, your next priority will easily be your family, and your finances will be the third priority. This understanding and order of priorities can remove all the complications in your life because you're sure of where you are today (a solid Believer in Christ), where your ultimate destination rests (heaven and eternity), and how to get there (trusting God by storing up treasures in heaven, not on earth). Your eternal C.F.P., your CONTINUALLY FAITHFUL PROVIDER, is your best advisor in all the different aspects of your life. Seek and listen to His counsel! The greatest commandment is "*Love the Lord your God with all your heart and with all your soul and with all your mind and with all your strength.*"[1] If you can focus on this verse in your every waking moment, your priorities will be the same as those of the happiest people on earth and in heaven! Walking closely with God can give you a peace "*which transcends all understanding.*"[2] That's the kind of peace I want in my life, a peace that I've barely even begun to taste. I have no idea how limitless the peace and protection provided by God really is. But I want to find out. I'm sure you do, too.

I have no idea how limitless the peace and protection provided by God really is. But I want to find out. I'm sure you do, too.

Refer to this book to help guide you in your finances. Use it as a tool to help you remember what a Roth IRA is. Read back over the chapter regarding family solutions when you feel like things aren't flowing as smoothly at home as you'd like them to. Refresh your perspective on faith when you feel like you're not getting anywhere in your Christian walk. Maybe something will help bring you back to the clarity that I hope now exists about each individual topic of finances, family, and faith. But remember, your priorities should be your faith, family, and then finances. Hopefully this book has been a useful guide for you and I hope some of my life experiences helped you see areas where you're doing well or areas where you could use some help.

One of the best things you can do when you close the covers of this book is pick up a Bible and start reading it. Like we talked about earlier, it's probably a good idea to set a S.M.A.R.T. goal for your Bible reading. The most profound and insightful author imaginable wrote that Book. Its contents will truly change your life, not just how you live. God loves you so much that Jesus sacrificed His life so that you may live. I urge you to truly live by growing through the Bible.

The Bible will help you see that your priorities should be your faith, then your family, and then your finances. You're now equipped to handle each individual priority. You can now put this book down with the confidence and belief that you can make good decisions.

Life is very complicated… but it doesn't have to be.

Things You Need To Do Now

1. **Put your FAITH first, then your FAMILY, and then your FINANCES in your order of priorities in life.** Give your heart, soul, mind, wallet, hopes, fears, and victories to God. Put the information and the processes outlined in this book to use. Read your Bible. Obtain the counsel of a professional in any areas in life where you need help. Marriage counselors, substance abuse counselors, financial counselors, legal counselors, family counselors, and faith counselors are available for you. Allow them to help you align your priorities to be your faith, your family, and then your finances. Trust God completely!

Acknowledgments

Readers of this book – Thank you for buying this book, and I pray that the information in this book has as much of a positive effect on your life as it has had on mine.

Mom – Thank you for giving me permission to share the stories of our lives with other people in this book. Your selfless willingness to share our good times and bad times will certainly help many readers. Some people unfortunately choose to hide from and to forget their past. I appreciate the fact that you're willing to share with others, just as you shared with me so generously throughout my life.

Thank you for showing me true strength and faith all during your life! You have endured more than any one person should have to endure in a lifetime, and I hope you see that your efforts are reaping dividends in who I am as a person, how I handle situations in my life, and in who your grandchildren will grow up to be. I rejoice over every situation that we've been through together, and I firmly believe that God was working for the good of many people through you, through us as family, and through the people we have come in contact with. I love you more than you'll know, I respect you more and more every day, and I'm proud of your being a winner!

Wendy and I sometimes feel overwhelmed with children, work, household, and personal issues. I can't imagine being a single parent trying to do everything by myself. Thank you for not ever giving up, for loving me, for supporting me, for coming to hear me speak, sing, play sports, and for crying so easily – are you crying right now?! Mom, I love you. Thank you, thank you, thank you!

Dad – Thank you for showing me how to let things "go in one ear and out the other." I wish I could not let things bother me as well as you can. I appreciate you taking me water skiing, and I really enjoyed our trips in the car on the way from Gaga's. I can't begin to tell you how much it meant to me when you drove to so many of my football games, especially the one that you attended only three weeks after having open-heart surgery. I know that you love me by the things that you've done for me! Even though when I was young I felt like the game of golf was my competition for your time and attention , I now enjoy playing the game with you and spending that time with you. I admire you for your ability to make (and keep) friends so easily, and I've only heard good things about you from people outside the family. I hope that we can spend our time in heaven playing the game of golf together!

Gaga – I know that you're in heaven, but I want these readers to know that I know you loved me even when I felt like I wasn't a very lovable child. Thank you for bringing food into my room and putting it right in front of my angry little face when I was hungry but didn't want to eat. Thank you for calling Mr. Langston to go find me when I'd run away before the school bus arrived. Thank you for teaching me patience; for teaching me how to really pinch pennies by giving me the exact change for a gallon of milk when you sent me to the grocery store on my bike; and thank you for always praying for me. I will always love you. I'll see you in heaven!

John Evans – God sent you to help save my life. You were a rock in my life when I needed a solid place to stand. Your Tuesday morning breakfasts with me showed me that you were someone who was willing to stay in my life and not leave. This book is a portion of my attempt to use the gifts that God has given me to help others. Thank you for showing me the good things that could come out of tough situations and for asking me over and over again how I "felt" and not what I "thought." There is a huge difference between the two. I "feel" a great deal of love and appreciation for your investment of time, effort, resources, and prayers into me. God bless you!

Wendy – I honestly could not have been given a better wife, a better companion, a better friend, and a better mother for our children than you. Thank you for enduring times with me when I'm so focused on work, ministry, music, or myself that I don't hear you talking. I promise I'm trying to work on that! I love that you know about football, that you can play basketball and football almost as well as I can (just kidding), and that you're living your life in search of a true relationship with God. I'm so glad that you didn't give up on me after we first married when I thought I didn't need God in my life – you set a great example for me and I love you for that. I look forward to many years with you watching our children grow, to keeping their boyfriends away, and to having us grow closer together every day. Thank you for being faithful, trustworthy, constant, reliable, supportive, and loyal. I love you more than any words can say!

Winston and Gail - thank you for helping give me the courage to write a book and for loving us as much as you do. McDonald & Associates - thank you for believing in me, this book, and our mission! Pam Owen, Todd Thompson, and Mary Ann Pelletier - thank you for your proofreading skills, words of wisdom, and constructive criticism. You helped make this a better book! I'd also like to thank Todd Sandroni for being such a great role model as a person, student, and athlete. Jim Langston - you were like a father to me and I appreciate you teaching me about work, family, responsibility, hunting, fishing, and honesty. Tag and Dot Gamblin - thank you for opening up your home to me so that I didn't have to move out of town. Dot, I think about you almost everyday as the greatest role model of a mother that ever existed. Tom Lamb, your graciousness and stability helped shape me and keep me out of situations that would have been far less than ideal. Aunt Katie - washing clothes at your house on Sunday afternoons with Bryan was a great relief to me at a time in my life when I was stressed out about school, money, the past, and who I was going to be in the future. Your hospitality, detergent, and ice cream is still greatly appreciated. Sue, thank you for taking good care of my dad. I know that you really love him. You are always in my prayers. Bryan, a relationship with God is everything! God - this is for You.

Endnotes

Chapter One

1 Kostigen, Thomas M., *What Money Really Means*, Allworth Press, April 2003 as reported in *Journal of Financial Planning*, March 2003, 29.

2 *Rocky Mountain News* as reported in the *Journal of Financial Planning,* March 2002, 20.

3 International Labor Organization as reported in the *Journal of Financial Planning,* November 2001, 24.

4 Nellie Mae Corporation as reported in the *Journal of Financial Planning,* November 2001, 24.

5 Nellie Mae Corporation as reported in the *Journal of Financial Planning*, November 2003, 25.

6 Greenspan, Alan in Federal Reserve-sponsored TV and radio ads as reported in the Journal of Financial Planning, August 2003, 19.

7 Jumpstart Coalition for Personal Financial Literacy as reported in the Journal of Financial Planning, August 2003, 19.

8 Proverbs 22:7, NIV

9 Proverbs 21:5, NIV

Chapter Two

1 Proverbs 12:15, NIV

2 The *Wall Street Journal* as reported in the *Journal of Financial Planning*, January 2003, 25.

Chapter Three

1 Certified Financial Planner Board of Standards Annual Report 2002, Denver, CO, 2.

2 Fidelity Investments as reported in the *Journal of Financial Planning*, March 2002, 20.

3 Bankrate.com as reported in the *Journal of Financial Planning,* August 2003, 19.

4 Cambridge Credit Index as reported in the *Journal of Financial Planning*, May 2003, 21.

5 CardWeb.com as reported in the *Journal of Financial Planning*, April 2003, 26.
6 Amerix as reported in the *Journal of Financial Planning*, October 2002, 28.
7 Consumer Federation of America as reported in the *Journal of Financial Planning*, November 2002, 28.
8 The Wall Street Journal as reported in the *Journal of Financial Planning*, March 2002, 20.

Chapter Four
1 National Council on Aging as reported in the *Journal of Financial Planning*, July 2003, 21.
2 www.ssa.gov
3 The *Wall Street Journal* as reported in the *Journal of Financial Planning*, July 2003, 21.
4 Samuelson, Robert J. as reported in the *Journal of Financial Planning*, May 2003, 21.
5 *The Wall Street Journal* as reported in the *Journal of Financial Planning*, November 2003, 25.
6 Centers for Disease Control and Prevention as reported in the *Journal of Financial Planning*, November 2002, 28.
7 2000 Annual Report of the Board of Trustees of the Federal Old-Age and Survivors Insurance Disability Insurance Trust Funds as reported in the *Journal of Financial Planning*, March 2001, 99.
8 Korcyzk, Sophie M. "Baby Boomers Head for Retirement." *Journal of Financial Planning*, March 2001, 116.
9 www.ssa.gov
10 *Journal of Financial Planning*, August 2003, AARP, 19.
11 www.ssa.gov

Chapter Five
1 U.S. Treasury Department as reported in the *Journal of Financial Planning*, October 2001, 30.
2 www.irs.gov
3 www.irs.gov
4 *http://www.frs.state.fl.us/frs/drop/dropsum.htm* (January 18, 2004)

Chapter Six

1 www.irs.gov

Chapter Seven

1 Mauboussin, Michael as reported from *Bloomberg Personal Finance* in the *Journal of Financial Planning*, May 2003, 20.

Chapter Eight

1 The College Board, Trends in College Pricing: 2001 as reported by American Council on Education website 9/17/03.

2 *USA Today* on 10/24/2001 from a report by the College Board: "Trends in College Pricing:2001."

3 IRS Publication 970

Chapter Nine

1 Douglas, Jennifer, "Long-Term Care Insurance: "Who Buys Long-Term Care Insurance in 2000?," prepared for the Health Insurance Association of America by LifePlans Inc., October 2000.

2 Lewin-VH1, in "Long-Term Care: Knowing the Risk, Paying the Price," Health Association of America, 1997, 12.

3 U.S. General Accounting Office, Testimony on Long-Term Care," Baby Boom Generation Increases Challenge of Financing Needed Services," March 27, 2001.

4 U.S. General Accounting Office, Testimony on Long-Term Care," Baby Boom Generation Increases Challenge of Financing Needed Services," March 27, 2001.

5 Ibid

6 Metlife Mature Market Group. 1997. Metlife Study of Employer Costs of Working Caregivers. Metropolitan Life.

Chapter Eleven

1 Federal Interagency Forum on Child and Family Statistics. America's Children: Key National Indicators of Well-Being 2003, Federal Interagency Forum on Child and Family Statistics,

Washington, DC: U.S. Government Printing Office, p. 7, *http://childstats.gov*.

2 Federal Interagency Forum on Child and Family Statistics. America's Children: Key National Indicators of Well-Being 2003, Federal Interagency Forum on Child and Family Statistics, Washington, DC: U.S. Government Printing Office, p. iii, *http://childstats.gov*.

3 Federal Interagency Forum on Child and Family Statistics. America's Children: Key National Indicators of Well-Being 2003, Federal Interagency Forum on Child and Family Statistics, Washington, DC: U.S. Government Printing Office, p. 9, *http://childstats.gov*.

4 United States Census Bureau, Census 2000.

5 Americans for Divorce Reform website

6 Carter, Jane & Susan Schecter (1997, November). Child Abuse & Domestic Violence: Creating Community Partnerships for Safe Families. Family Violence Prevention Fund.

7 Family Violence Project website, September 2002, *www.home.gwi.net/~circle/fvp/index.htm*

8 *http://www.vpcswi.org/statistics.html*, September 2003.

Chapter Twelve

1 Seixas, Judith S. and Geraldine Youcha, *Children of Alcoholism – A Survivor's Manual*, Harper & Rowe Publishers, New York, Copyright 1985.

2 Ibid, p 26–28.

3 Wegscheider, Sharon. *Another Chance: Hope and Health for the Alcoholic Family.*

4 Americans for Divorce Reform website, *www.divorcereform.org*.

Chapter Thirteen

1 Warren, Rick. *The Purpose Driven Life*, 2002. Zondervan, Grand Rapids, MI, 143.

2 Ibid, p. 127-128.

Chapter Fourteen

1 2 Corinthians 5:7, NIV
2 Hebrews 11:1, NIV
3 Dictionary.com
4 Laurie, Greg. *Impact – Equipping Believers to Impact Their World,* p 9, A New Beginning with Greg Laurie.
5 Luke 15:7, NIV.
6 Mark 12:30, NIV.
7 Luke 10:17, NIV.
8 Galatians 5:22-23, NIV.
9 1 Corinthians 12:7-9, NIV.
10 Jeremiah 29:11, NIV.
11 Strobel, Lee. *The Case for Christ. A Journalist's Personal Investigation of the Evidence for Jesus*. Zondervan, Grand Rapids, MI, Copyright 1988, 14.
12 *www.clarifyingchristianity.org*, Oct 2003.

Chapter Fifteen

1 Little, Paul. *Know What You Believe*, Cook Communications Ministries, Colorado Springs, CO, Copyright 1999, 138.
2 John 14:3, NIV.
3 Revelation 22:20 NIV.
4 Mark 9:43; Matthew 25:41.
5 Revelation 20:10.
6 Rev. 14:10-11.
7 Jude 13.
8 Little, Paul. *Know What You Believe*, Cook Communications Ministries, Colorado Springs, CO, Copyright 1999, 148.
9 Ibid, 17.
10 Matthew 22:37-39, NIV.
11 Acts Chapter 9, NIV.
12 Little, Paul. *Know What You Believe*, Cook Communications Ministries, Colorado Springs, CO, Copyright 1999, 140.

Copy or Tear This Page Out To Order More Copies of

"Finances, Family... and Faith"
An Understandable Guide to Life's Priorities"

or

Visit

www.walteronline.com

Order form on the back of this page

Order Form

Fax Orders: 850-271-9663. Fax this form.
Telephone Orders: 850-248-9606. Have your credit card ready.
Email Orders: **www.walteronline.com**
Postal Orders:
Priority Publishing Company
1602 New Jersey Avenue
Lynn Haven FL 32444 USA
(850) 248-9606
www.walteronline.com

Please send the following books or products. I understand that I may return any of them for a full refund, for any reason.

Quantity	Product

Your information:
Name: ______________________________
Address: ______________________________
City:____________________State:_____Zip:_______
Telephone: ________________________________
email address: ____________________________

Sales Tax: Please add ___% sales tax for products sent to Florida addresses.

Payment: Check Credit Card
Visa MasterCard Optima AMEX Discover
Card Number:__________________________________
Name on card:__________________Exp. date: _______

Copy or Tear This Page Out To Order More Copies of

"Finances, Family... and Faith"
An Understandable Guide to Life's Priorities

or

Visit

www.walteronline.com

Order form on the back of this page

Order Form

Fax Orders: 850-271-9663. Fax this form.
Telephone Orders: 850-248-9606. Have your credit card ready.
Email Orders: **www.walteronline.com**
Postal Orders:
Priority Publishing Company
1602 New Jersey Avenue
Lynn Haven FL 32444 USA
(850) 248-9606
www.walteronline.com

Please send the following books or products. I understand that I may return any of them for a full refund, for any reason.

Quantity	Product

Your information:
Name: ______________________________
Address: ______________________________
City:____________________State:_____Zip:_______
Telephone: ______________________________
email address: __________________________

Sales Tax: Please add ___% sales tax for products sent to Florida addresses.

Payment: Check Credit Card
Visa MasterCard Optima AMEX Discover
Card Number:_________________________________
Name on card:__________________Exp. date: _______